SHAKESPEARE ON LOVE & LUST

MAURICE CHARNEY

ON LOVE & LUST

COLUMBIA UNIVERSITY PRESS   NEW YORK

Columbia University Press
Publishers Since 1893
New York   Chichester, West Sussex
Copyright © 2000 Columbia University Press

Library of Congress Cataloging-in-Publication Data

Charney, Maurice.
Shakespeare on love and lust / Maurice Charney.
p. cm.
Includes index.
ISBN 0–231–10428–6 (cloth : alk. paper). – ISBN 0–231–10429–4
(paper : alk. paper)
1. Shakespeare, William, 1564–1616–Criticism and interpretation.   2. Love in
literature.   3. Gender identity in literature.   4. Lust in literature.
5. Sex in literature.   I. Title.
PR 3069.L6C48   2000
822.3′3–dc21   99-21631

Printed in the United States of America
Casebound editions of Columbia University Press books are printed on permanent
and durable acid-free paper.
c 10 9 8 7 6 5 4 3 2 1

for
Paul
artist and visionary

CONTENTS

Shakespeare is quoted throughout from the individual paperback volumes of *The Complete Signet Classic Shakespeare*, ed. Sylvan Barnet (New York: Harcourt Brace Jovanovich, 1972), except where otherwise noted. Sylvan Barnet is the general editor and the individual plays have different editors. Note that the line numbering of the individual volumes may be slightly different from the complete volume. The dates of Elizabethan and Jacobean plays are from Alfred Harbage, *Annals of English Drama 975–1700*, rev. S. Schoenbaum (London: Methuen, 1964). For proverbs, I refer to the numbering system in Morris Palmer Tilley, *A Dictionary of the Proverbs in England in the Sixteenth and Seventeenth Centuries* (Ann Arbor: University of Michigan Press, 1966). I have used throughout *The Harvard Concordance to Shakespeare*, by Marvin Spevack (Cambridge: Harvard University Press, 1973). I refer frequently to the *Oxford English Dictionary* (*OED*).

SHAKESPEARE ON LOVE & LUST

INTRODUCTION

The impetus for writing *Shakespeare on Love and Lust* came from reading Jean H. Hagstrum's monumental and eloquent study of love, *Esteem Enlivened by Desire: The Couple from Homer to Shakespeare* (1992). Starting with early Western antiquity, Hagstrum pursues his theme with relentless humanistic learning through classical Greece, Hellenistic-Roman culture, the Jewish and Christian Testaments, the earliest Christian centuries, the High Middle Ages, and the Renaissance, culminating in a long chapter on Shakespeare. This concluding chapter seemed to me the weakest in a splendid book, and in trying to explore its inadequacies I decided to write my own book about love in Shakespeare. Hagstrum is interested in all varieties of love, from friendship to its culmination up the Platonic ladder in love of God and *agapé*. He concentrates on the heterosexual couple whose love eventually leads to marriage. Shakespeare's conception of love doesn't fit Ficino's Platonic and neo-Platonic ideas, in which physical love is always transcended to something higher and more spiritual. Love in Shakespeare expresses itself in physical desire, and even at its most rapturous (as in *Romeo and Juliet*), never loses its sexual underpinnings.

Hagstrum's book, published in 1992, is fairly traditional and old-fashioned in its point of view. More recent studies have gone far beyond Hagstrum to explore areas in anthropology, history, economics, and psychology that are relevant to Shakespeare. The newer gender studies, for example, have shaken the received biological assumptions about male and female identities to center on gender as a historical and social construction. Two recent collections of essays are representative of new ways of thinking about gender: Deborah Barker and Ivo Kamps's *Shakespeare and Gender: A History* (1995) and Shirley Nelson Garner and Madelon Sprengnether's *Shakespearean Tragedy and Gender* (1996). The fact that all of the women's roles were played by boys in Shakespeare's theater is an obvious point that has interested modern critics of gender. When a young heroine like Rosalind in *As You Like It*, acted by a boy, then disguises herself as a man to pursue her love, Orlando, in the Forest of Arden, the gender complications are amusingly complex. This transvestite aspect of the love game in Shakespeare has stimulated lively commentary by gender critics such as Jean Howard and Stephen Orgel. One of Orgel's witty essays is called "Nobody's Perfect: Or Why Did the English Stage Take Boys for Women?" (1989), a question eloquently explored in *Impersonations: The Performance of Gender in Shakespeare's England* (1996). The book is designed to remind us of some of the anxieties about gender in the Elizabethan age. The Puritan attacks on the theater seem to be anchored in these provocative gender confusions.

In the case of Rosalind, there is an added complication in the fact that in her male disguise, she takes the name of Ganymede, the cupbearer of Jupiter—but a familiar Elizabethan representation, both in art and in literature, of the sodomite. Apart from the name Ganimede being used in Thomas Lodge's *Rosalynde* (1590), Shakespeare's source for *As You Like It*, there is no absolute necessity for the heroine to have a name that was a standard slang term for a homosexual. This is a teasing point explored in "Queering the Shakespearean Family" (1996), an illuminating essay by Mario Di Gangi. There has been a flurry of interest in the whole subject of the homoerotic in Shakespeare, most notably in the books by Mario Di Gangi, *The Homoerotics of Early Modern Drama* (1997), Valerie Traub, *Desire and Anxiety: Circulations of Sexuality in Shakespearean Drama* (1992), Bruce R. Smith, *Homosexual Desire in Shakespeare's England: A Cultural*

Poetics (1991), Gregory W. Bredbeck, *Sodomy and Interpretation: Marlowe to Milton* (1991), and Jonathan Goldberg, *Sodometries: Renaissance Texts, Modern Sexualities* (1992). None of these books attempts to prove that Shakespeare was a practicing homosexual, but by calling attention to the large amount of homoerotic material, they raise serious questions about the nature of love in his works. As a dramatist, he would naturally have been interested in exploring latent conflicts about the nature of love, or if not exploring them in any systematic way, at least profiting from the titillation that sexual ambiguities might stir up in an audience.

Feminist critics of Shakespeare have focused on love as a site of conflict with patriarchally oriented male critics. In the discussion of *Antony and Cleopatra*, for example, we have at least two perceptive attacks on traditional male criticism of the play in Linda Fitz's "Egyptian Queens and Male Reviewers: Sexist Attitudes in *Antony and Cleopatra* Criticism" (1977), and Linda Charnes's "What's Love Got to Do with It? Reading the Liberal Humanist Romance in *Antony and Cleopatra*" (1992). The most impressive of the early criticism of male assumptions about Shakespeare is in the collected essays of *The Woman's Part: Feminist Criticism of Shakespeare* (1980), edited by Carolyn Ruth Swift Lenz, Gayle Greene, and Carol Thomas Neely. This book offers a different, woman's perspective on the topic of love in Shakespeare, especially on the theme of misogyny.

The most powerful and intellectually stimulating discussion of misogyny is in Janet Adelman's psychoanalytic study, *Suffocating Mothers: Fantasies of Maternal Origin in Shakespeare's Plays, "Hamlet" to "The Tempest"* (1992). This is an imaginative, nondoctrinaire approach to male resistances to love. Male assumptions are also explored in Coppélia Kahn's *Man's Estate: Masculine Identity in Shakespeare* (1981). Among the most complex and wide-ranging of feminist discussions is Carol Thomas Neely's *Broken Nuptials in Shakespeare's Plays* (1993; first published in 1985). The nuptials are broken by deep-seated male fears and expectations, as, most obviously, those of Troilus in *Troilus and Cressida*. Lisa Jardine in *Still Harping on Daughters: Women and Drama in the Age of Shakespeare* (2nd ed., 1989) approaches feminist issues from a valuable historical point of view.

The above is only an exceedingly brief survey of some of the recent critics who have deepened our understanding of the topic of love and lust in Shakespeare. My approach is strongly based on what Shakespeare says about love and lust in his plays and poems, and emphasizes his language and imagery as they express a variety of attitudes and representations. I must confess that I don't have any developed ideology from which I look at the text; this book is not "committed" in any political sense. I pursue my own interest in Shakespeare as a writer of plays intended to be performed, as well as my fascination with intertextual relations among his works from different periods.

There is no overall doctrine of love that emerges from reading Shakespeare. He definitely doesn't follow the Platonic ideas of love in Ficino and in the devoted followers of Petrarch. Shakespeare seems eager to pursue dramatic and theatrical opportunities rather than to express a unified set of ideas about love. In other words, his works seem to be full of contradictions about the nature of love and the expected behavior of lovers. He often seems to be making fun of the absurdities of love and the pining lover as described so vividly in Lawrence Babb's book, *The Elizabethan Malady: A Study of Melancholia in English Literature from 1580 to 1642* (1951).

My first chapter explores the various conventions that Shakespeare draws on to portray people falling in love. He relies heavily on the Petrarchan assumptions that are fully exploited by Elizabethan writers of sonnets, but Shakespeare is also a notable satirist of these conventions. We are often presented with a contradictory situation in which a character like Romeo is suffering from an almost farcical love melancholy for Rosaline at the same time as his friends, especially Mercutio, are mercilessly making fun of him. *The Two Gentlemen of Verona* begins with Valentine ridiculing his friend Proteus, who is in love, but he himself will soon be smitten by the same amorous pangs that he has mocked. Lovers seem always to fall instantaneously in love and to express themselves with wild excess, which works well in the comedies. It suits Shakespeare's purposes to exploit the doubleness of love, both serious and absurd.

This leads into the subject of the second chapter, "Love Doctrine in the Comedies." I attempt here to understand the formulaic nature of comedy, which produces the inevitable happy ending out of a series of growing complications and perturbations. No problem is so serious that it cannot be resolved. The plots, which depend on mistaken identity, fortuitous meetings, and unforeseen couplings of circumstance, seem very mechanical and artificial. By necessity, "The course of true love never did run smooth," as Lysander tells us in *A Midsummer Night's Dream* (1.1.134); of course, there would be no dramatic interest in the unlikely event that true love, like a river, could run with nary a ripple. The love game has its own rules, and a little cheating is not amiss, as in *Much Ado About Noth-*

ing, if it manages to bring together a couple such as Beatrice and Benedick, who seem so well matched. Shakespeare's comedies are interested in the operations of analogy, so that pairs of lovers from different social spheres are set against each other, as in Plautus and Terence. The love theme suits comedy very well since it energizes the movement to the happy ending on all social strata, which features feasting, drinking, and rejoicing associated with marriage and the promise of children.

The assumptions are different in the problem plays and *Hamlet*, which are addressed in the third chapter. Of course, plays like *Measure for Measure* and *All's Well That Ends Well* use many of the devices of comedy. The bed trick, for example, is a fictional motif with a long history in folklore, but its melodramatic nature threatens the seriousness of love in these plays. It's as if the bed trick is deployed to take responsibility out of the protagonists' hands. *Troilus and Cressida* and *Hamlet* have many similarities in satirical tone and mood. In both plays romantic love is undercut and truncated in the face of a harsh and destructive reality. All of the problem plays and *Hamlet* are unsatisfying generically, from either a comic or a tragic point of view.

Chapter 4 is devoted to love doctrine in the tragedies. Love tragedy is genuinely difficult to write because of the feeling that, like Tristram and Isolde, the lovers fulfill themselves in death. Like Cleopatra, they defy this "vild world," which is "not worth leave-taking" (*Antony and Cleopatra* 5.2.297–98). The ending of this play is hardly tragic at all, as if love were a fulfillment for Antony and especially for Cleopatra. Her "Husband, I come" (287) seems ecstatic. Shakespeare tries valiantly to make *Romeo and Juliet* into a love tragedy by lugging in references to the inauspicious stars, but the lovers end without any clear complicity in their tragedy, "Poor sacrifices" (5.3.304) of the enmity engendered by the family feud. It is at best a scapegoat tragedy, if such a genre is possible. Only *Othello* seems to qualify as a successful love tragedy, and that may be because it is so securely anchored in the ordinary realities of domestic life. Pity and fear work with tremendous force in the play because Othello and Desdemona are characters with whom we can so strongly identify. We should also take account of the double consciousness of Othello, in which he seems proleptically to anticipate his own tragic doom. We feel the emotional pressure of act 4, scene 1, when he says: "My heart is turned to stone; I strike it, and it hurts my hand" (184–85). Shakespeare insists on making Othello a commentator on the intensity and magnitude of his own tragedy.

Chapter 5 is concerned with the enemies of love. It is axiomatic that all of Shakespeare's villains fit into this category. Richard, Duke of Gloucester's opening soliloquy in *Richard III* is almost a parody of a love discourse. His preoccupation with his own physical deformity is erotic in its intensity, and since he cannot "prove a lover," he is "determinèd to prove a villain" (1.1.28–30). Iago is Shakespeare's supreme enemy of love. He cannot even imagine the possibility of love, which in a sense poisons his own life, as in his unforgettable comment on Cassio: "He hath a daily beauty in his life / That makes me ugly" (*Othello* 5.1.19–20). In the comedies there are many reluctant male lovers, such as Bertram in *All's Well* and Malvolio in *Twelfth Night*, whom self-love blocks from love for another. The strongest (and almost parodic) example is Adonis in *Venus and Adonis*, who successfully resists the irresistible advances of the sweating Venus.

In our understanding of love in Shakespeare, much depends upon gender definitions, which are the subject of Chapter 6. Since the characteristics of gender are constructed socially and historically rather than physiologically, it is important to see how Shakespeare separates male from female qualities. Murderers generally do "man's work," as the Captain tells Edmund in *King Lear* (5.3.40). These traits become crucial in *Macbeth*, where Lady Macbeth speaks of unsexing herself from her role as woman and mother at the same time as she insists that her husband be manly and kill the king. The gender issues of *Macbeth* are replayed in *Coriolanus*, where Volumnia shapes the military (and therefore manly) values of her son Marcius. Tears in Shakespeare are always considered womanish, as in Laertes' bad pun for his drowned sister: "Too much of water hast thou, poor Ophelia, / And therefore I forbid my tears" (*Hamlet* 4.7.185–86). The issue of gender as a prepared role is nowhere more strikingly developed than in *The Taming of the Shrew*. Both Petruchio and Kate give us their exaggerated renditions of what they think it means to be a man or a woman.

Chapter 7, "Homoerotic Discourses," continues the topic of gender definitions. It is surprising how much same-sex love there is in Shakespeare, not in any doctrinal sense but as a dramatic expression of a wide variety of sexual impulses. This makes for what may seem to us like contradiction, but is actually a spirited defense of love as a spontaneous feeling outside of rigid, societal expectations. The point is made abundantly clear in *The Two Noble Kinsmen*, probably a collaborative play written with John Fletcher. Arcite says of his friend Palamon, with whom he is imprisoned: "We are one another's wife, ever begetting / New births of love" (2.1.139–40). This doesn't mean that Arcite is Shakespeare's favorite sodomite, nor is Emilia his favorite lesbian when she says: "the true love 'tween maid and maid may be / More than in sex dividual" (1.3.81–82). These are homoerotic comments, but they are not meant to be sexually definitive. The same is true of the innocent, schoolgirl attractions of Hermia and Helena in *A Midsummer Night's Dream* and Rosalind and Celia in *As You Like It*. Both of these pairs have no trouble at all in mustering up heterosexual attitudes when they are needed.

Chapter 8 sums up Shakespeare's riddling use of language in wordplay, puns, double entendres, and sexual innuendoes under the title, "Love and Lust: Sexual Wit." It is worth remembering that all love is sexual in Shakespeare—there is no ladder of love as in Ficino, where sexual attraction leads upward to spiritual enlightenment. Shakespeare is well aware of the doctrines of courtly love exploited by Petrarch and his followers, but, especially in the comedies, he is satirical about them rather than reverential. There is a great deal of bawdy in Shakespeare, as students are so delighted to discover, and not just in the bad puns and wordplay of clowns and servants. The language lesson in *Henry V*, which depends upon macaronic puns in French and English, is matched by the language lesson in *The Merry Wives of Windsor*. The paradoxes of sexuality are nowhere more vividly established than in Sonnet 129, whose couplet conclusion expresses Shakespeare's conflicted sense of the workings of love and lust:

> All this the world well knows, yet none knows well
> To shun the heaven that leads men to this hell.

CHAPTER ONE

FALLING IN

CONVENTIONS

Shakespeare follows the conventions for falling in love that derive from Petrarch's love poems to Laura collected in the *Canzoniere*, first published in Venice in 1470. These conventions were highly developed after Petrarch by both Italian and English writers of love poetry, especially sonnets.[1] Shakespeare is both a follower and a satirist of them. He draws on traditional Petrarchan postures and attitudes at the same time as he laughs at them, so that love in Shakespeare becomes complex and often contradictory.[2]

Let us begin with the convention of love at first sight.[3] Love enters through the eyes and it is spontaneous, irresistible, and absolute. Tilley lists as proverbial, with many references, "LOVE comes by looking (in at the eyes)" (L501). These assumptions are mockingly explored in *A Midsummer Night's Dream*. Love in the play is not a highly developed psychological force, but can be induced chemically by the distilled love-juice of the pansy, which makes a wonderfully efficacious aphrodisiac. Oberon, the King of the Fairies, invents an elaborate mythological origin for this potent drug. Cupid, the God of Love, loosed an arrow from his bow aimed at "a fair vestal thronèd by the west" (2.1.158), but it missed its mark and fell upon

> a little western flower,
> Before milk-white, now purple with love's wound,
> And maidens call it love-in-idleness. (166–68)

"Love-in-idleness" is the pansy, and the whole passage is perhaps a gracious compliment to Elizabeth, the Virgin Queen.[4] The juice of the pansy

> on sleeping eyelids laid
> Will make or man or woman madly dote
> Upon the next live creature that it sees. (170–72)

"Dote"[5] is the key word because it indicates love in the extreme, excessive fondness, which is produced immediately in the recipient. There is no progression or development.

Oberon is taking revenge on his wife, Titania, for denying him the Indian boy. There is a certain animus in Oberon as he squeezes the flower on Titania's eyelids and hopes to create a frightening and bestial illusion:

> What thou seest when thou dost wake,
> Do it for thy truelove take;
> Love and languish for his sake.
> Be it ounce [=lynx], or cat, or bear,
> Pard [=leopard], or boar with bristled hair,
> In thy eye that shall appear
> When thou wak'st, it is thy dear.
> Wake when some vile thing is near. (2.2.27–34)

The fairyworld in *A Midsummer Night's Dream* is not so gentle and pastoral as it is usually represented when the play is produced; it has a coarse, animal, amoral, and grotesque side.[6] The Fairies do not participate in the ethical delicacies and punctilioes of the human characters. This colors the representation of love in the play. Love is an irrational force, usually shown in the extreme, and we can see why the Duke at the end puts

"The lunatic, the lover, and the poet" together as "of imagination all compact" (5.1.7–8).

When Titania awakens from her sleep she immediately falls in love with Bottom, the Weaver, who wears an ass's head and is otherwise converted into an ass in form and behavior. Titania is already fully in love as she utters her first line: "What angel wakes me from my flow'ry bed?" (3.1.130). There is no development of her passion. From the beginning she is lost in ecstatic love rhetoric: "And thy fair virtue's force perforce doth move me / On the first view to say, to swear, I love thee" (141–42). Even Bottom is surprised: "And yet, to say the truth, reason and love keep little company together nowadays" (144–45). Titania takes her sudden infatuation even further in her desire to improve and purify Bottom: "And I will purge thy mortal grossness so, / That thou shalt like an airy spirit go" (161–62). The humor of the scene comes from Bottom's sweet imperturbability; not being anointed with the love-in-idleness flower, he can only wonder, with polite acceptance of her ministrations, at Titania's passion. Her last line before they sleep is "How I dote on thee!" (4.1.48). Oberon pities "Her dotage" (50) and vows to "undo / This hateful imperfection of her eyes" (65–66). Afterward, Titania wonders "What visions have I seen! / Methought I was enamored of an ass" (79–80).

This episode represents love at first sight as an irresistible physical experience. It has nothing to do with credible motivation, but deals in phantasms and illusions. The love is magically induced with a drug. The erotic experience of Titania and Bottom is duplicated in Lysander and Helena. The mischievous Puck seeks an Athenian "On whose eyes I might approve / This flower's force in stirring love" (2.2.68–69). Puck speaks of the love juice as a "charm," a word specifically associated with magic, and he anoints Lysander's eyes with the invocation: "When thou wak'st, let love forbid / Sleep his seat on thy eyelid" (80–81). Of course, the waking Lysander responds exactly as predicted with excessive passion for the poor and confused Helena: "And run through fire I will for thy sweet sake. / Transparent Helena!" (103–4). His former love for Hermia is now completely displaced: "Not Hermia but Helena I love: / Who will not change a raven for a dove?" (113–14). One of the effects of the love at first sight convention in this play is that the expressions of love become completely rhetorical. It is an amusing exercise in comic excess.

When the "error" (3.2.368) is finally corrected—"error" in this context means something like "illusion," or wandering of the mind, as in *The Comedy of Errors*—Lysander will once again be able to see correctly: "When they next wake, all this derision [=delusion] / Shall seem a dream and fruitless vision" (370–71). *A Midsummer Night's Dream* is partly a set of dream visions about love, which enters through the eyes and has an overpowering force. The lovers respond as if in a dream, and the crossing of the fairy world and the human world has interesting consequences. Titania is made to dote on Bottom as an ass, but Bottom doesn't exactly dote on Titania; in fact, he feels exceedingly cozy and comfortable in his animal role. Lysander dotes on Helena, but his love is so excessive that it is unconvincing to Helena, who continues to dote on Demetrius. As Lysander says in the first scene of the play:

> she, sweet lady, dotes,
> Devoutly dotes, dotes in idolatry,
> Upon this spotted and inconstant man. (1.1.109–11)

There is no moderation in love because it is not a reasonable passion. You either love too much or not at all.

The love at first sight convention operates throughout Shakespeare, though not always with the chemical, aphrodisiac force of *A Midsummer Night's Dream*. *As You Like It* shows us Rosalind falling in love instantaneously with Orlando as wrestler. She begins with fear for Orlando, unequally matched against the professional wrestler Charles, but when he wins she gives him a love token, presumably a chain: "Gentleman, / Wear this for me" (1.2.235–36). The fact that Orlando is a total stranger does not impede—in fact it encourages—the swiftness of love at first sight. Rosalind acknowledges her love at once: "Sir, you have wrestled well, and overthrown / More than your enemies" (244–45). After she leaves with Celia, Orlando echoes her words:

> What passion hangs these weights upon my tongue?
> I cannot speak to her, yet she urged conference.
> O poor Orlando, thou art overthrown!
> Or Charles or something weaker masters thee. (247–50)

Orlando's sudden "passion," or strong feeling, makes him tongue-tied, but he later proves extremely voluble as he fills the Forest of Arden with his mediocre poetry.

The love at first sight convention is mocked by Rosalind at the end of the play, when the plot complications are wound up with such remarkable celerity. Orlando's older brother Oliver is suddenly in love with Celia, Rosalind's childhood friend whom she calls sister. Rosalind mocks the very love conventions under which she operates:

There was never anything so sudden but the fight of two rams and Caesar's thrasonical brag of "I came, saw, and overcame"; for your brother and my sister no sooner met but they looked; no sooner looked but they loved; no sooner loved but they sighed; no sooner sighed but they asked one another the reason; no sooner knew the reason but they sought the remedy; and in these degrees have they made a pair of stairs to marriage, which they will climb incontinent, or else be incontinent before marriage: they are in the very wrath of love, and they will together; clubs cannot part them.

(5.2.29–40)

Notice how love begins by looking—through the eyes—and that it is always sexual. Celia and Oliver, in "the very wrath of love," can only be satisfied by immediate marriage and sexual consummation.

The love at first sight doctrine is more complex in *Twelfth Night*. Since people may fall in love against their better judgment, the power of love seems to be irresistible and outside of human agency. Olivia listens to Viola (disguised as Cesario) speaking Duke Orsino's love embassy: he loves "With adorations, with fertile tears, / With groans that thunder love, with sighs of fire" (1.5. 255–56). These are the tired, conventional aspects of the Petrarchan lover, of no interest to Olivia—and all of Duke Orsino's part as a lover seems right on the edge of parody. But the saucy, impertinent youth, Cesario, appeals without any conscious effort on his/her part to Olivia, although she tries valiantly to resist him. Her questions to herself are full of self-reproach: "Even so quickly may one catch the plague?" (296). She is drawn magnetically into the snares of love against her own conscious regard of what is good for her:

> Methinks I feel this youth's perfections
> With an invisible and subtle stealth
> To creep in at mine eyes. Well, let it be. (297–99)

"Well, let it be" shows resignation on Olivia's part, and she decides to send a ring as a love token to the departed Cesario. The ill-advised choice of messenger is Malvolio.

Olivia's final speech, in couplets, indicates that she has given herself up to what fate has in store for her. She is no longer capable of resisting love:

> I do I know not what, and fear to find
> Mine eye too great a flatterer for my mind.

> Fate, show thy force; ourselves we do not owe.
> What is decreed must be—and be this so! (309–12)

The eye, through which love enters, influences the mind, and Olivia feels that she is no longer master of herself—ourselves we do not "owe," or own. A delicious passivity carries her on an erotic wave. Of course, Olivia is mistaken about Cesario's gender, as Viola quickly surmises, with clear indications of how act 1, scene 5 is to be played by Olivia:

> She made good view of me; indeed, so much
> That sure methought her eyes had lost her tongue,
> For she did speak in starts distractedly. (2.2.19–21)

In the typical fashion of Shakespeare's comedies, Viola washes her hands of the difficulty: "O Time, thou must untangle this, not I; / It is too hard a knot for me t' untie" (40–41). The dilemma is solved by Viola's having a twin brother, Sebastian, who is suddenly dragooned into marrying Olivia.[7]

We may take a final, striking example of the love at first sight convention from an early play, *Henry VI, Part I*. As soon as Suffolk makes Margaret, daughter of Reignier, his prisoner, the stage direction reads: "*Gazes on her*" (5.3.45 s.d.). Suffolk is smitten at once by her irresistible beauty. Since he is married, he plots to offer Margaret as Queen to King Henry VI but to keep her as his paramour. In his asides, Suffolk confesses to his immediate and total infatuation:

> As plays the sun upon the glassy streams,
> Twinkling another counterfeited beam,
> So seems this gorgeous beauty to mine eyes. (62–64)

The eyes, like "the glassy streams," are a mirror to reflect back Margaret's "gorgeous beauty." A woman's beauty and the magnetic and involuntary attraction through the eyes are fairly traditional inducements to fall in love. Also traditional is Suffolk's conception of woman:

> She's beautiful and therefore to be wooed;
> She is a woman, therefore to be won. (78–79)

This is practically quoted verbatim from Demetrius's speech in *Titus Andronicus* just before he rapes Lavinia:

> She is a woman, therefore may be wooed;
> She is a woman, therefore may be won. . . . (2.1.82–83)

(Or perhaps Demetrius is quoting Suffolk.) When Suffolk kisses Margaret at the end of the scene, she says significantly: "That for thyself; I will not so presume / To send such peevish tokens to a king" (5.3.185–86).

Eyes are at the center of the love discourse in Shakespeare, and there are abundant references scattered everywhere in his works. In *The Merry Wives of Windsor*, for example, Falstaff justifies his love letter to Mistress Page by the fact that she has given him the eye:

> Page's wife, who even now gave me good eyes too, examined my parts with most judicious oeillades. Sometimes the beam of her view gilded my foot, sometimes my portly belly. (1.3.57–61)

In Falstaff's affected, gallicized speech, "oeillades" is a new-minted word for amorous and flirtatious glances or ogles. The discourse is similarly poeticized in Mrs. Page's eyebeam gilding, or turning to gold, his foot and portly belly, as if her gaze operated as a kind of Midas touch. In *King Lear*, Regan is bitterly aware that her sister Goneril is her rival for the love of Edmund:

> at her late being here
> She gave strange eliads and most speaking looks
> To noble Edmund. (4.5.24–26)

Goneril's "eliads" suggest that she is trying to ensnare Edmund with her eyebeams. In Renaissance thinking the eye was imagined to issue a powerful thread tying lovers to each other, as in Donne's poem, "The Extasie," written around the same time as the plays quoted here. Donne literalizes the meaning of "oeillades" or "eliads":

> Our eye-beames twisted, and did thred
> Our eyes, upon one double string. . . .[8]

The eyes are fetishized throughout Shakespeare as an object of amorous attention. In *Measure for Measure*, for example, Angelo's horrifying new awareness of his own sensuality centers on Isabella's speech and her eyes:

> What, do I love her,
> That I desire to hear her speak again,
> And feast upon her eyes? What is't I dream on? (2.2.176–78)

There is an Elizabethan expression, "to look babies" (under the verb "look" in sense 6a in the *OED*), which refers to an intense gaze of lovers in which they see their reflections in each other's eyes. This seems to be what Angelo is referring to in "feast upon her eyes." He is caught in his own excessive virtue: "O cunning enemy, that, to catch a saint, / With saints dost bait thy hook!" (179–80).

The most magnificent speech on the amorous powers of eyes is Berowne's long discourse in *Love's Labor's Lost*[9] after all four of the sworn members of the Academy of Navarre have unwittingly revealed that they are in love. In Berowne's 75-line oration, eyes are mentioned eight times (although some of the later speech seems to be a revision of the earlier part). Eyes have an educational function:

> For where is any author in the world
> Teaches such beauty as a woman's eyes? (4.3.311–12)

With the same meaning as in "looking babies," Berowne declares: "ourselves we see in ladies' eyes" (315), and love is "first learnèd in a lady's eyes" (326). Love "adds a precious seeing to the eye" (332) and "A lover's eyes will gaze an eagle blind" (333).

All of this ocular ideology is summed up toward the end of the speech, when Berowne reverses the barren and sterile premises of the Academy of Navarre, especially the injunction against seeing women:

> From women's eyes this doctrine I derive.
> They sparkle still the right Promethean fire;
> They are the books, the arts, the academes,
> That show, contain, and nourish all the world;
> Else none at all in aught proves excellent. (349–53)

The "right Promethean fire" is the creative impulse, poetic inspiration, which is what seems to be meant in the concluding couplet of Sonnet 23:

> O, learn to read what silent love hath writ.
> To hear with eyes belongs to love's fine wit.

So reading the author's "books be then the eloquence," and the eye of the reader is equated with the eye of the lover.

The love doctrine of eyes culminates in *The Merchant of Venice*. Portia is eager to give Bassanio broad hints for his choice of the right casket without violating her father's lottery for her marriage choice: "If you do love me, you will find me out" (3.2.41). But in the song that follows her speech, "Tell me where is fancy bred" (63), "bred" and "head" hint to Bassanio—they also rhyme with "lead." This song about the generation of "fancy," or love, clearly states that

> It is engend'red in the eyes,
> With gazing fed, and fancy dies
> In the cradle where it lies. (67–69)

When Bassanio finds Portia's painted portrait (or "counterfeit") in the leaden casket, the first item of physical attraction he comments on is the pair of remarkably lifelike eyes:

> Move these eyes?
> Or whether, riding on the balls of mine,
> Seem they in motion? (116–18)

The poetic conceit is filled out by the fancy that the painter must have been so dazzled by the beauty of the first eye that he was struck blind:

> Having made one,
> Methinks it should have power to steal both his
> And leave itself unfurnished. (124–26)

By contrast, in the Statue Scene (5.3) of *The Winter's Tale*, a much later play than *The Merchant of Venice*, Leontes feels a vivid sense of breath and body warmth coming from the statue of Hermione. He mentions eyes only in a single, familiar image: "The fixure of her eyes has motion in't, / As we are mocked with art" (67–68). This is Shakespeare's most often repeated criterion of excellence in painting and sculpture: that it imitates reality so successfully, is so lifelike in its sense of "motion" or movement that it "mocks" nature in executing an almost perfect mimesis.

The efficient cause of falling in love is women's beauty. The reverse proposition is also true, but male beauty is not developed as a specific theme in Shakespeare, except for Adonis in *Venus and Adonis* and the male figure to whom the *Sonnets* are addressed. Women seem to fall in love with maleness as a generalized property, rather than with specifically physical male traits. A good place to begin this discussion is with *The Rape of Lucrece*, since everything is so fixed and overdefined in this early poem. Tarquin the rapist is subdued against his better judgment by the spotless beauty and chastity of Lucrece, as Angelo is by the novice Isabella in *Measure for Measure*.

Lucrece's beauty is conventionally described in terms of Renaissance assumptions. In the second stanza of the poem, Collatine's praise of his wife is already enflaming Tarquin, a situation that clearly anticipates Posthumus and Iachimo in *Cymbeline*:

> Collatine unwisely did not let [=forbear]
> To praise the clear unmatched red and white
> Which triumphed in that sky of his delight. . . .   (10–12)

The war between red and white as an axiom of female beauty—the red lips and cheeks set against the white skin—is the most generalized stipulation, and has its roots in medieval thinking.[10] The poet rebukes Collatine for being "the publisher / Of that rich jewel he should keep unknown / From thievish ears" (33–35) because "Beauty itself doth of itself persuade / The eyes of men without an orator" (29–30). From a modern perspective, it is alarming in the poem how much Lucrece is considered a material possession or chattel of her husband, with specific aesthetic (and therefore valuable) characteristics.

The Rape of Lucrece uses lavish personification, which has the general effect of distancing its human subjects and making abstract the psychological issues. "This heraldry in Lucrece' face was seen, / Argued by Beauty's red and Virtue's white" (64–65). Tarquin is represented statically as a gazer or voyeur of "This silent war of lilies and of roses, / Which Tarquin viewed in her fair face's field" (71–72). The emphasis here is on his "still-gazing eyes" (84); Tarquin is convinced that Collatine's praise of Lucrece's beauty is inadequate. Like all of Shakespeare's lovers, Tarquin is "doting" (155), and the conclusion of the rather mechanical probing of his conscience is: "All orators are dumb when beauty pleadeth" (268).

Lucrece in her bed is described with the traditional attributes of an art object. The poem moves at a maddeningly slow pace as each item of female beauty is catalogued: "Her lily hand her rosy cheek lies under, / Coz'ning the pillow of a lawful kiss" (386–87). Notice how consistently the classic color scheme is maintained:

> Without the bed her other fair hand was,
> On the green coverlet; whose perfect white
> Showed like an April daisy on the grass,
> With pearly sweat resembling dew of night.   (393–96)

The descriptive rhetoric bears no relation to the exciting psychological scene, unless it is meant to build up an unbearable suspense. The poetic effects are ingeniously far-fetched, what the Elizabethans would call "conceits."[11] The "pearly sweat" of Lucrece's other hand seems almost comic in its mixed metaphor, like the frankly comic Venus of *Venus and Adonis*: "By this the lovesick queen began to sweat" (175). Similarly, Lucrece's eyes are imagined as marigolds, which "sheathed their light" (397) because they close at the advent of darkness.

In the scene of Lucrece's rape, great emphasis is placed on her breasts:

> like ivory globes circled with blue,
> A pair of maiden worlds unconquerèd,
> Save of their lord no bearing yoke they knew. . . .   (407–9)

The breasts are represented conventionally in the art terms of "ivory globes circled with blue," but they seem to belong to their lord Collatine rather than to Lucrece. Later, when Tarquin in a military maneuver puts his hand on her "bare breast," the "ranks of blue veins, as his hand did scale, / Left their round turrets destitute and pale" (440–41). Lucrece is a fortress under attack, and her beauty is specifically represented in a set of physical attributes that can be conquered: "Her azure veins, her alabaster skin, / Her coral lips, her snow-white dimpled chin" (419–20). Like Hamlet's description of the "rugged Pyrrhus," whose sword "seemed i' th' air to stick" (*Hamlet* 2.2.490), so Tarquin the voyeur delays any action, "His rage of lust by gazing qualified; / Slacked, not suppressed" (424–25). In the stanzas that follow Tarquin offers an elaborate but unconvincing (and simplified) explanation of how Lucrece's beauty has ensnared his will.

It's surprising how close the scene with Iachimo in Imogen's bed-chamber in *Cymbeline* is to *The Rape of Lucrece*. Collatine's boasting about Lucrece is matched by Posthumus's wager on Imogen, which we are sure he is bound to lose, if only by the tradition of the love wager as a folklore motif. When Iachimo the voyeur leaves the trunk in Imogen's bedchamber, he is astounded by her beauty. He specifically mentions Tarquin as his exemplar:

> Our Tarquin thus
> Did softly press the rushes ere he wakened
> The chastity he wounded.   (*Cymbeline* 2.2.12–14)

Again, Iachimo speaks in the familiar erotic vocabulary of the red and the white: "How bravely thou becom'st thy bed, fresh lily, / And whiter than the sheets!" (15–16). The thought of a kiss immediately conjures up the color red: "Rubies unparagoned, / How dearly they do't!" (17–18). The strong olfactory image in lily echoes the final scene of *Othello*: " 'Tis her breathing that / Perfumes the chamber thus" (18–19).

Iachimo's description of Imogen's beauty is much more successfully rendered than Tarquin's long-winded but highly conventional account of Lucrece. Iachimo uses sharply physical details:

> The flame o' th' taper
> Bows toward her and would underpeep her lids
> To see th' enclosèd lights, now canopied
> Under these windows, white and azure-laced
> With blue of heaven's own tinct. (2.2.19–23)

But the detail about Imogen's breast is the most memorable item in Iachimo's catalogue:

> On her left breast
> A mole cinque-spotted, like the crimson drops
> I' th' bottom of a cowslip. (37–39)

A five-spotted mole—recalling the "sink-a-pace" ("cinquepase") in *Twelfth Night* (1.3.126–27), a galliard of five steps—is a much more vivid touch than the "ivory globes circled with blue" in *Lucrece*. Iachimo centers on that mole in his inflamed account to Posthumus:

> under her breast—
> Worthy the pressing—lies a mole, right proud
> Of that most delicate lodging. By my life,
> I kissed it, and it gave me present hunger
> To feed again, though full! (2.4.134–38)

Like all good voyeurs, Iachimo is exciting himself by his own fantasy of erotic participation.

The scene of Iachimo in Imogen's bedchamber is so much modeled on *Othello* (as are many other details in *Cymbeline*) that it is worth looking at the parallel scene in which Othello is about to murder Desdemona. For the last time in the play, we see him as he was early in the action—in a kind of religious awe at his wife's beauty. Othello uses some of the same images of white and red for Desdemona's beauty that Tarquin used for Lucrece and that Iachimo will later use for Imogen. Othello hesitates naming his "cause" to the "chaste stars" (5.2.2). He comes to kill his wife, but right at the beginning he vows:

> Yet I'll not shed her blood,
> Nor scar that whiter skin of hers than snow.
> And smooth as monumental alabaster. (3–5)

Remember that Tarquin just before the rape is speaking of Lucrece's "azure veins, her alabaster skin" (419). Later Othello thinks of Desdemona in the image of the rose, which he smells on the tree by kissing her (5.2.15). Her "balmy breath" (16) is like Imogen's "breathing that / Perfumes the chamber" (18–19). The paradox in this scene is succinctly formulated by Desdemona: "That death's unnatural that kills for loving" (5.2.42). Othello tragically invokes Desdemona's beauty in order to maintain his guise as priestly sacrificer rather than murderer. He cannot successfully mediate between the roles of lover and revenger.

In *A Midsummer Night's Dream*, when Demetrius awakes after being anointed with the love juice, he launches immediately into accepted commonplaces about Helena's beauty:

> O, how ripe in show
> Thy lips, those kissing cherries, tempting grow!
> That pure congealèd white, high Taurus snow,
> Fanned with the eastern wind, turns to a crow
> When thou hold'st up thy hand: O, let me kiss
> This princess of pure white, this seal of bliss! (3.2.139–44)

Helena is skeptical of this "superpraise" of her parts (153); it is excessive and too conventional to be convincing. When Olivia in *Twelfth Night* removes her veil and shows her face, Viola as Cesario, the Duke's messenger, is similarly skeptical: "Excellently done, if God did all" (1.5.236), but once Olivia assures him/her that "'Tis in grain" (237), that is, that it is natural (or fast-dyed in grain), Viola then delivers her perfunctory conclusion: "'Tis beauty truly blent, whose red and white / Nature's own sweet and cunning hand laid on" (240–41). She doesn't mean to offer excessive praise of Olivia's beauty.

The red and the white are openly satirized in *Love's Labor's Lost* by

Moth, the diminutive page of Don Armado, when his master says, "My love is most immaculate white and red" (1.2.90). Actually, Don Armado, the fantastical Spaniard, is in love with Jaquenetta, a simple country wench. The ingenious Moth has a ballad ready for the occasion:

> If she be made of white and red,
> Her faults will ne'er be known,
> For blushing cheeks by faults are bred,
> And fears by pale white shown. (98–101)

Later in the play, Berowne praises his mistress Rosaline's blackness, with ironic exaggeration: "Is ebony like her? O wood divine!" (4.3.247) and "No face is fair that is not full so black" (252). Berowne is brazening it out, praising her unconventional beauty. Nowhere is this paradox about woman's beauty more openly satirized than in Sonnet 130, "My mistress' eyes are nothing like the sun." She doesn't measure up to the color criteria: "Coral is far more red than her lips' red; / If snow be white, why then her breasts are dun." Her cheeks cannot be compared with conventional roses: "I have seen roses damasked, red and white, / But no such roses see I in her cheeks." Despite all of these seeming faults, "I think my love as rare / As any she belied with false compare." Shakespeare is amusing himself by reversing the traditional Petrarchan conceits of his fellow Elizabethan sonneteers.

Another set of conventional images applies to love melancholy,[12] which is either one of the signs of falling in love or a symptom of a love that has been repelled or rejected. In the love game it was assumed, as in the school of courtly love,[13] that a mistress should resist the amorous advances of her lover in order to build up the intensity of his passion. This has nothing to do with love at first sight—it is only a caution against yielding too quickly to strong and irresistible feelings. Love melancholy is the subject par excellence of Robert Burton's masterpiece, *The Anatomy of Melancholy* (1625), but Burton is only gathering materials from much earlier authors, most of whom figure importantly in the Petrarchan tradition. Shakespeare generally makes fun of the traditional signs of love melancholy, especially in male lovers. He is sympathetic, but also amused. The most obvious example is Romeo in *Romeo and Juliet*, who has a torrid and unfortunate liaison with Rosaline before he meets Juliet. The point of this affair is that it is excessive, almost caricatural, and it indicates that Romeo must be a very adolescent young man to have such self-conscious and histrionic sorrows.

In the first scene of the play, Romeo has been out all night, shuns the company of his friends, and is otherwise melancholy. His father has observed him "With tears augmenting the fresh morning's dew, / Adding to clouds more clouds with his deep sighs" (135–36). When day breaks, the "heavy" (140), or melancholy, Romeo

> in his chamber pens himself,
> Shuts up his windows, locks fair daylight out,
> And makes himself an artificial night. (141–43)

At this point in the action, he speaks in a precious, affected style, which seems like mere posturing. His couplets indicate a heightened artificiality:

> Alas that love, whose view is muffled still,
> Should without eyes see pathways to his will! (174–75)

He indulges in oxymorons to define the nature of love rather than informing his friend Benvolio about his authentic feelings:

> Love is a smoke made with the fume of sighs;
> Being purged, a fire sparkling in lovers' eyes;
> Being vexed, a sea nourished with loving tears.
> What is it else? A madness most discreet,
> A choking gall, and a preserving sweet. (193–97)

The answer to all these vexed definitions of love is Benvolio's succinct and practical advice: "Examine other beauties" (231).

Hamlet too is a melancholy lover, and from the description Ophelia gives of his visit to her "closet," or withdrawing room, Polonius is not wrong to conclude: "This is the very ecstasy [=madness] of love" (2.1.102). Ophelia tells her father about a vivid scene we never see on stage, in which Hamlet burst in upon her while she "was sewing" (77). Hamlet has all the conventional signs of the melancholy lover:

> Lord Hamlet, with his doublet all unbraced [=unlaced],
> No hat upon his head, his stockings fouled,
> Ungartered, and down-gyvèd to his ankle,
> Pale as his shirt, his knees knocking each other,
> And with a look so piteous in purport,

As if he had been loosèd out of hell
To speak of horrors—he comes before me.   (78–84)

Ophelia has no way of knowing about the visit of the Ghost in act 1, scene 5, so there are no other explanations except that Hamlet is "Mad for thy love" (85), as her father says. In addition, Hamlet

raised a sigh so piteous and profound
As it did seem to shatter all his bulk
And end his being.   (94–96)

Why does Shakespeare throw us off by making Hamlet appear the typical melancholy lover? Or *does* he indeed throw us off? There is deliberate ambiguity in this scene.

In the earlier comedies, Shakespeare catalogues the typical signs of love melancholy. No speech is more explicit than that of Speed, Valentine's servant in *The Two Gentlemen of Verona*. In answer to his master's question, "Why, how know you that I am in love?", Speed proceeds to give an overly complete answer:

Marry, by these special marks: first, you have learned, like Sir Proteus, to wreathe your arms, like a malcontent; to relish a love song, like a robin redbreast; to walk alone, like one that had the pestilence; to sigh, like a schoolboy that had lost his A B C; to weep, like a young wench that had buried her grandam; to fast, like one that takes diet; to watch [=lie awake], like one that fears robbing; to speak puling, like a beggar at Hallowmas.   (2.1.17–25)

Most of these indications also apply to Romeo when he first appears in the play.

Speed's signs of melancholy are parodied in *Love's Labor's Lost* by Moth's specifications of how his master, Don Armado, can win his love, Jaquenetta, with a "French brawl," or dance:

jig off a tune at the tongue's end, canary to it with your feet, humor it with turning up your eyelids, sigh a note and sing a note, sometime through the throat as if you swallowed love with singing love, sometime through the nose as if you snuffed up love by smelling love, with your hat penthouse-like o'er the shop of your eyes, with your arms crossed on your thin-belly doublet like a rabbit on a spit, or your hands in your pocket like a man after the old painting; and keep not too long in one tune, but a snip and away. (3.1.11–22)

The same physical posturing keeps reappearing for the melancholy lover and also for the malcontent, a familiar type in late sixteenth- and early seventeenth-century literature.

Rosalind in *As You Like It* pokes fun at these somber and grotesque characteristics of the lover as she twits Orlando on his disappointingly healthy appearance. Her supposedly wise uncle taught her how to know the marks of a man in love:

> A lean cheek, which you have not; a blue eye and sunken, which you have not; an unquestionable spirit, which you have not; a beard neglected, which you have not. . . . Then your hose should be ungartered, your bonnet unbanded, your sleeve unbuttoned, your shoe untied, and everything about you demonstrating a care-less desolation. (3.2.366–74)

This catalog neatly describes Hamlet's "careless desolation" when he appears to Ophelia in her closet.

The condition of falling in love was overdetermined for Shakespeare and his contemporaries; its characteristics and certain signs were well established in the audience's mind. That's why falling in love lent itself so easily to satire and parody. Shakespeare is generally sympathetic to lovers, but he is also sensitive to their posturing and attitudinizing. Love rhetoric has a certain inherently comic cast, even in the tragedies, and Shakespeare has to work hard to make love fully believable and tragic, as in *Othello*. Love is irrational and excessive almost by definition, and that is why the lunatic, the lover, and the poet are equated by Duke Theseus in *A Midsummer Night's Dream*:

> Lovers and madmen have such seething brains,
> Such shaping fantasies, that apprehend
> More than cool reason ever comprehends. (5.1.4–6)

But as Hippolyta, Theseus's wife, objects, "the story of the night told over" produces a different conclusion and bears a different witness "than fancy's images." What she envisions is quite far from her husband's fears. All the irrational doings of the night grow "to something of great constancy; / But, howsoever, strange and admirable" (26–27); this "constancy," or consistency, is at an opposite pole from "fancy's images."

DOCTRINE IN THE COMEDIES

Shakespeare's plays are full of doctrinal statements about the nature of love and how it operates. The comedies tend to be optimistic about love, which generally leads to marriage and the promise of children. Comedy imposes generic requirements on love in these plays, which move inevitably to happy endings.[1] "Happy" has the Elizabethan connotation of "fortunate," a product of happenstance or good luck. The characters produce the happy ending naturally out of their good faith and credibility, so that true love is always fulfilled despite all of the blocking complications. The denouement needs plenty of knots in order to make the untying of the resolution not just satisfying and appropriate, but also astonishing and marvelous. There is a certain plot magic that answers the needs of the comic resolution.

Love lends itself particularly well to comedy because the happy ending of marriage is more or less envisaged from the start. Perturbations and difficulties are introduced to illustrate the principle that "The course of true love never did run smooth" (*A Midsummer Night's Dream* 1.1.135). The plot of a love comedy is essentially built on the overcoming of difficulties, so the marriage at the end is a triumph of wit, perseverance, and devotion. But this happy ending is prepared from the very beginning of the play. The outcomes of the tragedies are similarly foreshadowed; there can be no significant disturbance in nature like that announced in the first scene with the Witches in *Macbeth*. The problem of a comedy tends to be some outrageous and capricious edict, law, or belief that seems at the beginning to be totally unresolvable and arbitrary but is easily resolved at the end by some ingenious, mechanical means. All the knots that are tied in the plot at the beginning are untied at the end in the comic denouement, so that the play can end with the revelry of the marriage feast, with its accompanying drinking, dancing, singing, and lyrical assertions, especially about sex and future offspring.

Let us begin with *A Midsummer Night's Dream*, which is programmatic about love and its requirements. In the first scene, Egeus, the father of Hermia (like Brabantio in *Othello*), rejects his daughter's lover, Lysander, and claims that he has bewitched her:

> thou hast given her rhymes,
> And interchanged love tokens with my child.
> Thou hast by moonlight at her window sung,
> With feigning voice, verses of feigning love,
> And stol'n the impression of her fantasy
> With bracelets of thy hair, rings, gauds, conceits,
> Knacks, trifles, nosegays, sweetmeats, messengers
> Of strong prevailment in unhardened youth.
> With cunning hast thou filched my daughter's heart. . . .   (1.1.28–36)

This is an alarmingly specific catalogue of how to woo a young woman and win her love, but, putting aside hair bracelets, rings, gauds, conceits, knacks, trifles, nosegays, and sweetmeats, the basic persuasion is in the fact that Lysander has "stol'n the impression of her fantasy." In other words, he has won her fancy or imagination, which lies at the heart of all love. Egeus is an acute observer and what he describes is hardly bewitchment in the technical, legal sense. There is no mention of any magical charm. In *Othello* the "heavy" father Brabantio doesn't speak at all of love tokens, but of "chains of magic" (1.2.64), "foul charms" (72), "drugs or minerals" (73), and "spells and medicines bought of mountebanks" (61).

A Midsummer Night's Dream begins with dire pronouncements that we are sure can never be fulfilled. Egeus asserts his fatherly prerogatives: Hermia shall either marry Demetrius or be put to death. Out of kindness, Duke Theseus modifies this decree so that if Hermia doesn't marry according to her father's wishes, she must "endure the livery of a nun" (1.1.70). The choice is stacked, as the Duke himself enunciates it:

> But earthlier happy is the rose distilled [i.e., made into perfume],
> Than that which, withering on the virgin thorn,
> Grows, lives, and dies in single blessedness. (76–78)

The Duke doesn't see becoming a nun as much more advantageous than being put to death, so that the plot is laid for Hermia and Lysander to flee Athens to Lysander's widow aunt to get married.

None of the protests of Lysander and Hermia are effective at this point, even the fact that Demetrius made love to Helena,

> And won her soul; and she, sweet lady, dotes,
> Devoutly dotes, dotes in idolatry,
> Upon this spotted and inconstant man. (1.1.108–10)

Love is established right at the beginning as something wildly excessive. "Devoutly dotes, dotes in idolatry" applies to all of the lovers in the play except, perhaps, the mythological figures, Theseus and Hippolyta, although Titania, the Queen of the Fairies, dotes more than anyone on her beloved Bottom, transformed into an ass.

The restrictive pronouncements are the basis for Lysander's truism about the nature of love:

> Ay me! For aught that I could ever read,
> Could ever hear by tale or history,
> The course of true love never did run smooth. . . . (132–34)

This statement is the basis for love as a generator of plot in the comedies. The meanderings and turnings of true love as a river are necessary; if love ran smooth, there would be no play. The assumption is that the perturbations [2] of love are a prelude to the triumph of love in the end; they provide a kind of education in adversity. Presumably, the adventures of the lovers in the wood offer the kind of experience that will benefit their marriages. *A Midsummer Night's Dream*, like *As You Like It*, is a play that moves irresistibly to the celebration of weddings at the end. The wedding of Theseus and Hippolyta announced at the beginning draws with it the marriages of true love—Hermia and Lysander, Helena and Demetrius—which should have taken place at once when the play opened, but were necessarily postponed because "true love never did run smooth."

Lysander and Hermia cite specific examples of the ways in which love can be crossed: "Too high to be enthralled to low" (136), "Too old to be engaged to young" (138), love that "stood upon the choice of friends" (139). All of the possibilities added together, with "War, death, or sickness" (142) thrown in, make love a dangerous enterprise and set up a large theme of the play (including love in the "Pyramus and Thisbe" play that the Mechanicals put on). Love is fragile and subject to unanticipated difficulties:

> momentany [=momentary] as a sound,
> Swift as a shadow, short as any dream,
> Brief as the lightning in the collied [=blackened] night,
> That, in a spleen, unfolds both heaven and earth,
> And ere a man hath power to say "Behold!"
> The jaws of darkness do devour it up:
> So quick bright things come to confusion.   (143–49)

"Confusion," meaning destruction and utter ruin, is a much stronger word in this context than in its current sense. Lysander's love paradigm sounds tragic, but it engages the midsummer night's dream idea in which "quick" (or lively) and bright things are rescued by love from "confusion." It is after Lysander's speech that the lovers resolve to flee Athens.

Helena's soliloquy at the end of this first scene expands on the love doctrine of Lysander's speeches. Since she dotes on Demetrius, as Demetrius dotes on Hermia, she believes that love is infinitely unpredictable and subject to the sudden transformations that are the subject of Ovid's *Metamorphoses*, one of Shakespeare's favorite authorities on the workings of love (along with Ovid's *Art of Love*): [3]

> Things base and vile, holding no quantity
> [i.e., disproportionate to how they are valued by Love],
> Love can transpose to form and dignity.
> Love looks not with the eyes, but with the mind,
> And therefore is winged Cupid painted blind.

Nor hath Love's mind of any judgment taste;
Wings, and no eyes, figure unheedy haste:
And therefore is Love said to be a child,
Because in choice he is so oft beguiled.
As waggish boys in game themselves forswear,
So the boy Love is perjured everywhere. (232–41)

This is an unflattering representation of love as the boy Cupid, capricious and undependable, blind and waggish, loving, like Puck, to play jokes with a malicious intent—an alternative version of Lysander's speech asserting that "The course of true love never did run smooth."

Love is a creature of slippery fancy, so the mind can create whatever images it wants to, even those that contradict the evidence of the senses, especially the eyes—Cupid is represented as blind. The speeches in the first scene prepare us for the operations of love in the rest of the play. It is, after all, a dream, a product of fancy and imagination rather than of reason, and therefore strange, unpredictable, and unreliable. Yet everything does work out well and the play ends happily.

A Midsummer Night's Dream has a typical love plot that may serve as a paradigm for Shakespeare's comedies. The play begins with the impending marriage of Theseus and Hippolyta in "Four happy days" (1.1.2). The Duke announces that he wooed Hippolyta with his sword

And won thy love, doing thee injuries;
But I will wed thee in another key,
With pomp, with triumph, and with reveling. (17–19)

We are already preparing for the happy ending.

There are five love affairs in the play, each of which stands in an analogical relation to the others: Hermia and Lysander, Helena and Demetrius, Theseus and Hippolyta, Oberon and Titania, and Pyramus and Thisbe in the Mechanicals' play. Oberon and Titania, the King and Queen of the Fairies, who are often doubled in performance with Theseus and Hippolyta,[4] have their own domestic quarrel over the Indian boy. When Oberon places the love juice from the pansy in Titania's eyes, she instantly becomes enamored of Bottom, the weaver, who is disguised as an ass. This parodies the other love affairs in the play because Bottom in his transformation is so equitable and good-humored: "methinks I am mervail's hairy about the face; and I am such a tender ass, if my hair do but tickle me, I must scratch" (4.1.26–29). The *Pyramus and Thisbe* play, "very tragical mirth" (5.1.57), also parodies the other love actions in both its antiquated rhetoric and its histrionic confusions.

The mischievous Puck (Robin Goodfellow) seems deliberately to confuse the recipients of the love juice and thus to increase the perturbations and mistakings of the play, which are like the "errors" or wanderings of the mind or illusions of *The Comedy of Errors*. Puck delights in the absurdities of mortals, especially lovers:

> Shall we their fond pageant see?
> Lord, what fools these mortals be! (3.2.114–15)

"Fond" makes a perfect pun for Puck, since it means both foolish and doting. This is his idea of "sport": "those things do best please me / That befall prepost'rously" (120–21). When he is ordered by Oberon to repair his errors, he gets an extra measure of sport. He squeezes the love juice in Lysander's eyes with a song about his nonhuman detachment from love:

> And the country proverb known,
> That every man should take his own,
> In your waking shall be shown.
> Jack shall have Jill;
> Nought shall go ill;
> The man shall have his mare again, and all shall be well. (458–63)

Surely Shakespeare remembers Puck in his creation of Prospero's airy spirit, Ariel, who confesses to his master that his "affections / Would become tender" "were I human" (*The Tempest* 5.1.18–20). Puck delights in imitating the god Cupid, who is "a knavish lad" (*A Midsummer Night's Dream* 3.2.440).

Shakespeare seems to anticipate (or remember?) Puck's doggerel poem at the end of *Love's Labor's Lost*, when Berowne complains about the bad turn that the love action has taken:

> Our wooing doth not end like an old play;
> Jack hath not Jill. These ladies' courtesy
> Might well have made our sport a comedy. (5.2.875–77)

The "ladies' courtesy" in agreeing to marriage at the end of the play would have made the gentlemen's sport of wooing end as a typical comedy, but instead the marriages are put off for a twelvemonth and a day. As

Berowne says, "That's too long for a play" (879), but the delay is a form of penance for the sexist and misogynistic lords. Rosaline lectures Berowne on his scornful jesting:

> You shall this twelvemonth term from day to day
> Visit the speechless sick, and still converse
> With groaning wretches; and your task shall be
> With all the fierce endeavor of your wit
> To enforce the painèd impotent to smile. (851–55)

Berowne protests: "To move wild laughter in the throat of death?" (856), but Rosaline has a perfect, didactic answer:

> A jest's prosperity lies in the ear
> Of him that hears it, never in the tongue
> Of him that makes it. Then, if sickly ears,
> Deafed with the clamors of their own dear groans,
> Will hear your idle scorns, continue then,
> And I will have you and that fault withal;
> But if they will not, throw away that spirit,
> And I shall find you empty of that fault,
> Right joyful of your reformation. (862–70)

This is a special, bittersweet, time-delayed happy ending, which includes the moral reformation of the lords.

Love's Labor's Lost is cleverly constructed as a gender confrontation, in which the dominant male values at the beginning of the play are undercut. Berowne is the first ensnared in love, but his protests as a sworn enemy of Cupid are amusingly futile:

> O, and I, forsooth, in love!
> I, that have been love's whip,
> A very beadle to a humorous sigh,
> A critic, nay, a night-watch constable,
> A domineering pedant o'er the boy,
> Than whom no mortal so magnificent!
> This wimpled, whining, purblind, wayward boy,
> This senior-junior, giant-dwarf, Dan Cupid. . . . (3.1.175–82)

Berowne is thrown into love against his own conscious will. The concluding couplet of his soliloquy is an appeal for the audience's sympathy, especially from the men:

Well, I will love, write, sigh, pray, sue, groan.
Some men must love my lady, and some Joan.   (206–7)

By act 4, scene 3, all four of the lords are hopelessly in love, and Berowne steps forth "to whip hypocrisy" (150).

Act 5, scene 2, the long final scene of the play, is devoted to a reeducation of the men and the imposing of penances. The Princess and her ladies are aware in advance that the lords will come to them in a masque disguised as Muscovites, and are prepared to confute their histrionic and amorous endeavors. As the Princess says:

There's no such sport as sport by sport o'erthrown,
To make theirs ours, and ours none but our own.
So shall we stay, mocking intended game,
And they, well mocked, depart away with shame.   (143–46)

The comic climax is wittily engendered by plots set against plots, by the women's artifice in subverting male bravado.

The year's delay in the marriages is already anticipated by the chastened Berowne's forswearing of rhetoric:

Taffeta phrases, silken terms precise,
Three-pile hyperboles, spruce affectation,
Figures pedantical—these summer flies
Have blown me full of maggot ostentation.   (407–10)

Berowne promises a different style of wooing:

Henceforth my wooing mind shall be expressed
In russet yeas and honest kersey noes.
And to begin, wench—so God help me, law!—
My love to thee is sound, sans crack or flaw.   (413–16)

Rosaline's retort is perhaps the wittiest line in the play: "Sans 'sans,' / I pray you" (417). Compare Polonius's exchange with the Queen in *Hamlet*, who protests against his rhetorical artifice: "More matter, with less art." Polonius answers in a form of self-parody: "Madam, I swear I use no art at all" (2.2.95–96). Shakespeare seems to be aware that the word "sans" is an affected gallicism, as in Jaques' ornamental speech on the seven ages of man, which ends in "second childishness and mere oblivion, / Sans teeth, sans eyes, sans taste, sans everything" (*As You Like It* 2.7.165–66).

As You Like It introduces a good deal of satire and parody, which mitigates the arbitrary and capricious turns of love. It is a very different play from *A Midsummer Night's Dream*, which seems more earnest in its pursuit of Fancy's images, except in the wonderful interludes of the Mechanicals, who are all Stratford men like Christopher Sly and his friends in the Induction of *The Taming of the Shrew*.[5] Both *As You Like It* and *A Midsummer Night's Dream* successfully use analogies between different social classes of lovers, but Touchstone the Clown is a more active participant in the love game than the passive Bottom, who doesn't care to assert himself with the voracious Titania (who, in her amorous transports, is a little like Venus in *Venus and Adonis*).

There is an element of farcical exaggeration in *As You Like It*, as if to balance the love affair of Rosalind and Orlando against the absurdities of Phebe and Silvius and Touchstone and Audrey (with Celia and Oliver thrown in quickly at the end). In Jaques' Seven Ages of Man speech in the middle of the play, the figure of the lover is especially ridiculous, "Sighing like furnace, with a woeful ballad / Made to his mistress' eyebrow" (2.7.148–49). In the love triptych of the play, Phebe the shepherdess (who is none too beautiful) is paired with the super-doting shepherd Silvius, whom love has made "a tame snake" (4.3.71). If Rosalind and Orlando are in the center, then the clown Touchstone and his homely goatherd Audrey are on the other side. Silvius and Phebe enact the Pastoral Follies of the Forest of Arden. Silvius is foolishly, exaggeratedly in love with Phebe, as in his histrionic conversation with the old shepherd Corin:

> Or if thou hast not sat as I do now,
> Wearing [=wearying] thy hearer in thy mistress' praise,
> Thou hast not loved.
> Or if thou hast not broke from company
> Abruptly, as my passion now makes me,
> Thou hast not loved.
> O Phebe, Phebe, Phebe! (2.4.35–41)

At this point the lovelorn Silvius rushes off stage.

An added complication occurs in act 3, scene 5, when Phebe falls in love with Rosalind, disguised as Ganymede, a name Shakespeare takes over from his source in Thomas Lodge's *Rosalynde* (1590). The name is odd, nevertheless, because Ganymede was a familiar Elizabethan term for a sodomite, as in the opening scene of Marlowe's Dido play, where Jupiter is shown dandling Ganymede, the cupbearer of the gods. In his *Glossographia* (1670), Thomas Blount uses Ganymede as a cross-reference for "catamite," "a boy hired to be abused contrary to nature," and he defines Ganymede as follows:

> the name of a Trojan Boy, whom *Jupiter* so loved (say the Poets) as he took him up to Heaven, and made him his Cup-bearer. Hence any Boy, loved for carnal abuse, or hired to be used contrary to Nature to commit the detestable sin of *Sodomy*, is called *Ganymede*, or ingle. [6]

Phebe is impressed with Rosalind's chiding, especially about her lack of beauty: "For I must tell you friendly in your ear, / Sell when you can, you are not for all markets" (3.5.59–60). In Phebe's plan, Silvius will be her go-between to Ganymede, a position he is only too willing to slavishly take up:

> So holy and so perfect is my love,
> And I in such a poverty of grace,
> That I shall think it a most plenteous crop
> To glean the broken ears after the man
> That the main harvest reaps. Loose now and then
> A scatt'red smile, and that I'll live upon. (3.5.99–104)

This masochistic view of love is patently absurd, but Silvius is not to be shaken out of his groveling.

Phebe speaks in the extravagant and high-flown conceits of contemporary sonnet writers. Her image of the power of the eye in love is far-fetched and absurd, especially coming from a humble shepherdess:

> Thou [i.e., Silvius] tell'st me there is murder in mine eye:
> 'Tis pretty, sure, and very probable
> That eyes, that are the frail'st and softest things,
> Who shut their coward gates on atomies [=motes],
> Should be called tyrants, butchers, murderers.
> Now I do frown on thee with all my heart,
> And if mine eyes can wound, now let them kill thee.
> Now counterfeit to swound; why, now fall down;

Or if thou canst not, O, for shame, for shame,
Lie not, to say mine eyes are murderers. (3.5.10–19)

This is the ornate, conceited style of Richard II, especially when he is
in the depths of grief, but its elaborateness verges on parody. Later, Phebe
comes to quote a line from Marlowe's *Hero and Leander*, a verse epyllion
published in 1598:

Dead Shepherd, now I find thy saw of might,
"Who ever loved that loved not at first sight?" (3.4.81–82)

Curiously, of all his many lovers, Shakespeare chooses Phebe to express
his sophisticated anxieties about his rival, Christopher Marlowe, the
"Dead Shepherd," born like Shakespeare in 1564.

Rosalind herself is inordinately fond of high-flown love rhetoric, but
she seems also to be conscious of the artifice and the absurdity of her
poetic endeavors. As Ganymede she appeals to Orlando: "Come, woo
me, woo me; for now I am in a holiday humor and like enough to consent" (4.1.64–65), but at the same time she is making fun of the very love
poetry that her discourse is laved in:

Leander, he would have lived many a fair year though Hero had
turned nun, if it had not been for a hot midsummer night; for,
good youth, he went but forth to wash him in the Hellespont, and
being taken with the cramp, was drowned; and the foolish chron-
iclers of that age found it was "Hero of Sestos." But these are all
lies. Men have died from time to time, and worms have eaten
them, but not for love. (95–102)

She is alluding to Marlowe's *Hero and Leander*, the same poem that Phebe
quotes from earlier.

The frankly sensual relationship of Touchstone and Audrey parodies
the high-flown love scenes of Rosalind and Orlando. The clown begins
his wooing with complex puns:

I am here with thee and thy goats, as the most capricious poet,
honest Ovid, was among the Goths. (3.3.6–8)

"Goats" and "Goths" were homophones in Elizabethan pronunciation,
and the word "capricious" is derived from the Latin *caper*, a male goat.

This is a backhanded compliment to Shakespeare's master, Ovid, who was exiled among the Goths for the immorality of his verses, especially *The Art of Love*.

The whole scene collects puns by Touchstone, with Audrey playing dumb and setting up occasions for the clown's wit. He wishes that the gods had made Audrey "poetical,"

> for the truest poetry is the most feigning, and lovers are given to poetry, and what they swear in poetry may be said as lovers they do feign. (18–21)

Wooing to Touchstone is a verbal game, a wit combat, in which he has all the good lines. The upshot of the matter is expressed in a memorable couplet: "Come, sweet Audrey. / We must be married, or we must live in bawdry" (92–93). The goatherd is obviously named in order to make the rhyme with "bawdry."

Finally, as Touchstone explains to Duke Senior, his marriage is a realistic concession to the unromantic needs of the body:

> I press in here, sir, amongst the rest of the country copulatives, to swear and to forswear, according as marriage binds and blood breaks. A poor virgin, sir, an ill-favored thing, sir, but mine own; a poor humor of mine, sir, to take that that no man else will. Rich honesty dwells like a miser, sir, in a poor house, as your pearl in your foul oyster. (5.4.56–62)

Audrey is "ill-favored" (not good-looking), as Touchstone keeps reminding us, but love is the pearl in "your foul oyster." Thus Touchstone feels superior to the country copulatives, who are urged on by the "blood," or sexual instinct.

The romantic wooing of Rosalind and Orlando is set against the love affairs of Phebe and Silvius and Touchstone and Audrey. Satire and parody color our sense of the main couple, especially in relation to Orlando's bad poetry that he hangs on branches and carves on trees. Act 3, scene 2 begins with a ten-line Italianate sonnet of two quatrains and a concluding couplet, in which Orlando celebrates his mistress as Diana, "Queen of Night" (2). The couplet is a direction to himself, not unlike that of the mooning Silvius:

> Run, run, Orlando, carve on every tree
> The fair, the chaste, and unexpressive she. (9–10)

We remember that Polonius reads to the King and Queen Hamlet's feeble poem to Ophelia, along with Hamlet's apology:

> O dear Ophelia, I am ill at these numbers [=verses]. I have not art to reckon my groans; but that I love thee best, O most best, believe it. (*Hamlet* 2.2.120–22)

Why does Shakespeare make both Orlando and Hamlet such incompetent versifiers? Probably because he wants to emphasize their sincerity in love as opposed to the artifice of a professional dispenser of love songs. Hamlet claims that he lacks "art," or literary skill, to express his passion, and Orlando is similarly sincere in his artlessness.

Rosalind enters act 3, scene 2 reciting a doggerel tetrameter poem of Orlando with only a single rhyme:

> "From the east to western Ind,
> No jewel is like Rosalind.
> Her worth, being mounted on the wind,
> Through all the world bears Rosalind.
> All the pictures fairest lined
> Are but black to Rosalind.
> Let no face be kept in mind
> But the fair of Rosalind." (88–95)

Touchstone proceeds to parody these eight lines of mediocre verse in twelve bravura lines that also have only a single rhyme:

> If a hart do lack a hind,
> Let him seek out Rosalind.
> If the cat will after kind,
> So be sure will Rosalind.
> Wintred garments must be lined,
> So must slender Rosalind.
> They that reap must sheaf and bind,
> Then to cart with Rosalind.
> Sweetest nut hath sourest rind,
> Such a nut is Rosalind.
> He that sweetest rose will find
> Must find love's prick, and Rosalind. (101–12)

The allusion to "love's prick" is only Touchstone's mischievous devaluing of the expected images of love poetry.

Orlando is a dolt in love, and Rosalind leads the love game and wit combat by her intelligence and fertile imagination. The joking stance masks the real feelings of the protagonists, who are trying valorously to conceal their passion. Rosalind is at her best when she is Ganymede pretending to be Rosalind. Then she can fully exploit her coy artifice. Some of her speeches in act 4, scene 1 sound like Millamant in Congreve's *Way of the World* (1700) setting forth her provisos before she will consent to marry:

> Men are April when they woo, December when they wed. Maids are May when they are maids, but the sky changes when they are wives. I will be more jealous of thee than a Barbary cock-pigeon over his hen, more clamorous than a parrot against rain, more newfangled than an ape, more giddy in my desires than a monkey. I will weep for nothing, like Diana in the fountain, and I will do that when you are disposed to be merry; I will laugh like a hyen, and that when thou art inclined to sleep. (140–49)

This spirited, witty speech is meant to conceal "how many fathom deep I am in love" (197). Rosalind's "affection hath an unknown bottom, like the Bay of Portugal" (198–99).[7]

The play ends in a masquelike show, with Hymen, the God of marriage, blessing the lovers to the accompaniment of "*Still music*" (5.4.107 s.d.). The marriage pairs now include the miraculously converted Oliver (the older brother of Orlando) and Celia, the friend of Rosalind. The God Hymen speaks the hymn that opens the ceremony:

> Then is there mirth in heaven
> When earthly things made even
> Atone together. (108–10)

"Atone" is used in its literal sense of "to be made one." Hymen directs the "eight that must take hands / To join in Hymen's bands" (128–29). The marriages at the end of *As You Like It* are celebrated with appropriate solemnity, and the role of Hymen anticipates the fuller wedding masque for Ferdinand and Miranda at the end of *The Tempest*.

Close in time and spirit to *As You Like It*, *Twelfth Night* has a certain bittersweet tone, marking, as it does, the very end of the Christmas festivities. The last note in this play is the clown's wistful and melancholy song about the wind and the rain and the ages of man, which is taken up by the Fool in *King Lear* (3.2.74–77). The entrance of the shipwrecked Viola, with her breezy question: "What country, friends, is this?" (1.2.1), shifts the play into a different tone from the languorous beginning. She is the mysterious, romantic stranger who will change everything in the comic action. Olivia soon falls in love with her in disguise as Cesario, the Duke's messenger, but she, from an early moment in the play and for reasons that are never really explained, loves the Duke. It just so happens that she has a twin brother, who was also shipwrecked, who enters the play at act 2, scene 1, and whom Olivia seizes upon for her husband (equating him, by comic convention, with his twin, Cesario/Viola).

Shakespeare exploits the charming coincidences of the romantic and unbelievable plot. Like the twin Antipholus of Syracuse in *The Comedy of Errors* (2.2.181ff. and 213ff.), Sebastian wonders what is happening to him:

> What relish is in this? How runs the stream?
> Or I am mad, or else this is a dream.
> Let fancy still my sense in Lethe steep;
> If it be thus to dream, still let me sleep! (4.1.60–63)

But, like the true comic hero, he refuses to probe into his present predicament and decides to be ruled by Olivia. In his soliloquy in her garden, he reflects on what is occurring. He even thinks he may be going mad or that he is entangled in "some error" (4.3.10), but the pearl Olivia gives him is real and she herself seems to be fully in charge of her household. He makes no objection when she suddenly appears with a priest and sweeps him off to marriage:

> I'll follow this good man and go with you
> And having sworn truth, ever will be true. (32–33)

All the mysteries of the play are unraveled at the end, when the twins appear together and the Duke exclaims in wonder:

> One face, one voice, one habit [=costume], and two persons—
> A natural perspective that is and is not. (5.1.216–17)

So the action is resolved by a simple expedient; the twins are like the optical toys—"perspective glasses"—that people delighted to play with in the Renaissance.[8] The Duke gives his blessing to the union of Sebastian and Olivia, and he takes Viola/Cesario for his wife, which is what she longed for from the beginning. But Malvolio cannot be included in the final celebration and is resolved to "be revenged on the whole pack of you!" (5.1.380). Shakespeare seems determined to exclude at least one inappropriate person from each comic ending, like the malcontent Jaques in *As You Like It* and Caliban in *The Tempest*. The point seems to be that comedy and the green world and the feasting, dancing, and revelry of the marriage ceremony are not for everyone. To participate, you have to be in harmony with the spirit of comedy.

The merry war between the sexes is nowhere more explicitly developed than in the characters of Beatrice and Benedick in *Much Ado About Nothing*. They both begin the play as sworn enemies of love, which makes their infatuation, helped along by clever plotting, that much more astonishing. Beatrice's first line in the play is already mocking Benedick's manliness and military stature: "I pray you, is Signior Mountanto returned from the wars or no?" (1.1.29–30). "Montanto" or "montant" is a technical fencing term for an upright blow or thrust, with a sly pun on the sexual term, "mount." Beatrice is preoccupied with Benedick; she is introduced in the play as speaking about nothing else. In her second speech, she imagines Benedick the lady-killer challenging Cupid to a shooting match, which ends with energetic satire of his valor: "I pray you, how many hath he killed and eaten in these wars? But how many hath he killed? For indeed, I promised to eat all of his killing" (40–43). Beatrice's speeches have an absurd insistence, verging on direct insult: Benedick is "a very valiant trencherman" (49) and "no less than a stuffed man" (56–57). "Stuffed" seems to have derogatory connotations, like the modern British slang expression, "Get stuffed."

Leonato, the father of Hero and the Governor of Messina, explains that "There is a kind of merry war betwixt Signior Benedick and her. They never meet but there's a skirmish of wit between them" (58–61). As soon as Benedick arrives on the scene, Beatrice is impelled to provocative repartee, vowing that she is an enemy of love. She declares defiantly: "I had rather hear my dog bark at a crow than a man swear he loves me" (127–28), to which Benedick replies: "God keep your ladyship still in that mind, so some gentleman or other shall scape a predestinate scratched face" (129–31). Beatrice tries to outdo this by asserting: "Scratching could not make it worse and 'twere such a face as yours were" (132–33).

After the scolding, Beatrice leaves, and Benedick asserts his independence: he will live as a bachelor to avoid being a cuckold. He is immune to the pangs of love: "Prove that ever I lose more blood with love than I will get again with drinking, pick out mine eyes with a ballad maker's pen and hang me up at the door of a brothel house for the sign of blind Cupid" (241–45). Blind Cupid may have been a tradesman's sign in Shakespeare's time, for example, on the brothels in the Bankside near the theaters. [9] "Blood" in Benedick's assertion is ambiguous: not only would the lack of blood in the cheeks make one "look pale with love" (238), but semen was thought to be carried in the blood and "blood" was a general synonym for sexual desire, as in Antony's "You'll heat my blood" (*Antony and Cleopatra* 1.3.80), or get me excited.[10] It is obvious in the first scene of the play that Beatrice and Benedick protest too much.

The hyperbole of disdain is expanded in the early scenes of *Much Ado* in order to make the eventual love of Beatrice and Benedick that much more inflamed and furious. Beatrice is represented in act 2, scene 1 in the same key words that Shakespeare used for Kate in *The Taming of the Shrew.* Leonato says, "By my troth, niece, thou wilt never get thee a husband if thou be so shrewd of thy tongue" (18–19), and his brother Antonio says, "In faith, she's too curst" (20). She is not only antimarriage, but antimale as well: "Adam's sons are my brethren, and truly I hold it a sin to match in my kindred" (63–64). On the other side, Benedick is carried away by outrageous mythological comparisons: "She would have made Hercules have turned spit, yea, and have cleft his club to make the fire too. Come, talk not of her. You shall find her the infernal Ate in good apparel" (250–54). Disdain inspires both Beatrice and Benedick to rhetorical flights and witty excess. That's clearly predictive of the liveliness of their eventual union, as it is with Petruchio and Kate. Since they are so well suited for each other, Beatrice and Benedick lay themselves open to plotting to bring them together—they only need to be convinced by outside persuasion of what they know for certain in their own hearts. Don Pedro, who is the master of the plots, boasts: "If we can do this, Cupid is no longer an archer; his glory shall be ours, for we are the only love-gods" (2.1.380–82).

In a carefully staged scene, Leonato describes Beatrice's "enraged affection" (2.3.103–4) in such a way that Benedick will overhear every word. It is "most wonderful that she should so dote on Signior Benedick, whom she hath in all outward behaviors seemed ever to abhor" (97–99). She is in an "ecstasy" (153)—a very strong word for madness—of love and there is a danger that "she will do a desperate outrage to herself" (154–55). Benedick's soliloquy after the plotters leave shows how thoroughly he has been persuaded, and he proceeds by the erotic fury that characterizes lovers in Shakespeare's comedies. Love is an all-consuming fire, yet Benedick has a reserve of preening self-praise that reminds us of Malvolio in *Twelfth Night*. Benedick resolves to "be horribly in love with her" (231), but he rationalizes his passion as the product of humor or eccentricity: "Shall quips and sentences and these paper bullets of the brain awe a man from the career of his humor?" (236–38). When Beatrice appears to bid him to dinner, he postulates justifications to prove that she is in love with him: "If I do not take pity of her, I am a villain; if I do not love her, I am a Jew. I will go get her picture" (258–60). Presumably he is a Jew because he is a faithless infidel. By the way, where can Benedick obtain so quickly a painted miniature of his beloved (like the portraits in the Closet Scene of *Hamlet*, 3.4)? It is a symbolic step in the right direction for him to want Beatrice's "picture." That's what Bassanio finds in the lucky leaden casket of *The Merchant of Venice*: "Fair Portia's counterfeit!" (3.2.115), that is, her painted portrait.

In act 3, scene 1, Hero and Ursula, her waiting-gentlewoman, entrap Beatrice by their cunning speech. Echoing a theme from *Twelfth Night*, Hero says that Beatrice cannot love because "She is so self-endeared" (56). Malvolio too is "sick of self-love" (*Twelfth Night* 1.5.90), and so are Olivia and Duke Orsino. Therefore, the loving Benedick is doomed to be destroyed by his own silence:

> Consume away in sighs, waste inwardly.
> It were a better death than die with mocks,
> Which is as bad as die with tickling. (78–80)

Before they leave the stage, Ursula announces that Beatrice is "limed" (104), that is, caught like a bird in birdlime, a sticky substance smeared on branches by a fowler. Hero's concluding couplet about love is more triumphant:

> If it prove so, then loving goes by haps;
> Some Cupid kills with arrows, some with traps. (105–6)

It's interesting how this play mediates between two ideas of love: that love proceeds "by haps" and by Cupid's random arrows, and that love is a natural, psychological expression through which two people like Beatrice and Benedick, who really love each other and are perfectly suited for each other, are brought inevitably together.

Like Benedick in act 2, scene 3, Beatrice, who has overheard everything Hero and Ursula have said, ends her scene (3.1) by coming forward to speak an artful ten-line sonnet (two quatrains and a couplet). For the first time in the play she is tender and loving, ashamed of her previous pride and scorn:

> And, Benedick, love on; I will requite thee,
> Taming my wild heart to thy loving hand. (111–12)

The image is that of the taming of a wild bird by its keeper, associated with Hero's earlier comment:

> No, truly, Ursula, she is too disdainful.
> I know her spirits are as coy and wild
> As haggards of the rock. (34–36)

A haggard was a wild hawk, which most falconers preferred to train to hunt rather than a domesticated hawk. The image is crucial in Petruchio's plan to tame Kate (*The Taming of the Shrew* 4.1.182ff.), and it also figures importantly in Othello's conception of Desdemona: "If I do prove her haggard" (3.3.259). A haggard was valued for its wildness, which it presumably never lost.

Despite these revelations, the play doesn't end tamely. Once Benedick and Beatrice acknowledge their love, they are free to revert to their previous witty selves. They are both grudging about being in love, fierce about maintaining their independence, and scornful about the conventional accord of lovers. Beatrice asks impudently: "But for which of my good parts did you first suffer love for me?" (5.2.64–65), to which Benedick answers with politic reservations: "Suffer love! A good epithet. I do suffer love indeed, for I love thee against my will" (66–67). He concludes: "Thou and I are too wise to woo peaceably" (72). Unlike Orlando in *As You Like It*, Benedick "was not born under a rhyming planet, nor I cannot woo in festival terms" (40–41). Yet we do learn at the end of the play that Benedick has written "A halting sonnet of his own pure brain, / Fashioned to Beatrice" (5.4.87–88), and that Beatrice has written another, "stol'n from her pocket, / Containing her affection unto Benedick" (89–90).

They agree grudgingly to marry. As Benedick says regretfully:

> A miracle! Here's our own hands against our hearts. Come, I will
> have thee; but, by this light, I take thee for pity. (91–93)

Beatrice replies in kind:

> I would not deny you; but, by this good day, I yield upon great
> persuasion, and partly to save your life, for I was told you were in
> a consumption. (94–96)

So the wooing ends with amusing artifice. Benedick's last words advise
Don Pedro, Prince of Aragon, to marry, for, in the quasi-proverbial
apothegm: "There is no staff more reverend than one tipped with horn"
(123–24). Benedick cannot avoid the inevitable association of marriage
with cuckoldry. [11]

In the Claudio/Hero action of *Much Ado*, the plot is extravagantly
complicated by comic villainy. Don John, the bastard brother of Don
Pedro, the Prince of Aragon, is introduced into the play as a malcontent
and, in his own confession, "a plain-dealing villain" (1.3–30). Like other
bastards in Shakespeare, such as Edmund in *King Lear* and Faulconbridge in *King John*, Don John feels cheated by nature and out to get
his revenge on the world. His plot to calumniate the innocent Hero and
prevent her from marrying Claudio doesn't seem well motivated for
this comedy, and tends to draw it into the trammels of tragicomedy.
Certainly the rejection of Hero as a "rotten orange" (4.1.31) right at
the marriage ceremony seems excessively dire, as is Beatrice's command to Benedick: "Kill Claudio" (287). The villainy of Don John's
calumniation of Hero is partially undone by the mock-heroic capture of
Conrade and Borachio, Don John's plotters, by the clownish constables,
Dogberry and Verges. As Borachio confesses providentially to Don Pedro:
"What your wisdoms could not discover, these shallow fools have
brought to light" (5.1.231–33). Hero, supposedly dead, is revived to
marry Claudio in the final scene. "Another Hero!" (5.4.62) says Claudio
with wonder.

There are certain structural problems with the comic villainy in *Much
Ado*. First of all, it seems to convert the play into a romance, where
strange and wonderful events are pretty much routine. Then, the Hero
and Claudio action doesn't align well with the Beatrice and Benedick
relation. In most of Shakespeare's earlier comedies there is an admirable
harmony of the love actions, which stand in an important analogical relation to each other, as in *A Midsummer Night's Dream*. The danger of the
comic villainy in *Much Ado* is that it heats the plot up so torridly that it
is difficult to get rid of Don John and his paid conspirators, revive Hero,
reanimate Claudio, and produce the happy ending of comedy without

some sense of needless effort and overly hasty regenerations. Probably worst of all, Claudio and Hero remain an undeveloped pair of lovers alongside some of Shakespeare's most successful, witty players in love-game comedy: Beatrice and Benedick.

Berowne and Benedick are part of a group of venturesome male protagonists in Shakespeare's comedies. Bassanio in *The Merchant of Venice* is clearly one of them, since he begins the play as a fortune-hunter who needs financial backing for his wedding expedition to win the rich Portia of Belmont. Antonio finances this quest for his friend as he does other commercial ventures in Venice. Bassanio's voyage is a "hazard"—and the word is more important in this play than in any other play of Shakespeare (there are eleven examples in Spevack's *Shakespeare Concordance*)—a risky venture, just as the choice of caskets is a dangerous hazard for the suitors.

Bassanio's first speeches to Antonio are full of commercial imagery. He imagines himself as Jason in pursuit of the Golden Fleece:

> her sunny locks
> Hang on her temples like a golden fleece,
> Which makes her seat of Belmont Colchos' strond,
> And many Jasons come in quest of her. (1.1.169–72)

At the end of the successful Casket Scene, Gratiano, who will marry Nerissa, says to his victorious friend Bassanio: "We are the Jasons, we have won the Fleece" (3.2.241). The love action in Belmont is closely related to the bond action in Venice by its preoccupation with money and material rewards. As Portia says to her newfound husband: "Since you are dear bought, I will love you dear" (313). The pun on "dear"—combining expensively and lovingly—sums up the doubleness of this scene.

At the end of the play, Portia and Nerissa impose penances on their husbands like those at the end of *Love's Labor's Lost*. Both Bassanio and Gratiano have given away the rings that they have sworn to keep. No matter that they were given to Portia and Nerissa in disguise! Portia vows: "By heaven, I will ne'er come in your bed / Until I see the ring!" (5.1.190–91), and Nerissa concurs. The ring functions as an obvious sexual symbol, so that the husbands can be chastened for their infidelity at the same time as the disguises of Portia and Nerissa are revealed. Gratiano concludes the play with a minatory couplet:

> Well, while I live I'll fear no other thing
> So sore, as keeping safe Nerissa's ring. (306–7)

The men have lost some of the bravado with which they began the play.

The balancing love affair in the play between Jessica and Lorenzo also has something disquieting in it. They are both preoccupied with money and material goods. In act 2, scene 6, we see Jessica not only stealing away from her father's house, but also actively stealing her father's treasure. The scene of elopement is oddly mixed with a concern for loot. Jessica, from above, says to her love: "Here, catch this casket; it is worth the pains" (33), and: "I will make fast the doors and gild myself / With some moe ducats, and be with you straight" (49–50). Is Lorenzo responding to these gifts when he says, "For she is wise, if I can judge of her" (53)? Wise in what sense? We learn later from Tubal about Jessica's extravagance in Genoa: "Your daughter spent in Genoa, as I heard, one night fourscore ducats" (3.1.101–2). She is throwing money away in a pathological manner that stabs her father to the heart, especially when she exchanges her dead mother Leah's turquoise ring, a present to Shylock when he was a bachelor, for a monkey. Shylock, who knows the value of the ring, both sentimental and monetary, "would not have given it for a wilderness of monkey" (115–16).

The Merchant of Venice is a troubling comedy not only because of the revenge action of the bond and the pound of flesh, but also because of the imperfect love actions. When Shylock disappears in act 4, it is difficult for the play to recover its lyric tone. The extraordinary love speeches by Lorenzo and Jessica that open act 5 are not enough to reestablish the comic equilibrium. And Lorenzo's long and rhapsodic exposition on the powers of music only prepares us for the reentry of Portia and Nerissa and the contentious affair of the rings. Lorenzo invokes the music of the spheres that no mortal, except by miraculous intervention, can hear:

> There's not the smallest orb which thou behold'st
> But in his motion like an angel sings,
> Still quiring to the young-eyed cherubins;
> Such harmony is in immortal souls,
> But whilst this muddy vesture of decay
> Doth grossly close it in, we cannot hear it.   (60–65)

But the play ends more with "this muddy vesture of decay" than with the immortal harmony that only angelic creatures can hear.

It's a far cry from the sophistication of *The Merchant of Venice* and *Much Ado* to the relative simplicity of *The Two Gentlemen of Verona*, yet the early comedy is a useful reference point for some of the commonplaces about love that are satirized and parodied in later comedies.¹² *The Two Gentlemen of Verona* blithely collects familiar ideas that were in the air about love, ideas that are not tested at all in the play but merely put into action.

The play opens with a diatribe against love. Valentine, who is leaving Verona and going to Milan to broaden his perspective, makes fun of his friend Proteus, who is in love. The question then arises, will the play be designed to negate Valentine's objections? Is this like the outrageous propositions that begin most of Shakespeare's comedies and are eventually disproved by the action? Is the play a defense of love cunningly provoked to answer the bleak stipulations of the first scene? Part of the charm, or charming absurdity, of the play is that Proteus falls in love suddenly with Silvia, inspired as it seems by Valentine's amorous rhetoric:

> Is it mine eye, or Valentine's praise,
> Her true perfection, or my false transgression,
> That makes me reasonless to reason thus? (2.4.195–97)

These questions are never answered, and Proteus moves immediately to win his new love even if it involves betraying his deep-sworn friend, Valentine.

This conflict between the friends endows the play with a mechanistic quality. Proteus suddenly becomes a deep-dyed villain, willing to do in both his former love, Julia, and his friend Valentine. Love again becomes a destructive passion, as it was in the first scene of the play. Proteus's long soliloquy in act 2, scene 6 is like the explanatory soliloquy of the villain in tragedy. It is an awfully pat explanation for motives that could have been more fully explored. Everything is blamed on Love personified:

> Love bade me swear, and Love bids me forswear.
> O sweet-suggesting Love, if thou hast sinned,
> Teach me, thy tempted subject, to excuse it! (6–8)

The comparisons that Proteus invokes are fairly broad and conventional, and so is the imagery:

> And Silvia—witness Heaven, that made her fair!—
> Shows Julia but a swarthy Ethiope. (25–26)

This is obviously untrue because we have seen the beautiful Julia earlier in the play. In the final couplet, Love is presented as a baleful power whom Proteus calls upon to help him in his villainy:

> Love, lend me wings to make my purpose swift,
> As thou hast lent me wit to plot this drift! (42–43)

Act 2, scene 6 is set against the next scene, where Julia is resolved to leave Verona to pursue Proteus. This is the most lyrical scene in the play, and it represents love as a beautiful, tender, ecstatic passion. Julia speaks to her waiting-gentlewoman, Lucetta:

> Didst thou but know the inly touch of love,
> Thou wouldst as soon go kindle fire with snow
> As seek to quench the fire of love with words. (2.7.18–20)

The most moving descriptions and characterizations of love are spoken by Shakespeare's women, who define the nature of love and comment on its powers. Love is personified as "a gentle stream":

> He makes sweet music with th' enameled stones,
> Giving a gentle kiss to every sedge
> He overtaketh in his pilgrimage;
> And so by many winding nooks he strays,
> With willing sport, to the wild ocean. (28–32)

Of course, Julia has no idea of what Proteus is now thinking, so two radically different views of love are set side by side.

The turns and windings of the plot are brought to resolution in the pastoral setting of "Another part of the forest" in act 5, scene 4. Valentine, as leader of the outlaws, observes Proteus's outrageous conduct with Silvia. He is frantic in his pursuit, totally abandons any respect for Valentine—"In love, / Who respects friend?" (53–54)—and actually threatens to rape Silvia: "I'll force thee yield to my desire" (59). It is at this point that Valentine intervenes, Proteus apologizes for his misconduct, and the generous Valentine offers him Silvia as a proof of his friendship:

> And, that my love may appear plain and free,
> All that was mine in Silvia I give thee. (82–83)

This is carrying friendship[13] to an absurd degree of devotion.

Julia suddenly reveals herself, Proteus falls in love with her again, and everything speeds to the happy ending of comedy. In Valentine's final speech, all that was amiss is quickly restored without the need for any explanation at all:

> Come, Proteus; 'tis your penance but to hear
> The story of your loves discoverèd.
> That done, our day of marriage shall be yours;
> One feast, one house, one mutual happiness. (170–73)

In *The Two Gentlemen of Verona* the genre of comedy reasserts itself in the happy ending. Love is insubstantial, easily transformed from something negative to an exalted, beneficial state.

The most problematic of the comedies—at least in relation to contemporary criticism—is undoubtedly *The Taming of the Shrew*. It is clearly misogynistic, attacked by many (but not all) feminist critics of Shakespeare,[14] yet it also may be considered a conspicuously loving play, with Kate and Petruchio (like Beatrice and Benedick) admirably suited for each other. Can these two opposing points of view be reconciled? Obviously not, but there is a sense that Petruchio has met his match, as is evident in John Fletcher's sequel, *The Woman's Prize, or The Tamer Tamed* (1611), which reverses the roles of Petruchio and Kate. Fletcher and Shakespeare worked together for the King's Men company and may have collaborated on *The Two Noble Kinsmen*. Fletcher must have known Shakespeare's play, so his play functions as a kind of commentary on it.

We get hints of the other side of the Petruchio action throughout the play, but especially when Gremio says, "I warrant him, Petruchio is Kated" (3.2.245). Petruchio is a fortune-hunter, like Bassanio in *The Merchant of Venice*, but that doesn't mean he gets exactly what he is looking for—a rich marriage. Petruchio gets more than he bargains for, as does Bassanio. If we take *The Merchant of Venice* as parallel to *The Taming of the Shrew*, it was no part of Bassanio's intention to fall in love with Portia. That is pure lagniappe.

The first wooing scene (2.1) between Kate and Petruchio is a case in point. It is patently a wit combat, with Petruchio not so dominant as he seems to think. Kate gives as good as she gets, and the dialogue is not only witty but also provokingly sexual. Petruchio and Kate are clearly the only intelligent characters in the play. Notice how spontaneously and effortlessly the love game unfolds. Petruchio's plan, as he explains it to Baptista, Kate's father, does not exactly forecast the way things will turn out:

I am as peremptory as she proud-minded.
And where two raging fires meet together
They do consume the thing that feeds their fury.   (131–33)

In his soliloquy right before Kate enters, Petruchio again enunciates his plan, as if it is necessary to keep the audience (as well as himself) informed of how things are expected to go in order to rule out randomness. Petruchio seems to be reassuring himself and assuaging his fears with his soliloquies:

Say that she rail, why then I'll tell her plain
She sings as sweetly as a nightingale.
Say that she frown, I'll say she looks as clear
As morning roses newly washed with dew.   (170–73)

But Kate is not so simple as to be taken in by all these mechanistic contraries. She definitely has a mind of her own.

In the lively scene Kate is full of insulting puns and double entendres. She calls Petruchio a "movable" (197), or piece of furniture, a "joint stool" (198), or a stool made by a joiner or carpenter, to which Petruchio replies: "Thou hast hit it; come sit on me" (198). The next two lines are made to match each other as witty ripostes:

KATE   Asses are made to bear and so are you.
PETRUCHIO   Women are made to bear and so are you.   (199–200)

The whole scene reverberates with clashing rejoinders, ending with an obscene reference to the wasp and its sting. Petruchio calls her an angry "wasp" (209) and Kate replies: "If I be waspish, best beware my sting" (210).

This begins a chain of associations:

PETRUCHIO   Who knows not where a wasp does wear his sting?
   In his tail.
KATE   In his tongue.
PETRUCHIO   Whose tongue?
KATE   Yours, if you talk of tales, and so farewell.
PETRUCHIO   What, with my tongue in your tail?   (213–16)

This is grossly sexual, as is his reply to Kate's question:

KATE What is your crest? A coxcomb?

PETRUCHIO A combless cock, so Kate will be my hen. (223–24)

The sexual references and the nonstop punning energize the scene. Kate and Petruchio obviously enjoy each other's company, and this scene shows her as not just shrewd, curst, froward, and toward, as she is repeatedly described in the play, but also witty, sportive, intelligent, and gamesome—not unlike Petruchio at his best. There is not a little irony in Petruchio's comment: "in a twink [=twinkling] she won me to her love" (303). His last line before he exits is "kiss me, Kate" (317), which echoes like a refrain in the play. Why does he want to kiss her if he is only after her dowry?

What does "taming" mean in this play? Obviously, one thing to Petruchio and another to Kate. Yet there is also a sense that Petruchio doesn't understand the implications of taming, just as Christopher Sly in the Induction is not really tamed by the rich lord who transforms him from a drunken tinker, or Bottom the Weaver is not really tamed by Titania, the Queen of the Fairies, in *A Midsummer Night's Dream*. He is only "translated." Perhaps if "taming" is understood as a histrionic word, then some of the taming backfires on Petruchio, as Kate becomes more and more masterful at the love game.

Petruchio's long soliloquy in act 4, scene 1 is awfully naive about Kate as we perceive her in the play. She is not at all as he imagines her:

Another way I have to man my haggard [=wild hawk captured after maturity],
To make her come and know her keeper's call,
That is, to watch her as we watch these kites
That bate and beat and will not be obedient. (187–90)

Petruchio wishes that it will all be as simple as he projects, but he himself graciously undergoes all of the instructional torments intended for Kate, including not eating, not sleeping, and not participating in the pleasures of the wedding night. He emerges from the ordeal as hungry and sleepless and deprived of affection and sex as Kate. He is tamed too and different from the blustering fortune-hunter at the beginning of the play.

At the end of act 5, scene 1, Kate and Petruchio are seen as a loving couple, but still politely brawling like Benedick and Beatrice in *Much Ado*. When Petruchio enunciates his favorite verbal formula, "kiss me, Kate" (142), Kate objects: "What, in the midst of the street?" (143), but yields tenderly anyhow: "Nay, I will give thee a kiss. Now pray thee, love, stay" (148). Notice that she addresses her husband as "love." Petruchio is delighted:

> Is not this well? Come, my sweet Kate.
> Better once than never, for never too late. (149–50)

He needs to have his loving relation to his wife demonstrated over and over again.

This leads directly into the last scene of the play, with the wager among the men and Kate's groveling oration about a wife's duty to her husband, ideas already expressed in *The Comedy of Errors*. This speech has really annoyed feminist critics, but in context it is something different from its literal meaning. It is not ironic but sportive. Kate knows finally how to play the good wife, and the wager is almost perfectly suited for Petruchio and Kate to demonstrate their connubial harmony and to win a lot of loot. Kate speaks of wifely obedience as if she were reading a speech from a contemporary marriage manual: a husband "craves no other tribute at thy hands / But love, fair looks, and true obedience" (5.2.152–53). Kate offers the physiological argument about women's bodies in relation to women's temperament, as if it weren't one of the most tedious and specious of clichés:

> Why are our bodies soft and weak and smooth,
> Unapt to toil and trouble in the world,
> But that our soft conditions [=qualities] and our hearts
> Should well agree with our external parts? (165–68)

Never in the play has it seemed that Kate's body is "soft and weak and smooth" or that she depends on her "soft conditions." This is all a convenient gamester's fiction.

The bet is won and Petruchio says again, this time with real pride and astonishment: "Why, there's a wench! Come on and kiss me, Kate" (180). His last speech goes even further in his admiration for his new wife: "Come, Kate, we'll to bed" (184). This doesn't mean, as critics trained in motive-hunting might say, that the marriage has not yet been consummated, but it does indicate that Petruchio, the fortune-hunter, thinks he has gotten a much better deal than he bargained for, and a wife that puts Kate's prim sister, Bianca, to shame, as well as Hortensio's much-labored-for Widow. *The Taming of the Shrew* is after all only a play-within-a-play, put on for Christopher Sly's benefit and meant to convince him of the magical nature of the world that now opens up for him. I don't think we are meant to take the presented play too literally and to substitute what the characters say for what they mean. Both Christopher Sly's play and the play of Petruchio and Kate are alike in being full of games and deceptions. Petruchio and Kate emerge from their extensive love combat with new understandings of reality. They are strongly attracted to each other, have fun in each other's company, and wind up as an affectionate married couple. No one could have predicted this conclusion at the beginning of the play.

Shakespeare's late romances are characteristically different from his earlier comedies. They specialize in effects of magic and sudden transformations. The dead are brought back to life, as is the pregnant Thaisa in *Pericles*, who gives birth to Marina, and Hermione in *The Winter's Tale*, who is revived as a polychromed statue by Julio Romano after a sixteen-year gap. She is then reunited not only with her husband Leontes but also with her daughter Perdita, the "lost one." The late romances produce effects that are marvelous and create a mood of admiration and astonishment in the audience. This is the conventional happy ending of comedy with a special twist. Love endures all sorts of calamities, even death, and in the end families that were sundered are reunited with overflowing joy and harmony. The comic effects in the late romances transcend the fallible human limitations of the earlier comedies.

Of course, Shakespeare uses romantic themes in all of his comedies, for example, the shipwrecks in *The Comedy of Errors* and *Twelfth Night* and the twins who are separated from each other. The reuniting of the twins in both of these plays is an effect of wonder—"A natural perspective that is and is not" (5.1.217), says the Duke in *Twelfth Night*—and Adriana, the wife of Antipholus of Ephesus in *The Comedy of Errors*, exclaims: "I see two husbands, or mine eyes deceive me" (5.1.332). But these romantic effects are incidental in these plays and not central, as in the late romances, where love can become a magical, almost religious experience.

In *The Winter's Tale* the jealousy of Leontes is essentially unexplained, although the background that leads up to it—the friendship of Leontes and Polixenes as boys and their sense of perfect innocence—is understandable. This past of Leontes and Polixenes is re-created in their children, Perdita and Florizel, who fall naturally into a perfect love. The play is divided into a Before and After at act 4, where Time, the Chorus, enters to tell us that sixteen years have passed. The sheep-shearing festi-

val of act 4, scene 4 opens with Florizel and Perdita as nubile youths who
are in love with each other. Perdita, the lost daughter of Leontes, is now
the supposed daughter of the humble shepherd who found her, while
Florizel is in disguise as Doricles, a shepherd, although Perdita knows that
he is the son of the king, Polixenes. Perdita is dressed as the Queen of the
sheep-shearing feast, and act 4, scene 4 opens with Florizel addressing her
as Flora, the Roman goddess:

> These your unusual weeds [=garments] to each part of you
> Do give a life; no shepherdess, but Flora,
> Peering in April's front. This your sheep-shearing
> Is as a meeting of the petty gods,
> And you the Queen on't.   (1–5)

Everything is immediately mythologized and the scene is set self-consciously out of Ovid's *Metamorphoses*.

Perdita is worried about the social gap between herself and Florizel,
and she fears that the King will soon appear—as he does—and expose
their idyllic love affair. Florizel blithely draws examples from Ovid of the
gods transforming themselves to pursue their mortal loves:

> The gods themselves,
> Humbling their deities to love, have taken
> The shapes of beasts upon them. Jupiter
> Became a bull, and bellowed; the green Neptune
> A ram, and bleated; and the fire-robed god,
> Golden Apollo, a poor humble swain,
> As I seem now.   (25–31)

Florizel doesn't do any bellowing or bleating, but these Ovidian examples are not exactly flattering to Perdita, since in Ovid the maidens were
all forced, if not actually raped, by the gods. Despite his lascivious examples, Florizel protests his innocence:

> my desires
> Run not before mine honor, nor my lusts
> Burn hotter than my faith.   (33–35)

Lust is suppressed in Shakespeare's romances, except for in characters
such as Caliban in *The Tempest* and Cloten in *Cymbeline*.

Perdita, disguised and goddesslike, distributes flowers to Polixenes. It is in this scene that she makes her well-known disquisition against "streaked gillyvors" (82), or pinks, which are products of art rather than nature, art being the gardener's skill in producing unusual hybrids. Perdita is a partisan of the simplicity and purity of nature. She compares the flowers with cosmetics and the moral obliquity of being "painted":

> I'll not put
> The dibble in earth, to set one slip of them;
> No more than were I painted, I would wish
> This youth should say 'twere well, and only therefore
> Desire to breed by me. (99–103)

Perdita slips easily into the mythological mode in seeking flowers for Florizel and the shepherdesses of the feast:

> O Proserpina,
> For the flow'rs now, that, frighted, thou let'st fall
> From Dis's wagon! (116–18)

The story of Proserpina comes from Ovid's *Metamorphoses*, Book V, and also echoes the flowers that the mad Ophelia distributes in *Hamlet* (4.5).

The point of the Sheep-shearing Scene is that love is mythologically elevated. Perdita is dressed as Queen of the Feast, but both she and Florizel imagine themselves enacting a role "In Whitsun pastorals" (134), the May-games of Whitsuntide, especially the Robin Hood plays. Both lovers are histrionic, particularly Perdita:

> Methinks I play as I have seen them do
> In Whitsun pastorals; sure this robe of mine
> Does change my disposition. (133–35)

The robe is a costume for Perdita's prepared part.

As the transcendent and aesthetic mood rises, Florizel delivers the most magnificent love speech of the play:

> What you do
> Still betters what is done. When you speak, sweet,
> I'd have you do it ever; when you sing,
> I'd have you buy and sell so; so give alms,

Pray so; and for the ord'ring your affairs,
To sing them too. When you do dance, I wish you
A wave o' th' sea, that you might ever do
Nothing but that—move still, still so,
And own no other function. (135–43)

The speech's style epitomizes the mood of the late romances: complex, lyrical, hypnotic, with the irregular pauses of speech and the musical manipulation of the caesura. Here Shakespeare captures an extraordinary feeling of sibilance. Perdita and Florizel are made to seem like unearthly, mythological creatures.

The Statue Scene at the end of the play (5.3) continues the mood of wonder, marvel, and adoration. Through Paulina's art, the painted statue of Hermione by Julio Romano is brought to life. Much in the scene depends upon Renaissance doctrines of mimesis, or imitation, with art and nature set against each other the way they were in the Sheep-shearing Scene (4.4). The aim of art is to imitate nature, but in such an expert way that all distinction between the two is obliterated. Paulina says of the statue:

> prepare
> To see the life as lively mocked, as ever
> Still sleep mocked death. . . . (18–20)

The whole scene teases Leontes, but it also acts to increase his expectation and suspense. The ending of the play is devoted to reinvoking Leontes' intense love for his wife and thus returning the play, despite everything that has happened (including the deaths of Mamillius and Antigonus), to its harmonious beginning.

The scene is staged as a magical, quasi-religious event. Music is crucial, as in Paulina's wonderful lines full of abrupt caesuras:

> Music, awake her: strike.
> 'Tis time; descend; be stone no more; approach;
> Strike all that look upon with marvel; come;
> I'll fill your grave up. Stir; nay, come away. . . . (98–101)

There is an intrinsic play on "stone," which is the material of the statue but also an emotional word. A hard heart, one that has turned to stone, is the opposite of a heart that is warm and compassionate, as in Othello's powerful exclamation at a moment when his feelings for Desdemona are supremely ambiguous: "my heart is turned to stone; I strike it, and it hurts my hand" (*Othello* 4.1.184–85).

Paulina the wonder-worker bids the statue come alive: "be stone no more." Leontes, transfixed, feels that the stone has become warm: "What fine chisel / Could ever yet cut breath?" (5.3. 78–79). Paulina operates as if by magic, but she insists throughout that this is not unlawful black magic but a process that is guided by "faith" (95): "her actions shall be holy as / You hear my spell is lawful" (104–5). The play ends happily with Leontes reunited with his wife Hermione, his daughter Perdita restored to her parents, Perdita troth-plight to her love, Florizel, and, for good measure, the good Camillo pledged to the good Paulina.

Unlike *The Winter's Tale*, *The Tempest* is one of the few plays of Shakespeare to observe the unity of time (*The Comedy of Errors* is another), but in both plays all the events of the comic action are carefully choreographed and stage managed. Prospero, by the help of magic, has devised an elaborate scheme not only to be revenged on his brother Antonio, who has usurped the kingdom of Milan, but also to marry his daughter Miranda to Ferdinand, the son of Alonso, King of Naples (who helped Antonio seize his dukedom). The revenge and marriage themes are brought together as Prospero, through his magical art, stages the tempest that shipwrecks the entire marriage party, coming from the wedding of Alonso's daughter Claribel in Tunis, on the shore of Prospero's island in the Mediterranean. Shakespeare undoubtedly modeled his description of this island on travelers' reports about Bermuda.

When Miranda first sees Ferdinand in act 1, scene 2, she cannot believe that he is a human being and not a spirit, since the only men she has ever looked on are her father and the deformed slave Caliban, who tried to rape her:

> What is't? A spirit?
> Lord, how it looks about! Believe me, sir,
> It carries a brave form. But 'tis a spirit. (410–12)

"Brave" means handsome, beautiful, and it is frequently used in this play (there are eighteen examples of "brave" and related words in Spevack's *Concordance*). Prospero assures his daughter that Ferdinand is human, "A goodly person" (417), but Miranda goes on to hyperbolize him as "A thing divine; for nothing natural / I ever saw so noble" (419–20).

For his part, Ferdinand thinks Miranda "the goddess / On whom these airs attend" (422–23). Prospero is proud of his work, aided by Ariel, because the couple has fallen in love instantaneously: "At the first sight / They have changed eyes" (441–42). As prudent father, Prospero charms Ferdinand's sword and takes him prisoner deliberately to slow down the pace of the wooing:

> They are both in either's pow'rs. But this swift business
> I must uneasy make, lest too light winning
> Make the prize light. (451–53)

Even when Ferdinand has proved himself loyal and true, Prospero lectures him on the dire consequences of breaking his daughter's "virgin-knot" (4.1.15)[15] before marriage. He is remarkably didactic and moralistic.

The happy ending cannot occur until Prospero gives up his magic. When he has all his enemies in his power at the beginning of act 5, Ariel offers extraordinary advice:

> Your charm so strongly works 'em,
> That if you now beheld them, your affections
> Would become tender. (5.1.17–19)

Ariel, a creature of the air, projects what he would feel if he were not a spirit: "Mine would, sir, were I human" (20). This persuasion is irresistible and Prospero, like Duke Vincentio in *Measure for Measure*, renounces a well-merited vengeance:

> Though with their high wrongs I am struck to th' quick,
> Yet with my nobler reason 'gainst my fury
> Do I take part. The rarer action is
> In virtue than in vengeance. (25–28)

Prospero abjures his "potent art" (50):

> I'll break my staff,
> Bury it certain fathoms in the earth,
> And deeper than did ever plummet sound
> I'll drown my book. (54–57)

By thus giving up his magical powers, he becomes a fallible, erring mortal again.

At the end, a tableau is discovered of "Ferdinand and Miranda playing at chess" (171 s.d.), a symbol of concord in marriage, as in Sonnet 116:
"Let me not to the marriage of true minds / Admit impediments." For
Miranda the sight of all these courtly people is astonishing, and she is full
of ecstatic admiration:

> O, wonder!
> How many goodly creatures are there here!
> How beauteous mankind is! O brave new world
> That has such people in't!   (181–84)

Her father cannot resist a final, ironic comment: " 'Tis new to thee"
(184).

Alonso, Ferdinand's father, thinks of Miranda as a goddess: "Is she the
goddess that hath severed us / And brought us thus together?" (187–88),
but Ferdinand assures him "she is mortal; / But by immortal providence
she's mine" (188–89). The son begs his father's forgiveness for marrying
without his consent, and Alonso, like Lear, humbles himself before his
child: "How oddly will it sound that I / Must ask my child forgiveness!"
(197–98).

The play ends with a sense of benediction and divine blessing. The
old counselor Gonzalo speaks the wisdom of romance:

> In one voyage
> Did Claribel her husband find at Tunis,
> And Ferdinand her brother found a wife
> Where he himself was lost; Prospero his dukedom
> In a poor isle; and all of us ourselves
> When no man was his own.   (208–13)

This is not only the happy ending of comedy, but also a blessed, religious
event. Everything that was lost is now found, everything that was blemished or deformed—or thought to be blemished or deformed—is now
restored to its natural shape and luster. The ship that was thought to be
"split" (223) is now "tight and yare and bravely rigged as when / We first
put out to sea" (224–25), and everyone's garments are now as fresh and
handsome as if newly washed. The final, magical impression is that the
tempest was merely an illusion.

Whatever perturbations and disturbances it suffers, love in the comedies always turns out well, usually ending in marriage or the promise of

marriage. The happy ending is implicit in the idea of comedy, although there are all different kinds of happiness, including the bittersweet variety of *Twelfth Night*. Witty and intelligent women dominate the comedies, educating the men, deflating their pretensions and bravado, and even setting them penances, as at the end of *Love's Labor's Lost*. The comic plots favor gender-based situations, which lend themselves to amusing turns and counterturns contrary to conventional expectations. The audience is shamelessly teased and titillated.

CHAPTER THREE

DOCTRINE IN THE PROBLEM PLAYS & *HAMLET*

In Shakespeare's so-called "problem plays,"[1] love tends to be thwarted and unfulfilled. Both *Measure for Measure* and *All's Well That Ends Well* are tragicomedies, in which the dire issues of the earlier parts are suddenly resolved by bed tricks. *Troilus and Cressida* is a harsh, satirical play that is difficult to classify generically, although it ends like a tragedy with the death of Hector and a foreshadowing of the fall of Troy. All three of these plays are basically different from the comedies in their tone and mood. What happy endings there are, as in *Measure for Measure* and *All's Well*, seem grudging and unsatisfying, as if produced solely to satisfy the technical demands of the tragicomic resolution. *Hamlet* resembles *Troilus and Cressida* in its bitterness and satirical tone, and is sometimes included with the problem plays.[2] It is not a love tragedy, but disappointed love is a significant factor in its tragic thrust.

Measure for Measure begins as a tragedy but ends happily for all, as a comedy, with the abandonment of the strict Old Testament *lex talionis*, the law of "measure for measure," which is sometimes translated as the law of an eye for an eye. But there is a distinct feeling that the later part of the play doesn't really influence our sense of the earlier part, which remains dire and unresolved. Dramatic productions in general tend to have difficulty reconciling tragedy and comedy in a single, satisfying tragicomic ending. Love in this play is compromised, frustrated, and unsatisfactory, as it is in others that are also claimed as problem plays: *All's Well That Ends Well* and *Troilus and Cressida*. In *Measure for Measure* love is inchoate and undeveloped, in a way that is genuinely disturbing.

I am thinking particularly of the Angelo/Isabella sequence. "Lord Angelo is precise" (1.3.50), an expression usually applied to Puritans or Precisians; as the Duke says, he "scarce confesses / That his blood flows" (51–52). Then why did the Duke appoint him as his deputy to enforce the letter of the law in Vienna? The early part of the play makes it seem that the Duke is testing the "prenzie Angelo" (3.1.94)—a word that has never been defined and may simply be a mistake, although it sounds appropriate here, like a diminutive of "apprentice."

"Blood" is a key word in this play because blood carries the sexual impulses as well as emotions in general. The coldness of Angelo's blood reflects his calculating nature. Elsewhere in the play, Lucio says that he is

> a man whose blood
> Is very snow-broth; one who never feels
> The wanton stings and motions of the sense. . . . (1.4.57–59)

"Sense" is a synonym for "sex." Lucio is a general calumniator, but he is also a person of surprising insights into both the Duke and Angelo, of whom Lucio is sure "that when he makes water his urine is congealed ice" (3.2.112–13).

On the other side is Isabella, the condemned Claudio's sister, whom we first encounter in the play about to enter the nunnery of St. Clare. She too is to be tested, as we see in her strange first line: "And have you nuns no farther privileges?" (1.4.1), which she explains as: "I speak not as desiring more, / But rather wishing a more strict restraint" (3–4). These lines immediately establish a link with Angelo, who is also strict and literal-minded. Lucio convinces Isabella to plead with Angelo for her brother Claudio's life—he has been sentenced to die for fornication, although he has legally married Juliet on a pre-contract. Again, we are confronted with a problematic situation. Lucio's opening line, greeting Isabella, is jarring, especially in a nunnery: "Hail, virgin—if you be" (16). Everything in the play seems designed to set us on edge and to disorient our judgment.

When Isabella sets to work, under Lucio's tutelage, to persuade Angelo, everything she says seems to have a double meaning (as do Angelo's answers). Shakespeare works brilliantly here to establish an undertone of sexual innuendo in discourse that is literally innocent and straightforward. We are made painfully aware of the pulsing double entendre by Angelo's aside: "She speaks, and 'tis / Such sense, that my sense breeds with it" (2.2.141–42). "Sense" is what is sensible to reason, but it is also a synonym for "sex." When Isabella says, "Hark how I'll bribe you" (145), Angelo can't believe what he is hearing, but Isabella only means that she will bribe him "with such gifts that heaven shall share with you" (147). And so it goes. Everything is made clear in Angelo's soliloquy, which ends this scene. He doesn't understand what is happening to him, and he is unusually uncomfortable in the Petrarchan role of lover:

> What, do I love her,
> That I desire to hear her speak again,
> And feast upon her eyes? (176–78)

This is, of course, what lovers do: feast upon each other's eyes and "look babies." But Angelo hardly belongs with the lovers of the comedies.

Act 2, scene 4 opens with Angelo's soliloquy, which continues the soliloquy at the end of act 2, scene 2. It is clear that he has minimal self-knowledge. All the sexual events that overwhelm him seem to penetrate the armor of his self-awareness and astonish him. In the soliloquy of 2.4, he is fatalistic about what is happening: "Blood, thou art blood" (15); in other words, there is no resisting evil sexual impulses. The euphemisms Angelo uses for sexual indulgence betray his own naiveté: "saucy sweetness" (45), "sweet uncleanness" (54), "the treasures of your body" (96). "Treasure" is the same euphemism that Laertes uses to warn his sister Ophelia not to accept Hamlet's advances: "your chaste treasure open / To his unmastered importunity" (*Hamlet* 1.3.31–32). But Angelo, whatever we may think of him as a murderous hypocrite, is smitten with Isabella— "Plainly conceive, I love you" (141).

He is extraordinarily inept as a lover and does everything wrong, including speaking in a stilted and legalistic style:

> Be that you are,
> That is, a woman; if you be more, you're none;
> If you be one, as you are well expressed
> By all external warrants, show it now,
> By putting on the destined livery. (134–38)

What is "the destined livery" of a woman, as opposed to the habit of the sisters of St. Clare? Angelo's threat of force in his final speech is a counsel born of frustration, and is even more counterproductive than his bungling love speeches: "Fit thy consent to my sharp appetite, / Lay by all nicety and prolixious blushes" (161–62). This only angers Isabella.

Under Angelo's influence, Isabella also turns harsh and legalistic. She assumes, incorrectly of course, that her brother Claudio will be glad to hear of her resolve and will happily lay down his life—as if he had a real choice—to preserve his sister's honor. Isabella's motto, expressed in a couplet, doesn't show much Christian charity:

> Then, Isabel, live chaste, and, brother, die:
> "More than our brother is our chastity." (184–85)

Of course, the polarized choice is never necessary in the play, as the Duke solves the moral dilemma with his ingenious bed trick. But it is worth considering how provocative Isabella is in the course of this scene. She speaks with a sexual innuendo of which she seems totally unaware:

> were I under the terms of death,
> Th' impression of keen whips I'd wear as rubies,
> And strip myself to death as to a bed
> That longing have been sick for, ere I'd yield
> My body up to shame. (100–4)

Regardless of her overt meaning, "Th' impression of keen whips" must impress the inflamed Angelo, as well as the image of Isabella stripping herself "to death as to a bed." In the final scene of the play, Isabella speaks of Angelo's "concupiscible intemperate lust" (5.1.98). How does she know it is that bad without supplying some measure of her own fantasies? And in kneeling to plead for Angelo's life, she thinks "A due sincerity governèd his deeds, / Till he did look on me" (449–50). Does she imagine herself so irresistible to men?

There is no use in exaggerating points in the dramatic action that are fairly obvious, but the Duke's wooing of Isabella in the final scene is more puzzling than anything in the Isabella/Angelo action. After pardoning Claudio, the Duke suddenly says to Isabella: "for your lovely sake, / Give me your hand, and say you will be mine" (5.1.493–94). This is astounding even in a context where the knots of the denouement are so quickly untied. Isabella says nothing. At the end of his final speech, the Duke once more addresses her with the hope of wrapping things up as in an old comedy:

> Dear Isabel,
> I have a motion much imports your good,
> Whereto if you'll a willing ear incline,
> What's mine is yours, and what is yours is mine. (537–40)

Isabella still says nothing. In many dramatic productions, much is made of Isabella's dealing in pantomime with the Duke's offer—she refuses it, of course. There is no possibility of her returning to the nunnery rather than accepting the Duke, but there is no way of wordlessly working out an enormous moment of truth for Isabella. If Shakespeare wanted to express these meanings, he would certainly have done it in the language of the play and not in pantomime and a series of wordless gestures.[3]

The problem plays rely on tragicomic themes that are not easily amenable to resolution, like the knots that can be so cleverly untied in the denouement of comedy. There are no happy endings in the problem plays, and the management of the action is much less confident than in the comedies. *Measure for Measure* feels dire at the beginning as we await the execution of Claudio for fornication under the strict new laws of Vienna as enforced by Angelo. In *All's Well* Bertram abandons his new bride and flees Paris under the foolish guidance of Parolles. When Cressida in *Troilus and Cressida* returns to the Greek camp and Achilles prepares to enter the field of battle, we feel that fate is moving against the Trojans and that they will ultimately be defeated. These events are much more serious than the usual perturbations and complications of comedy.

As a case in point, I'd like to look at how the bed trick is used in *Measure for Measure* and *All's Well That Ends Well*.[4] This is an old medieval and folkloric motif based on the idea that in bed all women are alike and that one woman can easily be substituted for another without doing any harm. It is a comic device because in the end everything turns out for the best, yet there are certain unsavory, sexist assumptions about the bed trick because it is founded on the idea that women are sexual objects without any distinctive subjectivity. In *Measure for Measure*, the Duke proposes the bed trick in almost the exact middle of the play, when it seems as if there is no way to prevent Claudio's execution under Angelo's tyrannous administration of the law. The Duke's *deus ex machina* solution to the plot difficulties sounds almost too good to be true:

> to the love I have in doing good a remedy presents itself. I do make myself believe that you may most uprighteously do a poor wronged lady [i.e., Mariana] a merited benefit; redeem your brother from the angry law; do no stain to your own gracious person; and much please the absent Duke, if peradventure he shall ever return to have hearing of this business. (3.1.200–7)

The Duke doesn't hesitate to work in ironic self-praise in his last line.

In act 4, scene 1, Isabella seems pleased with her surrogate role in the bed trick, and she dwells on the erotic details of the assignation in Angelo's garden as she recites them to the Duke and Mariana:

> He hath a garden circummured with brick,
> Whose western side is with a vineyard backed;
> And to that vineyard is a planchèd [=planked] gate,
> That makes his opening with this bigger key.
> This other doth command a little door
> Which from the vineyard to the garden leads.
> There have I made my promise
> Upon the heavy middle of the night
> To call upon him. (28–36)

The imagery of the keys that unlock various gates and doors in the "heavy middle of the night" is loaded with erotic associations, just as Isabella's dialogue with Angelo is in act 2, scene 4. It's the lingering on the details that leads us to believe that Isabella is enjoying her role in the bed trick. She can act out a surreptitious sensual role without any direct participation.

In *All's Well That Ends Well*, Helena lays out the details of the bed trick in act 3, scene 7. She has managed to marry Bertram, at the King's behest, but he has fled from her without consummating their marriage. Once in Florence, Bertram lustfully pursues Diana, daughter of the Widow. Helena, in disguise, has followed her husband to Italy, and now importunes the Widow to allow her to substitute herself for Diana in Bertram's bed:

> You see it lawful then. It is no more
> But that your daughter, ere she seems as won,
> Desires this ring; appoints him an encounter;
> In fine, delivers me to fill the time,
> Herself most chastely absent. (30–34)

Everything is aboveboard, everyone will benefit by the deceptions, yet some moral stigma clings to the bed trick.

Helena insists on paying large sums of money to assuage any guilt attached to the arrangement:

> Take this purse of gold,
> And let me buy your friendly help thus far,
> Which I will over-pay and pay again
> When I have found it. (14–17)

And further, "To marry her I'll add three thousand crowns / To what is passed already" (35–36). This sounds like a necessary bribe. At the end of the scene, Helena revels in the ambiguity of fulfilling the riddling and impossible conditions that Bertram has set for the renewal of their marriage:

> Let us assay our plot, which, if it speed,
> Is wicked meaning in a lawful deed,
> And lawful meaning in a lawful act,
> Where both not sin, and yet a sinful fact. (44–47)

The "wicked meaning" is obviously Bertram's supposed adultery with Diana, but the whole bed trick is cloaked with such overtones.

At the end of the play, Helena claims her husband because she has fulfilled all the conditions stipulated in his letter:

> There is your ring,
> And, look you, here's your letter. This it says:
> "When from my finger you can get this ring,
> And is by me with child," &c. This is done.
> Will you be mine, now you are doubly won? (5.3.310–14)

Helena seems to claim her right to Bertram on a technicality drawn out of folklore. The specified conditions function like an oracle—compare the almost impossible oracle in *Pericles*. The ring play is specifically like the ending of *The Merchant of Venice*.

Troilus and Cressida is similar to *Measure for Measure* in its representation of love. In both plays, love is unsatisfactory and unfulfilled. Even though Troilus and Cressida do consummate their love, through the good offices of Pandarus, the passion is brief and unenduring, and there are already strong hints of the destruction of Troilus's romantic longing. The problem seems to lie with his conception of love.[5] Why does he need Pandarus to pimp for him? This immediately undercuts his own fantasy-laden sense of love. There is a discordant tone in Troilus's first speeches in the play. When he tells Pandarus that he is "mad / In Cressid's love" (1.1.53–54), Pandarus is imagined to answer

> she is fair,
> Pour'st in the open ulcer of my heart
> Her eyes, her hair, her cheek, her gait, her voice. . . . (54–56)

It is odd to hear Troilus, the lover, speaking of his heart as an "open ulcer," and it is even odder to hear Cressida's lovable qualities described as being poured into it. There is another grotesque image at the end of Troilus's speech: "Thou lay'st in every gash that love hath given me / The knife that made it" (64–65). Is love appropriately imagined as a knife that makes gashes in the body of the lover?

In the great love scene of act 3, scene 2, Troilus attempts to define the nature of love, and especially of sexual passion, in terms that are not only strange but also occasionally inept. Before Pandarus enters with Cressida at line 40, Troilus indulges himself in description of his exalted erotic state. He begins as a lost soul on the banks of the River Styx that leads into the underworld of Hades. He appeals to Pandarus to ferry him across:

> O, be thou my Charon,
> And give me swift transportance to those fields
> Where I may wallow in the lily beds
> Proposed for the deserver. (9–12)

In his imagination of sexual pleasure, Troilus speaks only of himself and not at all about Cressida, and his speeches have a naive and narcissistic quality like those of Angelo to Isabella. "Wallow" is an odd word for what Troilus proposes to accomplish in the "lily beds" of the Elysian Fields.

The next exclamation is to "gentle Pandar": "From Cupid's shoulder pluck his painted wings, / And fly with me to Cressid" (13–14). It is hard to imagine Pandarus in the play as being "gentle," and even more preposterous to imagine him with Cupid's "painted wings." The "giddy" Troilus, in a soliloquy, plunges into "Th' imaginary relish" of sexual fulfillment, which "is so sweet / That it enchants my sense" (18–19). What will the actual experience be like, "When that the wat'ry palate tastes indeed / Love's thrice-repurèd nectar" (20–21)? Troilus fears that he will not be able to cope with the intense ecstasy of the triple-distilled nectar of love, that he will either die or experience

> some joy too fine,
> Too subtle, potent, tuned too sharp in sweetness
> For the capacity of my ruder powers. (22–24)

The imagery is extravagant, overwrought, even grotesque, and it all centers on Troilus's vain attempt to conceptualize his sexual feelings. There is no corresponding timorousness of young love in Cressida, and these preliminary speeches bode ill for the success of the love affair.

Pandarus, the go-between, is consistently vulgar in this scene, and since everything is done through his arrangement, the romantic tone of Troilus is singularly out of place. Cressida is always coy and witty, but she is obviously much more sophisticated sexually than Troilus. He complains to her of the disparity between will and execution:

> This is the monstrosity in love, lady, that the will is infinite and the execution confined; that the desire is boundless and the act a slave to limit. (82–83)

Cressida's answer is a witty disclaimer about the nature of love:

> They say all lovers swear more performance than they are able, and yet reserve an ability that they never perform, vowing more than the perfection of ten and discharging less than the tenth part of one. They that have the voice of lions and the act of hares—are they not monsters? (86–91)

There is an odd disparity between the lovers, as if they were not in the same world of discourse.

Cressida is wary in this scene, as if she is afraid to speak too openly. She confesses that she has loved Prince Troilus "night and day / For many weary months" (116–17), but she also says that she was "Hard to seem won" (119), as if only too aware of the dangers of saying all:

> But, though I loved you well, I wooed you not;
> And yet, good faith, I wished myself a man,
> Or that we women had men's privilege
> Of speaking first. (128–31)

She is still excessively careful not to be too demonstrative and never to speak of "Love's thrice-repurèd nectar," as Troilus does. There is even a certain doubleness in her comments:

> Perchance, my lord, I show more craft than love,
> And fell so roundly to a large confession
> To angle for your thoughts. But you are wise,
> Or else you love not, for to be wise and love
> Exceeds man's might; that dwells with gods above. (154–58)

This is ambiguous at best, and Cressida remains inscrutable.

There is no way of forgetting Cressida's chilling soliloquy at the end of act 1, scene 2, which is in the position of the conventional villain's soliloquy in Shakespeare. Cressida is extraordinarily calculating in this speech, presented entirely in formal couplets. It is Pandarus and not Cressida who offers Troilus "love's full sacrifice" (294). Cressida is coy: "Yet hold I off. Women are angels, wooing; / Things won are done, joy's soul lies in the doing" (298–99). Everything is stated in end-stopped, didactic, two-line apothegms. In the love game, desire is more important than fulfillment, which only ends the pursuit: "Men prize the thing ungained more than it is" (301). Sex is an illusion, mostly a foolish male illusion; the soliloquy is firmly anchored in a cynical, female perception of reality: "That she was never yet, that ever knew / Love got so sweet as when desire did sue" (302–3). This soliloquy doesn't provide the basis for Ulysses' later comment, when Cressida is in the Greek camp, that she is one of the "sluttish spoils of opportunity / And daughters of the game" (4.5.62–63). But it does suggest that Cressida is not a natural and foolish romantic about love the way Troilus is—we are certain that he will be bitterly disappointed. Her soliloquy alerts us to the fact that love and desire are manipulable passions rather than the spontaneous overflow of powerful feelings.

Helen and Paris provide the quasi-mythological background against which the affair of Troilus and Cressida is played. The ostensible cause of the Trojan War is that Paris, the son of Priam, has carried off Helen, the wife of Menelaus. The big scene with Helen (3.1) comes right before the love scene of Troilus and Cressida in 3.2. Helen is shown as a highly sophisticated, urbane, and languorous lady, like Cleopatra. As everyone acknowledges, she is "the mortal Venus, the heartblood of beauty, love's invisible soul" (33–34). In her witty conversation with Pandarus, she requests that he sing: "Let thy song be love. This love will undo us all. / O Cupid, Cupid, Cupid!" (111–12). She calls upon Cupid as if he were her tutelary deity. The song is teasingly sexual, which Paris interprets as: "hot blood begets hot thoughts, and hot thoughts beget hot deeds, and hot deeds is love" (128–29).

Pandarus interprets the song even more grossly:

> Is this the generation of love—hot blood, hot thoughts,
> and hot deeds? Why, they are vipers. Is love a generation
> of vipers? (130–32)

There is something about Helen that tends to poison the atmosphere, as if to establish in advance that the Trojan War is wrong and will end in tragedy for Troy. At the end of the scene, Paris asks Helen to "disarm great Hector" (153) with her "white enchanting fingers" (150), an action like Cleopatra's arming of Antony in *Antony and Cleopatra* 4.4. She is, fatally, the armorer of Antony's heart.

Hamlet has many similarities with *Troilus and Cressida* in its discordant, satirical tone and its sense of great hopes and expectations that are lost or destroyed. Hamlet and Troilus are both young men who are discontented with the world as it is. Love in *Hamlet* is frustrated and bitter. His aborted relation with Ophelia is played off against his perception of his mother's incestuous marriage to Claudius, his father's brother. This relation is endowed by Hamlet with a torrid and disgusting sexuality, especially in the Closet Scene (3.4) between Hamlet and Gertrude. We know from Hamlet's soliloquy at the end of act 3, scene 2 that he intends the scene with his mother to be hortatory:

> Let me be cruel, not unnatural;
> I will speak daggers to her, but use none. (403–4)

He has to steel himself not to murder her: "let not ever / The soul of Nero enter this firm bosom" (401–2). Nero was the Roman emperor who had his mother murdered, and Gertrude thinks of it as a real possibility in the Closet Scene. Her call to Polonius for help precipitates his murder.

We have no doubt that Hamlet intends to be cruel to his mother and to "speak daggers to her." His attack is predominantly sexual: she is incestuous, adulterous, a creature of loathsome lust. Hamlet shows his mother two painted portraits; the first is of his dead father,

> A combination and a form indeed
> Where every god did seem to set his seal
> To give the world assurance of a man. (3.4.61–63)

The other is of Gertrude's new husband, Claudius,

> like a mildewed ear
> Blasting his wholesome brother. Have you eyes?
> Could you on this fair mountain leave to feed,
> And batten on this moor? Ha! Have you eyes? (65–68)

Hamlet cannot understand how the menopausal Gertrude can conjure up sexual pleasure:

> You cannot call it love, for at your age
> The heyday in the blood is tame, it's humble,
> And waits upon the judgment. . . . (69–71)

In characteristic fashion, Hamlet sets his mother apart from the "heyday in the blood," or sexual appetite, that is typical of the young. The whole scene turns on the fantasies of inflamed adolescence.[6]

Hamlet's accusations are alarmingly sexual, somewhat like Iago's calumniations of Desdemona in *Othello* and Leontes' of Hermione in *The Winter's Tale*. Hamlet says with disgust and anger,

> Nay, but to live
> In the rank sweat of an enseamèd bed,
> Stewed in corruption, honeying and making love
> Over the nasty sty— (92–95)

"Seam" is a word for fat or grease, most familiar in cooking. "Rank" means disgusting in smell, like "rancid." The marriage bed is a "nasty sty" and the lovers are imagined as a couple of pigs. Has Hamlet actually spied on his mother and her new husband, or is he just indulging his sexual imagination? Sometimes Claudius and Gertrude are played on stage or in film as a lustful couple, but this overliteralizes an obvious point. The same problem arises in *The Winter's Tale*, when Leontes speaks of his wife and his friend Polixenes "meeting noses," "Kissing with inside lip," and "Horsing foot on foot" (1.2.285–88). We never see any of this in the stage action. That's the point of Leontes' insane jealousy: that it is generated from his own frantic thoughts.

Hamlet can't let go of his obsessive, primal scene imaginings. Even after the Ghost of his father appears to warn him against being so harsh with his mother—"Leave her to heaven / And to those thorns that in her bosom lodge" (1.5.86–87), as the Ghost says in an earlier scene—Hamlet cannot cease speaking daggers to Gertrude. It obviously serves him as an important mode of expression and a release of pent-up emotions. He is preoccupied with sexual sermonizing: "go not to my uncle's bed, / Assume a virtue, if you have it not" (3.4.160–61).

But a score of lines further he is again dwelling on his mother's sexual depravity:

> Let the bloat King tempt you again to bed,
> Pinch wanton on your cheek, call you his mouse,
> And let him, for a pair of reechy [=smoky] kisses,
> Or paddling in your neck with his damned fingers,
> Make you to ravel all this matter out. . . .   (183–87)

"Mouse" is a lover's diminutive, which the Citizen's Wife uses quite frequently in Beaumont and Fletcher's *The Knight of the Burning Pestle* (1607). We never see the "bloat King" "paddling" in Gertrude's neck, which is presumably substantial enough to lend itself to paddling. Iago uses "paddle"—"Didst thou not see her paddle with the palm of his hand?" (*Othello* 2.1.253–54)—and so does the jealous Leontes: "But to be paddling palms and pinching fingers, / As now they are" (*The Winter's Tale* 1.2.115–16). Hamlet is tormented by his own lewd thoughts about his mother and Claudius.

It is against this corrupted background of "a mother stained" (4.4.57) that we have to understand Hamlet's relation with Ophelia. It is already clear from his first soliloquy (1.2) that his mother's hasty marriage has disillusioned him about women. "Frailty, thy name is woman" (146), that Gertrude should "post / With such dexterity to incestuous sheets"

(156–57), is the theme of this speech. The word "incest"[7] is repeated over and over again in the play, especially in these early scenes. It is interesting that Hamlet imagines even the previous, good Gertrude, married to the elder Hamlet, as a strongly sexual creature:

> Why, she would hang on him
> As if increase of appetite had grown
> By what it fed on. . . . (143–45)

Appetite and feeding make strongly negative images for love, equating it with lust, as in Antony's complaint about Cleopatra: "I found you as a morsel cold upon / Dead Caesar's trencher [=wooden dish]" (*Antony and Cleopatra* 3.13.116–17), or Troilus's lament about Cressida:

> The fractions of her faith, orts of her love,
> The fragments, scraps, the bits, and greasy relics
> Of her o'ereaten faith, are given to Diomed.
> (*Troilus and Cressida* 5.2.155–57)

The grievous falling-off of Hamlet's mother makes him disillusioned and bitter about the possibility of love.

In her extraordinary passivity, Ophelia is different from the heroines of comedy. Laertes' advice to his sister in act 1, scene 3 is given as if to a child:

> For Hamlet, and the trifling of his favor,
> Hold it a fashion and a toy in blood,
> A violet in the youth of primy nature,
> Forward, not permanent, sweet, not lasting,
> The perfume and suppliance of a minute,
> No more.   (5–10)

Hamlet's love for Ophelia is devalued: it is "a toy in blood," a sexual trifle or fancy. There is an active danger that the naive and unsophisticated Ophelia will her "chaste treasure open / To his unmastered importunity" (31–32). "Chaste treasure" is vulgar, the direct representation of sexuality in monetary terms. Ophelia is disempowered. Her father is even more imperious than her brother in giving her advice; to her pathetic "I do not know, my lord, what I should think" (104), Polonius says only: "Marry, I will teach you. Think yourself a baby" (105).

Ophelia's eventual fate is already evident in these early scenes. Beginning with her report of the melancholy Hamlet's visiting her in her closet, Polonius jumps to the conclusion, "This is the very ecstasy of love" (2.1.102), and he reports to the King and Queen his certain conviction that Hamlet is mad for love. Ophelia doesn't take part in these judgments. After the "To be, or not to be" soliloquy in act 3, scene 1, Hamlet bitterly turns on Ophelia, who has been on stage for all of his speech. "Get thee to a nunnery" (121) is an angry imperative to remove her from marriageable women: "Why wouldst thou be a breeder of sinners?" (121–22). "Nunnery" was used ironically in Shakespeare's time to mean a brothel. The scene is full of a wild misogyny that connects with earlier parts of the play. It is hard to believe that Hamlet is speaking specifically of Ophelia as she appears on stage when he inveighs against women's cosmetics: "I have heard of your paintings, well enough. God hath given you one face, and you make yourselves another" (144–46). This seems more like a generalized attack on women than a specific insult to the pitiful Ophelia, who is so abashed by Hamlet's savagery.

In the play scene too, Hamlet's bawdy talk with Ophelia is meant to demean her. Under the guise of madness, his free speech is grossly sexual: "Lady, shall I lie in your lap?" (3.2.115). He protests disingenuously: "Do you think I meant country matters?" (119). There is an obvious pun on "country" as an imagined adjectival form of "cunt." There is certainly an undertone of this meaning in Iago's sexualized Venice:

I know our country disposition well:
In Venice they do let heaven see the pranks
They dare not show their husbands. (*Othello* 3.3.201–3)

A few lines further Iago speaks of Desdemona's "country forms" (237).

Hamlet is consistently sexual with Ophelia. He threatens her as a voyeur of her sexual escapades: "I could interpret between you and your love, if I could see the puppets dallying" (3.2.252–53). Ophelia tries to maintain a tone of witty banter: "You are keen, my lord, you are keen" (254). But Hamlet cuts off the discourse with male bravado: "It would cost you a groaning to take off mine edge" (255–56). Compare the odd sexual word "disedge," used only once by Shakespeare in *Cymbeline*. Imogen is thinking of her husband Posthumus, who has rejected her and tried to kill her through Pisanio:

I grieve myself
To think, when thou shalt be disedged by her
That now thou tirest on [=feeds voraciously]. . . . (3.4.94–96)

Hamlet is exhilarated by the discoveries of the Play Scene and lets go everything else, like the trivialities of love.

Ophelia eventually goes mad and sings snatches of popular ballads that are markedly bawdy. After monumental repression, she seems finally to be expressing herself. When she drowns, wittingly or unwittingly, the Queen speaks sentiments we weren't aware of earlier in the play:

> I hoped thou shouldst have been my Hamlet's wife.
> I thought thy bride bed to have decked, sweet maid,
> And not have strewed thy grave. (5.1.246–48)

Ophelia emerges as a tragic victim of frustrated love and repression on the part of both Hamlet and her father and brother. She exists in a context where love cannot flourish. Her most moving speeches are those that express pity for others: the melancholy Hamlet, who appears in her closet and whom she believes "Blasted with ecstasy" (3.1.163); and her dead father. Her last lines in act 3, scene 1 are a beautifully formed couplet: "O, woe is me / T' have seen what I have seen, see what I see!" (163–64). These are among the most haunting lines in the play.

None of the problem plays nor *Hamlet* has a happy ending like those of comedy. In *Measure for Measure* and *All's Well*, the tragicomic issues are resolved by the bed trick, but without any sense of fulfillment or satisfaction. All four of the plays discussed in this chapter are harsh and satirical; the feeling of love is defective, and women are represented in a strongly disillusioned and bitter way. None of these plays is either a love comedy or a love tragedy. Love itself is problematical and unfulfilled: the marriages in *Measure for Measure* and *All's Well* either exist to satisfy some legal formality or are glaringly imperfect, and in *Troilus and Cressida* and *Hamlet* the love relationships are doomed to failure almost from the start.

CHAPTER FOUR

DOCTRINE IN THE TRAGEDIES

Love does not lend itself well to Shakespearean tragedy[1] for the same reasons that make it especially rewarding in comedy. In other words, love ending in marriage is a natural theme of comedy. All the perturbations and troubles that block the fulfillment of love in a Shakespearean comedy are overcome in the happy ending. Moreover, the difficulties that stand in the way of love are decidedly not tragic, in the sense that they are not profound, not related to the nature of things, not insuperable, not deeply established in character or situation. Love comedies emphasize that the original problems are capricious and arbitrary and can be resolved with sufficient imagination, ingenuity, energy, and good fortune. Love is conceived as a positive good, which makes its fulfillment almost comic by definition. Closely allied with beauty in all of its manifestations, love is understood to be something celebratory.

All these popular assumptions work against the possibility of love tragedy. In Denis de Rougemont's book, *Love in the Western World*, the Tristram and Isolde story is used as a paradigm for the love relation. The basic thesis is that the death of the lovers—the *Liebestod*—is a fulfillment and a consummation of their passion. Their deaths celebrate the strength and intensity of their devotion to each other: "The approach of death acts as a goad to sensuality. In the full sense of the verb, it aggravates desire."[2] While death is ordinarily the ending of tragedy (as marriage is the usual ending of comedy), death for love does not feel truly tragic. The lovers are doomed through no "fault"—Aristotle's *hamartia*, or tragic flaw—of their own, but because of some barrier in the world around them. The union of true lovers is not possible, or not even desirable, in this world or in this life because the world is inadequate to their high, ideal demands. Death for love may be terribly sad, but it is the only end possible for those who love deeply enough. They are love's martyrs in one aspect but grand, heroic figures in another. If the lovers are glorified by their death, then their end cannot properly be tragic.

In the Swedish movie *Elvira Madigan* (1967) by Bo Widerberg, the beautiful heroine, who is a slack-wire performer, and the dashing young officer seem to have nothing else to do but love each other. Their careers, such as they are, are subordinated to their hopeless passion. They cannot survive in this crude and materialistic world, as is clear in the lush romantic image of the cherry blossoms falling on them as if to seal their fate. However, their mutual deaths are not so much tragic as infinitely sad and sorrowful because they seem to enter into another life in which they will finally achieve happiness. There is no place for them among earth's practical and unpoetic creatures. They are too beautiful and too much in love with each other to live in this world without being involved in disastrous compromises.

The same romantic assumptions apply to Nagisa Oshima's *In the Realm of the Senses* (1976), a highly erotic Japanese film that shows the lovers engaged in endless sexual couplings that ultimately lead to their deaths, probably by suicide. They fulfill themselves—neurotically, to our eyes—but beautifully nevertheless. Although their end fills us with sadness at the wasted potential, death seems the only option available to them, considering the intensity of their passion. Their deaths are not brought on by any flaws or weaknesses in their character, according to the precepts for tragedy in Aristotle's *Poetics*, but rather because they are totally unsuited for life in this world. They are not tragic in any strict definition of the term, but rather doomed. We feel the conventional pity and fear for their fate, but we also feel a certain instinctive admiration for the intensity of their passion and their commitment to each other. The death of the lovers has some quality of celebration that is not appropriate for tragedy.

I am not claiming that Shakespeare has affinities with Bo Widerberg, Nagisa Oshima, or the creators of the Tristram and Isolde story, but Shakespeare's love tragedies have inherent difficulties in their conception of tragedy. Love tragedy raises special genre problems. It seems a distinct branch of tragicomedy because the union of lovers at the end represents a positive, upward movement, but historically, there are many melodramatic tragicomedies in which the tragedy is suddenly reversed at the climax and a happy ending is tacked on. *Othello* seems to be the only Shakespearean love tragedy that at the end is truly tragic, although there are still ways in which *Othello* as a domestic play departs from conventional expectations.[3]

Romeo and Juliet raises acutely some of the problems of love tragedy.[4] It is a fairly early play, usually dated around 1595, from the same period as *A Midsummer Night's Dream* and *Richard II*, which it resembles in its intense lyricism. The play begins as a comedy, with the mooning Romeo, a somewhat absurd victim of melancholy, in love with Rosaline. The feud between the houses of Montague and Capulet is represented in the first scene as a rather farcical conflict of comic servants, Sampson and Gregory for the Capulets and Abram and Balthasar for the Montagues. As the action progresses, only Tybalt, the "ratcatcher" and the "King of Cats" (3.1.76, 78), seems to take the feud seriously, and he is represented as a rather laughable, histrionic malcontent/revenger, plucked out of old plays like Kyd's *The Spanish Tragedy* (1587).

His dialogue with his uncle Capulet at the ball, where Romeo first sees and falls in love with Juliet, illustrates how isolated a figure Tybalt is and how fanatical he is about a feud no one else seems to believe in. Tybalt recognizes Romeo immediately and calls for his rapier:

> Now, by the stock and honor of my kin,
> To strike him dead I hold it not a sin. (1.5.60–61)

Capulet takes pains to curb his nephew's ardor and to insist on Romeo's worth and integrity:

> Content thee, gentle coz, let him alone.
> 'A bears him like a portly [=of good deportment] gentleman,
> And, to say truth, Verona brags of him

To be a virtuous and well-governed youth.
I would not for the wealth of all this town
Here in my house do him disparagement. (67–72)

Capulet obviously doesn't think of Romeo as his mortal enemy. He calls the swordsman Tybalt "a saucy boy" (85) and a "princox" (88).

Until the death of Mercutio in 3.1, the love interest overpowers the sense of doom and astrological disaster that the lovers are constantly speaking about. They understand fully what an extraordinary experience it is to be in love. Juliet seems the epitome of the radiant young woman of comedy: innocent, intelligent, warm-hearted, witty, lyrical. Romeo is not unlike Shakespeare's male lovers in the comedies, who are overwhelmed by love at first sight and seem much less resourceful in coping with love than the women.

Mercutio's Queen Mab speech in act 1, scene 4 prepares us for the great love scene that follows. Queen Mab, the Fairy Queen, is like Titania in *A Midsummer Night's Dream*, and the fairy world invoked is similar in both plays, which Shakespeare wrote around the same time. According to Mercutio, Queen Mab has strong control over dreams: "she gallops night by night / Through lovers' brains, and then they dream of love" (70–71). In other words, love is a product of fantasy, fancy, and imagination, as expressed in dreams:

> True, I talk of dreams;
> Which are the children of an idle brain,
> Begot of nothing but vain fantasy;
> Which is as thin of substance as the air,
> And more inconstant than the wind. . . . (96–99)

Romeo's love scene with Juliet in act 1, scene 5 surpasses all the love scenes in the comedies by the intensity of its lyric expression. It is hyperbolic in conception. As soon as Romeo sees Juliet and before he has even spoken with her, he is exploding with inexpressible love, far greater than what can be expected by the love-at-first-sight convention:

> O, she doth teach the torches to burn bright!
> It seems she hangs upon the cheek of night
> As a rich jewel in an Ethiop's ear—
> Beauty too rich for use, for earth too dear! (46–49)

How can Romeo proceed so quickly into such ecstatic exclamatory couplets? There is no development, no buildup, nowhere to go from here, since Romeo is already at the climax of his affection even before Juliet is allowed to enter the dialogue.

Their wooing is highly artificial, as they speak in perfectly formed, sonnetlike quatrains that answer each other. The images are far-fetched, ingenious conceits, common in sonnets of the period. Romeo introduces the religious/erotic theme with a clever pun:

> If I profane with my unworthiest hand
> This holy shrine, the gentle sin is this:
> My lips, two blushing pilgrims, ready stand
> To smooth that rough touch with a tender kiss. (95–98)

Juliet continues the conceit by addressing Romeo as "Good pilgrim" (99) and modestly speaking of hands rather than lips: "And palm to palm is holy palmers' kiss" (102). The witty Juliet translates "palmer," a religious pilgrim who carries a palm branch, into one who uses his palms for touching his loved one. The fourteen-line sonnet proper ends with a couplet and a kiss, then another couplet is tacked on.

The extreme stylistic artifice is produced by the intensity of their passion, but Romeo and Juliet manage to bring it off and make it convincing. The fact that the lovers use conventional imagery doesn't seen to matter; it is empowered by the strength of their feelings. Act 2, scene 2 serves as a climax for the wooing; the lines are illuminated by their exalted images. Romeo sees Juliet as an angelic being:

> O, speak again, bright angel, for thou art
> As glorious to this night, being o'er my head,
> As is a wingèd messenger of heaven
> Unto the white-upturnèd wond'ring eyes
> Of mortals that fall back to gaze on him
> When he bestrides the lazy puffing clouds
> And sails upon the bosom of the air. (26–32)

This is not so much about love as about the actions of the angelic orders in relation to a worshipful mankind. There is a great deal of religious imagery converted to erotic needs, which fits perfectly the mood of adoration. Juliet asks Romeo to "swear by thy gracious self, / Which is the god of my idolatry" (113–14), so even Juliet recognizes that her doting love is a kind of worshipping of Romeo, as if he were a god.

Juliet is strikingly similar to the heroines of Shakespeare's comedies. She leads the love game. While Romeo is frantic with grief in act 3, scene 3 and acting in a distracted, grotesque way, Juliet is always trying to cope with the difficulties of her position. She seems to grow up in the course of the action, to become more mature and self-directed, a development that is not equally true of Romeo. This is carefully articulated in act 3, scene 5, which begins with the beautiful wedding night of the lovers on the upper stage ("*aloft*"), but continues with Juliet's father's wildly tyrannical discourse about his daughter's proposed match to Paris.

Old Capulet's "fingers itch" (165) as he speaks to Juliet with a harshness that is akin to direct abandonment:

> Wife, we scarce thought us blest
> That God had lent us but this only child;
> But now I see this one is one too much,
> And that we have a curse in having her. (165–68)

Lady Capulet is similarly unresponsive to Juliet's plea, "O sweet my mother, cast me not away!" (200). She says coldly: "Talk not to me, for I'll not speak a word" (204). The Nurse too refuses to give Juliet "comfort" (214). In her soliloquy at the end of the scene Juliet is no longer a protected teenager but absolutely alone to confront her fate: "If all else fail, myself have power to die" (244).

The consequences of this speech are worked out in the long soliloquy in act 4, scene 3, when she is about to take Friar Lawrence's sleeping potion, which will induce a seeming death. Juliet in this scene is quite different from the witty, charming, innocent, childlike character earlier in the play; she is moving to some important tragic awareness. The whole soliloquy turns on her fears, especially her fear of death. She sees clearly that "My dismal scene I needs must act alone" (19), and she has a dagger ready if the potion doesn't work. She imagines vividly the burial vault when she will awake:

> loathsome smells,
> And shrieks like mandrakes torn out of the earth,
> That living mortals, hearing them run mad. . . . (46–48)

She is afraid of the despair that might encourage her to take her own life, yet at the end she acts as if to protect Romeo from Tybalt's ghost: "Stay,

Tybalt, stay! / Romeo, Romeo, Romeo, I drink to thee" (57–58). The repetition of Romeo's name is a wonderful, loving touch for the actor to dwell on, as Juliet drinks from the vial. Her sleep/death is another consummation of her love.

In the construction of *Romeo and Juliet*, Shakespeare carefully establishes the feud as a blocking action to the course of true love, but it is not until Tybalt's killing of Mercutio in 3.1 that the play turns abruptly to tragedy. The scene begins with Mercutio's witty banter, in which he endows the mild Benvolio with the qualities of a testy duelist like Tybalt. When Tybalt enters with his companions right afterward, Mercutio is provocative. To Tybalt's "A word with one of you," Mercutio replies: "And but one word with one of us? Couple it with something; make it a word and a blow" (39–41). Romeo enters and Tybalt challenges him to fight by calling him a villain, but Romeo, now in love with Tybalt's cousin Juliet, demurs. Mercutio cannot bear this "calm, dishonorable, vile submission" (74) and draws on Tybalt, while Romeo, trying to stop the fray, holds back Mercutio, who is mortally stabbed under Romeo's arm. His first words are: "A plague a' both houses" (92), which is repeated as a refrain in the next eighteen lines as the play is suddenly catapulted into tragedy. Romeo's killing "the furious Tybalt" (123) when he returns to the stage to seek out Romeo completes the movement to tragedy.

Before Tybalt reenters the scene, Romeo complains that Juliet's "beauty hath made me effeminate / And in my temper soft'ned valor's steel!" (116–17). This is Antony's problem in relation to Cleopatra in *Antony and Cleopatra*, and love versus honor is a familiar topic in the continuing debate about the nature of love. Romeo already predicts the dire consequences of what has happened:

> This day's black fate on moe days doth depend;
> This but begins the woe others must end. (121–22)

This only continues the enumeration of portents and evil omens that began in the Prologue, which speaks of "A pair of star-crossed lovers." Shakespeare goes to great lengths, even in the comic action, to give the play a tragic coloring, as if he were particularly anxious to work against the assumption of the audience that they are watching a comedy.

The introduction of inauspicious signs sometimes seems not only inappropriate but also mechanical and artificial. After Mercutio's magnificent Queen Mab oration, Romeo is troubled by unmotivated forebodings. His anxieties precede his meeting with Juliet in the next scene:

> my mind misgives
> Some consequence yet hanging in the stars
> Shall bitterly begin his fearful date
> With this night's revels and expire the term
> Of a despisèd life, closed in my breast,
> By some vile forfeit of untimely death. (1.4.106–11)

Why does Romeo have these fears—only to help Shakespeare out in his heroic effort to inject a feeling of tragedy into this play?

Likewise, Juliet surprises us with her trepidations in the magnificent Orchard Scene:

> Although I joy in thee,
> I have no joy of this contract tonight.
> It is too rash, too unadvised, too sudden;
> Too like the lightning, which doth cease to be
> Ere one can say it lightens. (2.2.116–20)

But love in Shakespeare is traditionally represented as sudden, immediate, and lightninglike. It comes at once and is not the product of mature deliberation. It is hard to know, therefore, what Juliet's fears are based on, unless, like Tom Stoppard's Rosencrantz and Guildenstern, she has already read the play and knows how it will turn out. She has no way of discerning at this point that the comedy of love culminating in marriage will take a bad turn and end in tragedy. Admittedly, there is the feud between the Capulets and the Montagues, but that seems to be dissipating, so it seems another comic plot device to prevent the course of true love from running smooth.

Friar Lawrence also does much to develop the sense of fatality in the love affair. In the scene before Mercutio's death in 3.1, the lovesick Romeo comes to ask the Friar to perform the marriage ceremony. Already Romeo is speaking of "love-devouring death" (2.6.7), as if his love for Juliet were naturally associated with death. Friar Lawrence continues in the same vein:

> These violent delights have violent ends
> And in their triumph die, like fire and powder,
> Which, as they kiss, consume. The sweetest honey
> Is loathsome in his own deliciousness
> And in the taste confounds the appetite.

Therefore love moderately: long love doth so;
Too swift arrives as tardy as too slow. (9–15)

"Love moderately" is surely bad advice in the context of all the love affairs in Shakespeare before *Romeo and Juliet*. It is a contradiction in terms. Shakespeare is making such a strenuous effort to pull the play into tragedy that the many portentous statements about the love of Romeo and Juliet seem misconceived. The tragedy of the lovers seems generated by their intense and abrupt passion rather than by the feud between the houses. This is an idea that the play is promoting in many different, misguided ways.

Romeo too is made to fear the absoluteness and suddenness of his love. Shakespeare makes a continuous association of love and death—the *Liebestod*—in this play despite a comic context of search and fulfillment. Inauspicious astrological signs are inserted into *Romeo and Juliet* like the portents in the early scenes of *Julius Caesar*. Even before he meets Juliet, Romeo fears that "this night's revels" shall inevitably lead to "some vile forfeit of untimely death" (1.4.109–11). There is no real basis for his feelings, except that we onlookers know the play will take a sudden turn toward tragedy. I am arguing that this turn, or peripeteia, is overprepared, as if Shakespeare were worried that the audience would not properly accept the way the play moves into tragedy. Romeo and Juliet love each other deeply and truly, and they want naturally to get married and consummate their passion as soon as possible, like all the other lovers in Shakespeare's comedies. There is nothing wrong with any of this.

What we have to fall back on is the fact that love in itself does not produce the tragedy in *Romeo and Juliet*. The protagonists are always represented as pure and innocent and devoted to each other. They are clearly victims of the feud between the houses. This explanation is explicitly set forth in the Prologue. In his didactic sonnet, the Chorus begins with the "Two households" in fair Verona and their "ancient grudge," whose causes are never explained. It is "From forth the fatal loins of these two foes" that "A pair of star-crossed lovers take their life." "Star-crossed" means astrologically fated or unlucky; it doesn't imply that there is anything wrong with the lovers or that they do anything to incur disastrous consequences. According to the Chorus, the death of the lovers is necessary to end the feud between their families. Their "misadventured piteous overthrows / Doth with their death bury their parents' strife," "And the continuance of their parents' rage, / Which, but their children's end, naught could remove." It sounds as if Romeo and Juliet are specifically marked as scapegoats.

This idea is taken up again at the end of the play. Capulet announces that Romeo and Juliet are "Poor sacrifices of our enmity" (5.3.304), and the Prince deals with the love death as a sacrifice:

> Capulet, Montague,
> See what a scourge is laid upon your hate,
> That heaven finds means to kill your joys with love.   (291–93)

So the tragedy by rights belongs to Capulet and Montague rather than to Romeo and Juliet, who are required to die for love because true love is not possible in a world of senseless blood feuds. They are "Poor sacrifices" of the feud, victims and scapegoats, rather than tragic protagonists.

Antony and Cleopatra illustrates even better than *Romeo and Juliet* the generic difficulties of love tragedy. The play was written late in Shakespeare's career, certainly after *Hamlet, Othello, King Lear,* and *Macbeth,* perhaps just before *Timon of Athens* and *Coriolanus,* both of which are rather imperfect tragedies. The point of this tentative chronology is to place *Antony and Cleopatra* in 1606 or 1607, just before Shakespeare's great romances, *Pericles, Cymbeline, The Winter's Tale,* and *The Tempest.* There are, in fact, many romance elements in *Antony and Cleopatra.* Perhaps its genre is better described as romantic tragedy than either tragedy or tragicomedy. Wonder, awe, and marvelous astonishment apply better to its upbeat ending than the pity and fear associated with Aristotle's definition of tragedy. The endings of *Antony and Cleopatra* and *Romeo and Juliet* celebrate the unions of true lovers, who seem, in their deaths, to be superior to the base, materialistic world they leave behind. Dryden's version of *Antony and Cleopatra, All for Love, or The World Well Lost* (1678), simplifies and dichotomizes the generic issues, but his play seems even less a tragedy than Shakespeare's. To die for love, as Antony and Cleopatra do, is made to seem a triumphant act.

One of the difficulties arises from the fact that Shakespeare's Cleopatra is never convincingly tragic. She is allied to comedy, but she is not at all like young heroines such as Rosalind, Beatrice, and Viola. She is more like Cressida, Helen, and even Venus in *Venus and Adonis* in her lustfulness, her wiles, and her satiric energy. She herself says that she is "with Phoebus' amorous pinches black, / And wrinkled deep in time" (1.5.28–29). How old is that? We can't say exactly, but she is definitely not a young ingenue. She has already had a variety of previous lovers.

Agrippa tells us, "She made great Caesar lay his sword to bed; / He plowed her and she cropped" (2.2.233–34). Cleopatra clearly has children. Octavius mentions Caesarion (3.6.6), the son that came of her union with Julius Caesar, Octavius's adoptive father.

The key to love in *Antony and Cleopatra* is the character of Cleopatra, who has either been foolishly idealized as a transcendent being or excoriated as a temptress violating all the postulates of Christian doctrine. In the play she is neither of these, and it is good to have feminist critics such as Linda Charnes writing about Cleopatra and calling sexist male critics to task for their infatuation.[5] Like Cressida in *Troilus and Cressida*, Cleopatra is a mixed character. The conversation of Antony and Enobarbus in act 1, scene 2 is instructive. When Antony announces, "I must with haste from hence" (133), Enobarbus immediately answers, "Why, then we kill all our women" (134). Enobarbus is the great exemplar of the Roman general, for whom it is unimaginable to be in love. He admires women from a distance, and when Antony says bitterly: "Would I had never seen her!" (154), Enobarbus answers in a way that seems extraordinarily superficial and uninvolved:

O, sir, you had then left unseen a wonderful piece of work, which not to have been blest withal would have discredited your travel. (155–57)

Cleopatra is clearly a three-star attraction, which, in the Michelin rating system, is worth not just a detour but a special trip.

In their talk, Enobarbus is the one who praises the value of women, not Antony, who feels tragically divided from himself in his love affair. Enobarbus speaks as a fully qualified participant in the love game, with all of its histrionic excesses:

Cleopatra, catching but the least noise of this, dies instantly; I have seen her die twenty times upon far poorer moment. I do think there is mettle in death, which commits some loving act upon her, she hath such a celerity in dying. (141–46)

There is obvious erotic play on the word "die," which was used familiarly for "orgasm"—there is even an echo of this in Antony's "I am dying, Egypt, dying" (4.15.18). In 1.2, Antony gives Enobarbus's arguments short shrift—"She is cunning past man's thought" (147)—but Enobarbus protests at length:

Alack, sir, no; her passions are made of nothing but the finest part
of pure love. . . . This cannot be cunning in her; if it be, she makes
a show'r of rain as well as Jove. (148–49, 152–53)

There is no way that he can convince Antony; they have totally different
conceptions of love.

This conversation in act 1, scene 2 provides a good basis for understanding Enobarbus's celebrated description of Cleopatra as she appears
on her barge on the river Cydnus when she first meets Antony. This is a
pictorial set piece, but remarkably little is said about Cleopatra herself:

> For her own person,
> It beggared all description: she did lie
> In her pavilion, cloth-of-gold of tissue,
> O'erpicturing that Venus where we see
> The fancy outwork nature. . . . (2.2.203–7)

Enobarbus uses the familiar Marlovian trick of invidious comparison:
Cleopatra's beauty goes beyond even the painting of Venus herself.
There is a peculiar stasis in the imagery, as if all conscious effort to
describe the scene were useless. The "pretty dimpled boys," who stand on
each side of Cleopatra "like smiling Cupids" (208), fan her

> With divers-colored fans, whose wind did seem
> To glow the delicate cheeks which they did cool,
> And what they undid did. (209–11)

This is a characteristic image in the play, where the effort of fanning both
cools and sets aglow Cleopatra's cheeks; the yoking of opposites produces
an effect that cancels itself out.

After the Battle of Actium, Antony speaks contemptuously of her las-
civiousness in the repulsive terms used for leftovers at a meal:

> I found you as a morsel cold upon
> Dead Caesar's trencher: nay, you were a fragment
> Of Gneius Pompey's, besides what hotter hours,
> Unregister'd in vulgar fame, you have
> Luxuriously picked out. (3.13.116–20)

Luxuria, or Lust, is one of the seven deadly sins, and the food terms—
"cold morsel" and "fragment"—are all unappetizing. Cleopatra is defi-

nitely not a young, virginal heroine; rather, she is a witty, clever, and highly mannered woman, tempting Antony with her histrionic artifice.

Enobarbus sums up her attractions right after his grand oration about how she first met Antony in her barge on the Cydnus:

> Age cannot wither her, nor custom stale
> Her infinite variety: other women cloy
> The appetites they feed, but she makes hungry
> Where most she satisfies. . . . (2.2.241–44)

"Infinite variety" is an archetypal description of a comic heroine because it connotes artifice as well as natural magnificence. In other words, Cleopatra has tricks that earn her Antony's affectionate title, "My serpent of old Nile" (1.5.25). Throughout the play serpents are associated with the fruitful river and with hot and teeming Egypt. We remember that Cleopatra kills herself with the bite of the asp, which she has found, by experiment, to be the easiest way to die. In a typical image of excess at both ends of the scale, she "makes hungry / Where most she satisfies." She doesn't "cloy" the appetite like other women—and the image is strongly sexual—but stimulates it. These are formulas for endlessly prolonged love.

This yoking of opposites is repeated at the end of Enobarbus's speech:

> vilest things
> Become themselves in her, that the holy priests
> Bless her when she is riggish. (2.2.244–46)

"Riggish" means wanton or horny, another strongly sexual word, but we should beware of those "vilest things" that realize their apotheosis in Cleopatra. She is a strange mixture of opposites.

If we go back to act 1, scene 5, we see the Cleopatra who is afterward described by Enobarbus. I think we need to understand that her dramatic character is only partly set out in words; to put this another way, she enacts on stage much more than is said about her in the words of the play. This is a scene in Egypt in Cleopatra's palace, where we see her alone with her waiting gentlewomen, Charmian and Iras, and the eunuch Mardian. She is bored during her separation from Antony, and her roving desire seeks out substitute objects of gratification. The boredom is strongly expressed in sudden changes of mood and interest. At the beginning of the scene, she is presumably yawning when she says:

Ha, ha.
Give me to drink mandragora. . . .
That I might sleep out this great gap of time
My Antony is away. (1.5.3–6)

Mandragora, used as a sleeping potion, is a narcotic prepared from the root of the mandrake. Iago has a gloating comment on Othello in which mandragora figures importantly:

Not poppy nor mandragora,
Nor all the drowsy syrups of the world,
Shall ever medicine thee to that sweet sleep
Which thou owedst yesterday. (*Othello* 3.3.327–30)

Mandragora was thought to have magical properties connected with sexual activity, as in Machiavelli's cynical play *Mandragola* (c. 1518).

Cleopatra teases the eunuch Mardian with the fact that he is "unseminared" (1.5.11)—a sexual, not an academic, term. She takes no pleasure "In aught an eunuch has" (10). Mardian has "fierce affections" (17) and thinks "What Venus did with Mars" (18), but in actuality he "can do nothing / But what indeed is honest to be done" (15–16). Cleopatra delights in twitting him on his incapacity, but this conversation leads immediately to thoughts of the absent Antony and breathless questions about him:

O, Charmian,
Where think'st thou he is now? Stands he, or sits he?
Or does he walk? Or is he on his horse?
O happy horse, to bear the weight of Antony! (18–21)

This is overtly sexual, as is Petruchio's wisecrack to Kate: "Women are made to bear and so are you" (*The Taming of the Shrew* 2.1.200). We remember this line later when Cleopatra is lifting up the dying Antony into her monument: "Here's sport indeed! How heavy weighs my lord!" (4.15.32). "Sport" is also a sexual word.

Act 2, scene 5 is in the same mode as act 1, scene 5. Again, Cleopatra is in her palace with Charmian and Iras and her servant Alexas. She begins with a histrionic, musical-comedy line: "Give me some music: music, moody food / Of us that trade in love" (1–2). She is hardly a trader in love, or prostitute, preparing an erotic atmosphere ("moody food") for her clients. The phrasing is not just heightened but faintly ridiculous. It echoes Duke Orsino's affected opening speech in *Twelfth Night*:

> If music be the food of love, play on,
> Give me excess of it, that, surfeiting,
> The appetite may sicken, and so die. (1.1.1–3)

The Duke is merely sentimentalizing on the high-strung emotions of love, just as Cleopatra is dabbling in music, in which she quickly loses interest. In line 3, she is already on to something else: "Let it alone, let's to billiards." This is not known to be an ancient Egyptian game, but Cleopatra is again diverted by the presence of Mardian the Eunuch. She teases him on his sexual inadequacies: "As well a woman with an eunuch played / As with a woman" (5–6), and in the adolescent sexual pun, "And when good will is showed, though't come too short, / The actor may plead pardon" (8–9).

But Cleopatra quickly tires of obvious jokes and goes on to another passing fancy: "Give me mine angle" (10). In violent, gamelike terms, she imagines fishing, and the scene is set histrionically: "My music playing far off, I will betray / Tawny-finned fishes" (11–12). Are Egyptian fish "tawny-finned," or is Cleopatra merely indulging her fantasy? She herself is tawny, "with Phoebus' amorous pinches black" (1.5.28). Her fancy culminates in an aggressive image of hooking Antony:

> My bended hook shall pierce
> Their slimy jaws; and as I draw them up,
> I'll think them every one an Antony,
> And say, "Ah, ha! y'are caught!" (2.5.12–15)

What is the analogy that Cleopatra conjures up between the slimy jaws of the tawny-finned fishes and her lover Antony, finally caught? She recalls the time, described in Plutarch, when she changes clothes with him:

> Ere the ninth hour, I drunk him to his bed;
> Then put my tires and mantles on him, whilst
> I wore his sword Philippan. (21–23)

This is the disgraceful effemination of which the Roman soldiers accuse Antony. In the love game, Cleopatra imagines herself as the dominant partner.

When the Messenger enters with the news for which Cleopatra has been waiting, she explodes in a sexual fury:

> O, from Italy!
> Ram thou thy fruitful tidings in mine ears,
> That long time have been barren. (23–25)

But when the unlucky Messenger announces that Antony is now married to Octavia, Caesar's sister, Cleopatra turns violent. She "*Strikes him down*" (61 s.d.), "*She hales him up and down*" (64 s.d.), presumably pulling him by his hair about the stage, and, finally, we have an astounding direction for a female character: "*Draw a knife*" (73 s.d.). Cleopatra is eventually ashamed of her passionate outburst, and at the end of the scene we have the most mysterious line in the play: "Pity me Charmian, / But do not speak to me" (118–19). Why does Cleopatra ask this? Is it because she considers herself in an entirely different world of discourse, in the sense that nothing Charmian could possibly say would be relevant to the grief she feels? This is like Mae West's cryptic remark: "Beulah, peel me a grape."

Antony is much more convincingly tragic than Cleopatra. The conflict in the play is set up so that the first words spoken are the condemnatory judgments of the Roman soldier Philo: "Nay, but this dotage of our general's / O'erflows the measure" (1.1.1–2). Antony, the great Roman general, is now in his dotage—he dotes foolishly, like an old man in love—and he forgets his spectacular, heroic aspect:

> Those his goodly eyes
> That o'er the files and musters of the war
> Have glowed like plated Mars, now bend, now turn
> The office and devotion of their view
> Upon a tawny front. (2–6)

Cleopatra is "tawny"—described as "sun-burnt" elsewhere, "with Phoebus' amorous pinches black" (1.5.28–29)—as the tawny-finned fish she is trying to catch. In a characteristic gesture, Antony moves from Mars to Venus and thereby risks destroying himself. Cleopatra's "front"—either her forehead or the front of her body—is radically different from the battlefront, where Antony was once preeminent.

Before his shameful transformation, Antony was a model Roman soldier in his courage, fortitude, and Stoic endurance. Caesar recalls the heroic Antony after the retreat from Modena:

Thou didst drink
The stale of horses and the gilded puddle
Which beasts would cough at. (1.4.61–63)

In Caesar's judgment the ability to drink the "stale" (piss) of horses is heroic. Further,

On the Alps,
It is reported thou didst eat strange flesh,
Which some did die to look on. (66–68)

Consuming "strange flesh" appeals to Caesar as a hyperbolic accomplishment of a true Roman warrior, as opposed to Antony as he is now:

he fishes, drinks and wastes
The lamps of night in revel; is not more manlike
Than Cleopatra, nor the queen of Ptolemy
More womanly than he. . . . (4–7)

Antony has lost his manhood in Egypt, and this is at the heart of the Roman conception of Antony's tragedy.

The sense of tragedy develops and deepens in the course of the action, especially after Antony's decisive defeat at the Battle of Actium through Cleopatra's perfidy. At this point he is acutely aware of his dotage in love. In act 3, scene 11, there is a stage direction with important symbolic overtones: he "*Sits down*" (24 s.d.). He presumably doesn't stand up until Cleopatra enters and he becomes reconciled with her. Antony is full of self-accusations: "I have offended reputation, / A most unnoble swerving" (49–50). This is like the cashiered Cassio's complaint, "O, I have lost my reputation! I have lost the immortal part of myself, and what remains is bestial" (*Othello* 2.3.261–63). Antony is powerfully aware of his shame, and he doesn't try to mitigate his guilt.

Once, however, Antony hears Mardian's report of Cleopatra's death— false as it turns out to be—he moves away from tragedy and toward the final recognition of love and a consummation in which he will join his mistress in death. This movement begins literally with his unarming in act 4, scene 14: he is now "No more a soldier" (42). The soliloquy that follows is a kind of celebratory romantic afterpiece to Antony's tragedy: "I will o'ertake thee, Cleopatra, and / Weep for my pardon" (44–45). All

labor is now otiose and ceases to matter. Antony's appeal to his supposedly dead queen is ecstatic and has no element of tragedy at all:

> I come, my queen. . . . Stay for me.
> Where souls do couch on flowers, we'll hand in hand,
> And with our sprightly port make the ghosts gaze. . . .   (50–52)

His discovery that Cleopatra is not dead but has deceived him once more
does not produce the expected effect—in fact, it produces no effect at all,
only the resigned "Too late, good Diomed" (128). One sign of the failure
of tragedy at this point is the fact that Antony botches his suicide. His
sword is "made weak by my affection" (3.11.67), and he prays Diomedes
to "give me / Sufficing strokes for death" (4.14.116–17).

Cleopatra's final scene is similarly heightened and untragic. Although
she chooses to die "after the high Roman fashion" (4.15.86), we learn
from Plutarch that she has experimented with the easiest way to die, by
the bite of the asp. Her death scene is made as aesthetically beautiful as
possible, and she dies grandly in full regalia:

> Give me my robe, put on my crown, I have
> Immortal longings in me. Now no more
> The juice of Egypt's grape shall moist this lip.   (5.2.280–82)

The speech sounds like impressive organ music as it rolls mellifluously
from Cleopatra's lips.

Death is represented in erotic terms: "the stroke of death is as a lover's
pinch, / Which hurts, and is desired" (295–96). Cleopatra announces,
"Husband, I come: / Now to that name my courage prove my title!"
(287–88). This is the first time that she has proclaimed herself Antony's
wife, and the line self-consciously echoes Othello's "Strumpet, I come"
(*Othello* 5.1.34). Later the asp is represented as a love child: "Dost thou
not see my baby at my breast, / That sucks the nurse asleep?" (309–10).
She is sexually eager to meet "the curlèd Antony" (301), freshly barbered,
before his dead wife Octavia can claim "that kiss / Which is my heaven
to have" (302–3). The long death scene is an erotic, domestic, and aesthetic fulfillment for her. It is not tragic at all, but has the kind of marvelous, awesome longing we associate with romance. It looks ahead to
the series of romances that Shakespeare will soon write.

Obviously, Shakespeare was still uncertain in *Romeo and Juliet* about
how to write a love tragedy. The tragic action is deflected from the

blameless and innocent lovers onto their parents and the deadly blood feud. The love tragedy of Antony and Cleopatra is more clearly celebratory and romantic. Charmian intends to make it so when she finishes Cleopatra's final sentence: "What should I stay—" with "In this vild world?" (5.2.313–14). Caesar's world cannot compare to the world the lovers will find in each other's arms after death,

> Where souls do couch on flowers, we'll hand in hand,
> And with our sprightly port make the ghosts gaze:
> Dido and her Aeneas shall want troops,
> And all the haunt be ours. (4.14.51–54)

In this world,

> The quick comedians
> Extemporally will stage us, and present
> Our Alexandrian revels. (5.2.216–18)

When Iras falls and dies after her mistress's kiss, Cleopatra concludes: "If thus thou vanishest, thou tell'st the world / It is not worth leave-taking" (297–98). In both plays love seems to have its own rules that make the endings sad, in the sense of enormous waste, but that also set them apart from tragedy. There may be pity but there is no fear. The lovers triumph in death and achieve a spiritual union impossible in this vile world.

Othello is probably Shakespeare's only successful love tragedy. There is no sense of romantic triumph at the end of the play, and the conventional effects of Aristotelian tragedy, pity and fear, are felt in abundance. We fear the fate of Desdemona and Othello because we sympathize with them and feel that their fate could plausibly have been ours. For these effects to work it is necessary to think of the action as not merely the triumph of Iago's rhetorical skills, but also the failure of a certain kind of love. The two motives work together and answer the question of why Iago finds Othello such an easy victim. It is the one tragedy by Shakespeare that is not about kings and princes and heads of state set in a remote time or place, but about ordinary people, who are neither exalted nor base in social position. It is a domestic tragedy, starting from the traditionally comic base of the cuckolded husband, or the husband who imagines himself a cuckold.

In his final speech, Othello asks his Venetian compatriots to "Speak of me as I am" (5.2.338). Before he stabs himself, he offers an acute self-appraisal:

Then must you speak
Of one that loved not wisely, but too well;
Of one not easily jealous, but, being wrought,
Perplexed in the extreme; of one whose hand,
Like the base Judean, threw a pearl away
Richer than all his tribe; of one whose subdued eyes,
Albeit unused to the melting mood,
Drops tears as fast as the Arabian trees
Their med'cinable gum. (339–47)

This is Othello once more asserting his large stature as the tragic protagonist. What does it mean to love "not wisely, but too well"? This seems a
contradiction in terms, but Othello dotes on Desdemona, which has its
own inherent dangers. He speaks of her as the pearl of great price that he
foolishly threw away, and he talks finally of his womanish tears, inappropriate to a great military chief but a final memorial to his love for Desdemona. It is all inexpressibly sorrowful.

Othello dies, like Romeo, with a final amorous couplet:

I kissed thee ere I killed thee. No way but this,
Killing myself, to die upon a kiss. (354–55)

In Romeo's final speech, he also wants to end his life with a kiss. His last
words are: "Thus with a kiss I die" (5.3.120), and just before that,

And, lips, O you
The doors of breath, seal with a righteous kiss
A dateless bargain to engrossing death! (*Romeo and Juliet* 113–15)

Othello is no young lover like Romeo, yet in both there is a sense of sacrifice for love. Othello aggrandizes the power of love, as in his speech at
the beginning of Iago's temptation:

Excellent wretch! Perdition catch my soul
But I do love thee! And when I love thee not
Chaos is come again. (3.3.90–92)

He foresees the approach of his own disaster, which looms at the other
side of a love of great magnitude. This is one of the ways of understanding what it means to love "not wisely, but too well."

All of these strains are already implicit in act 1, scene 3, which describes Othello's wooing of Desdemona.[6] This is unlike most wooing scenes in Shakespeare's comedies, where women take the lead or are at least equal partners (as in *Romeo and Juliet*). In *Othello*, Desdemona is represented as a passive, hero-worshipping recipient of Othello's exotic life story. The romantic, heroic tale does not speak of love at all. It is not witty and personal, as wooing speeches tend to be in the comedies, but grave and portentous:

> Where I spoke of most disastrous chances,
> Of moving accidents by flood and field,
> Of hairbreadth scapes i' th' imminent deadly breach,
> Of being taken by the insolent foe
> And sold to slavery, of my redemption thence
> And portance in my travel's history. . . . (133–38)

Desdemona's reaction is not so much as a lover but rather as one of those "wonder-wounded hearers" (*Hamlet* 5.1.260) that Hamlet speaks of at the beginning of his wit-combat with Laertes. Othello admires the effect of his powerful narrative on the young daughter of Brabantio:

> My story being done,
> She gave me for my pains a world of kisses.
> She swore in faith 'twas strange, 'twas passing strange;
> 'Twas pitiful, 'twas wondrous pitiful.
> She wished she had not heard it; yet she wished
> That heaven had made her such a man. (157–62)

The conclusion is satisfying in the narrative context, but has its own lurking perils:

> She loved me for the dangers I had passed,
> And I loved her that she did pity them. (166–67)

In relation to the comedies, this doesn't seem like an adequate basis for love. We speculate that there must be something else we haven't heard about.

Desdemona is soon protesting that she wants to accompany her husband to Cyprus, and she alleges reasons that are directly sexual;

So that, dear lords, if I be left behind,
A moth of peace, and he go to the war,
The rites for why I love him are bereft me. . . . (250–52)

This echoes Juliet's impatience for the physical pleasures of the wedding night:

Spread thy close curtain, love-performing night,
That runaways' eyes may wink, and Romeo
Leap to these arms untalked of and unseen.
Lovers can see to do their amorous rites,
And by their own beauties. . . . (*Romeo and Juliet* 3.2.5–9)

This connection of Desdemona and Juliet as lovers and as brides is part of a strong emphasis in Shakespeare on the "amorous rites" of love.

What is surprising, however, is that Othello demurs. He protests that his love is spiritual, not physical, and that he is too old for the pleasures of young love. This is an excuse that no one ever makes in the comedies, even the old pantaloon Gremio in *The Taming of the Shrew*. Only Malvolio, the foolish suitor of his mistress in *Twelfth Night*, stands so apart from sex. Othello's speech to the Venetian senators is fatal to his status as a lover. He wants his new wife to accompany him to Cyprus for reasons opposite to hers:

I therefore beg it not
To please the palate of my appetite,
Nor to comply with heat—the young affects
In me defunct—and proper satisfaction;
But to be free and bounteous to her mind. . . . (256–60)

He protests that he is not vulnerable to "light-winged toys / Of feathered Cupid" (263–64). Clearly, Othello, by declaring himself so directly an enemy, opens himself to Cupid's revenge. Why does he want to appear so much like the chaste opponent of love, Adonis? Desdemona is no rapacious Venus, but there is already a sense that her vigorous sexuality threatens Othello.

Iago hears Othello's speech to the Venetian senators and makes use of it later, as he puts together bits and scraps of dialogue that he hears throughout the play. At the end of act 1, scene 3, Iago is already developing two of his major themes with the gull Roderigo: that Desdemona is young and lustful, a typical Venetian woman, and that Othello is old and perhaps impotent. For Iago love does not exist; there is only lust, for which love is a euphemism: "we have reason to cool our raging motions, our carnal stings or unbitted lusts, whereof I take this that you call love to be a sect or scion" (325–28). The supposed love of Othello and Desdemona "is merely a lust of the blood and a permission of the will" (330–31). Even Roderigo has trouble believing such cynical counsel. Desdemona's love for Othello is only a passing, sexual infatuation: "She must change for youth; when she is sated with his body, she will find the errors of her choice" (346–48). Iago offers the argument from nature, that it is unnatural for the young and beautiful Desdemona to love a middle-aged black man. One of the fascinations of Iago's reasoning is that he not only seems spontaneous and improvisatory, but also makes up facile arguments that tickle his own sense of cleverness and superiority.

In the next scene (2.1), Iago continues to instruct Roderigo in the sexual lore of which he claims to be a master. It is no wonder that in Iago's satirical analysis of the romantic situation, the promiscuous and lecherous Desdemona is now in love with the "handsome, young" (244–45) Cassio:

> Mark me with what violence she first loved the Moor but for bragging and telling her fantastical lies. To love him still for prating? Let not thy discreet heart think it. Her eye must be fed. And what delight shall she have to look on the devil? When the blood is made dull with the act of sport, there should be a game to inflame it and to give satiety a fresh appetite, loveliness in favor, sympathy in years, manners, and beauties; all which the Moor is defective in. (220–29)

Iago cannot let go of his persistent preoccupations: that the Moor is black ("the devil"), that he is much older than Desdemona (no "sympathy in years"), and that his speech is full of "bombast circumstance, / Horribly stuffed with epithets of war" (1.1.12–13). Iago considers himself a plain speaker, honest, gruff, and forthright, as a soldier should be.

Iago is not only the instructor of the foolish Roderigo in affairs of the heart, but he is also, more important, the mentor of Othello. This is the core of the love tragedy, because Othello is so unsure of himself, so full of doubts about why the beautiful and young Desdemona should have fallen in love with him, so deeply penetrated with a sense of his own unworthiness that it is easy for Iago to inflame him and to make him insanely jealous. As if he were his big brother, the worldly Iago lectures the innocent Othello on the complexities of love:

> I know our country disposition well:
> In Venice they do let heaven see the pranks
> They dare not show their husbands; their best conscience
> Is not to leav't undone, but kept unknown.   (3.3.201–4)

Bemused, Othello can only answer with a naive question, "Dost thou say so?" (204), and Iago continues his attack:

> She did deceive her father, marrying you;
> And when she seemed to shake and fear your looks,
> She loved them most.   (206–8)

Sophisticated Iago already has Othello under his spell. He can only agree with something he should have known long before but has now only realized: "And so she did" (208).

Othello's foolish naiveté is most evident when he demands from Iago "ocular proof" that will confirm his "love a whore" (356–57). He wants to "see't" (361), to be "satisfied" (387). This opens the floodgates of Iago's pornographic imagination:

> How satisfied, my lord?
> Would you, the supervisor, grossly gape on?
> Behold her topped?   (391–93)

This resembles his sexual calumniations in the first scene of the play: "Even now, now, very now, an old black ram / Is tupping your white ewe" (1.1.85–86). There is nothing easier for Iago to supply than "ocular proof." First, there is his ambiguous homoerotic image of being together in bed with Cassio, who thinks him Desdemona:

> Then kiss me hard,
> As if he plucked up kisses by the roots
> That grew upon my lips; laid his leg o'er my thigh,
> And sigh, and kiss. . . .   (3.3.419–22)

But Desdemona's handkerchief, a gift from Othello picked up by Emilia, works even better as a sexual symbol. Othello blows all his "fond love" (442) to heaven and vows revenge.

Act 4, scene 1 of *Othello* is an extraordinary demonstration of the use of anticipation in tragedy. Not only is Othello persuaded by Iago to murder Desdemona, but he also feels proleptically what he will feel at the end of the play, when he understands the magnitude of his crime. It is worth looking at the doubleness of some of Othello's speeches, which Iago, for the first time in the play, is without any power either to understand or to manipulate. When Iago tells him about the handkerchief that Cassio now wants to give to Bianca, his courtesan, Othello replies with rage: "I would have him nine years a-killing!" (180). But then he immediately thinks of Desdemona: "A fine woman, a fair woman, a sweet woman" (180–81). This is a random thought, without any preparation in the text, and Iago is nonplussed: "Nay, you must forget that" (182).

Othello, overwrought by passion, continues in this paradoxical and contradictory way:

Ay, let her rot, and perish, and be damned tonight; for she shall not live. No, my heart is turned to stone; I strike it, and it hurts my hand. O, the world hath not a sweeter creature! She might lie by an emperor's side and command him tasks.   (183–87)

Why does Othello suddenly strike his heart, and why does he discover that it has turned to stone? The heart is the seat of compassion, and it is compassionate to think that "the world hath not a sweeter creature" than Desdemona. Yet Othello is determined to kill her. There is no reconciling of these opposites, and Iago is at a total loss for the first time in the play: "Nay, that's not your way" (188).

The double perspective is amplified by Othello's loving recollections:

Hang her! I do but say what she is. So delicate with her needle. An admirable musician. O, she will sing the savageness out of a bear! Of so high and plenteous wit and invention—   (189–92)

Of course, we never hear anything further in the play about Desdemona's needlework, and, unlike Ophelia, she never sings except for the moving "Song of Willow" in 4.3. "Plenteous wit and invention" are terms for the creative faculties, but we never see any of Desdemona's poems or paintings. Othello is already mourning his loss and thinking sorrowfully

of the time when he will have no wife. The impatient Iago now inter-
rupts a line of reasoning that is going against his plans: "She's the worse
for all this" (193). It is a foolish and ineffective line, one of his few
gaucheries in the play.

Othello cannot be stopped in the direction he is moving. Desdemona
is "of so gentle a condition" (195), a high-born lady of exquisite manners.
Iago protests feebly: "Ay, too gentle" (195), meaning yielding and unre-
sistant. But Othello brings his tormented and divided thoughts to their
dramatic conclusion:

> Nay, that's certain. But yet the pity of it, Iago. O Iago, the pity of
> it, Iago. (197–98)

This functions in the minds of the audience as an anticipatory comment
on the love tragedy. It rouses pity abundantly, so necessary for tragedy
according to Aristotle's *Poetics*, and fear too. What do we pity? Certainly,
the sense of inevitability that Othello himself is committed to even
though he secretly feels that it is entirely wrong. We have pity for the
innocent Desdemona, who is going to her doom through no fault of her
own, only through Iago's malicious calumniation. This appeal to Iago for
pity is entirely misdirected, and perhaps that is also pitiable, that the noble
Othello could be so totally mistaken in his confidants.

Act 4, scene 3 continues the mood that dominates act 4. The pity is
generated so actively because there is a prevailing sense that there is nothing either Othello or Desdemona can do to stop the inevitable tragedy.
All possibility of explanation, revelation, reconciliation has been sum-
marily cut off. Now Othello and Desdemona can only suffer and wait for
the imminent moment when they will act out their roles as murderer and
victim. Act 4, scene 3 follows the so-called Brothel Scene, in which Othello pretends that his wife is a prostitute and that Emilia is her bawd. He
shows the same sorrowful doubleness as in the previous scene:

> O thou weed,
> Who art so lovely fair, and smell'st so sweet,
> That the sense aches at thee, would thou hadst never been born!
> (4.2.66–68)

In the scene that follows, Desdemona is already painfully aware of
her impending death. As she says to Emilia: "If I do die before, prithee
shroud me / In one of these same sheets" (4.3.24–25), that is, her

wedding sheets, with which she now makes her bed. Desdemona cannot put out of her mind her mother's maid, Barbary, who had a lover who proved mad and forsook her. "She had a song of 'Willow' " (28) and "she died singing it" (30). So Desdemona sings the sorrowful ballad of "Willow," a tree associated with forsaken love. The song literally announces her fate.

At the end of this scene, Desdemona's innocence is reasserted for the audience right before the catastrophe. Her strange conversation with Emilia sounds like Juliet speaking to the Nurse in *Romeo and Juliet*. She asks naively:

> Dost thou in conscience think, tell me, Emilia,
> That there be women do abuse their husbands
> In such gross kind? (62–64)   .

Desdemona cannot even conceive what infidelity and adultery are. Emilia is witty and worldly, and playfully suggests that she might do such a deed "for all the world" (69). But Desdemona remains incredulous: "Beshrew me if I would do such a wrong for the whole world" (80–81) and "I do not think there is any such woman" (86).

When Othello enters to strangle his wife in the last scene of the play, he comes in the guise of a priest performing a religious ritual; it is a sacrifice, not a murder. He kisses her three times while she is sleeping, but he also smells her as if she were a rose:

> When I have plucked the rose,
> I cannot give it vital growth again;
> It needs must wither. I'll smell thee on the tree. (5.2.13–15)

The rose is aligned metaphorically with the lighted torch he carries, as a symbol of human life. Love and death, the *Liebestod*, are closely allied in Othello's mind:

> O balmy breath, that dost almost persuade
> Justice to break her sword. One more, one more!
> Be thus when thou art dead, and I will kill thee,
> And love thee after. One more, and that's the last! (16–19)

This is different from the triumphant union of love and death in *Antony and Cleopatra*, yet the scene is imbued with a hieratic sense of love. Desdemona comes to the heart of the paradox when she says: "That death's unnatural that kills for loving" (42).

When the truth of the plot is revealed after Desdemona is dead, it is as if Othello knew it all along. He is self-condemned and self-damned:

> O ill-starred wench!
> Pale as thy smock! When we shall meet at compt,
> This look of thine will hurl my soul from heaven,
> And fiends will snatch at it. (269–72)

Desdemona is "ill-starred"—remember Romeo's "inauspicious stars" (*Romeo and Juliet* 5.3.111)—and Othello dies with a fourth kiss:

> I kissed thee ere I killed thee. No way but this,
> Killing myself, to die upon a kiss. (354–55)

There is some sense of fulfillment in Othello's end, "For he was great of heart" (357), and the vile world, as it is presently constituted, "is not worth leave-taking" (*Antony and Cleopatra* 5.2.298).

Of all Shakespeare's plays, only *Romeo and Juliet*, *Othello*, and *Antony and Cleopatra* can be considered love tragedies. But *Romeo and Juliet* has trouble developing the tragedy from what are essentially comic materials. The feud is like the perturbations of comedy until it becomes deadly with the murder of Mercutio. Romeo and Juliet are like the intensely lyrical and playful lovers of comedy, so that their final tragic status seems thrust upon them. The ending of *Antony and Cleopatra* is so positive and upbeat that it seems to project the play into romance rather than tragedy. Like Tristram and Isolde, the lovers achieve a transcendence in their deaths that is not possible in this "vile world." Only *Othello* evokes the kind of pity and fear that is postulated for tragedy in Aristotle's *Poetics*. We not only pity the protagonists caught in the web of Iago's ingenious calumniations, but we also fear the tragic fate of people like ourselves, who are neither royal nor base but in between. The fact that *Othello* is based on a traditionally comic story of the cuckolded husband is an additional twist in its tragic status.

ENEMIES OF Love

Love discourse in Shakespeare is set against indifference, if not down-right hostility, to love. Significant dramatic conflict is generated as love seeks to triumph over obstacles and to fulfill itself, as it does in the happy endings of the comedies. In the tragedies love generally ends in disrup-tion, failure, and death, as if it cannot properly succeed in a tragic world. The enemies of love are many in Shakespeare's works, but we shall con-centrate on characters who forswear love in order to pursue other, power-related objectives. The whole code of manliness, both in war and in civil life, is opposed to love because it is believed to feminize the heroic character. Ideas of love in Shakespeare depend strongly on gender con-cepts, on how masculine and feminine are defined. As George Meredith argues in his "Essay on Comedy" (1877), love can only flourish in a soci-ety where women are highly valued.[1]

Shakespeare's early verse epyllion, *Venus and Adonis*, based on Marlowe's *Hero and Leander*, presents the love debate in a simplified and polarized form. The poem is mythological because it deals with the loves of gods and goddesses, but they are represented in completely human terms. That is part of the poem's witty irony. The sexually rapacious Venus, the goddess of love, despite her inflamed and even grotesque desire, has no magical and godlike powers with which to seduce Adonis.[2] He is reluctant and recalcitrant and basically not interested in love as an activity—he much prefers hunting the boar, as he tells us in the first lines of the poem:

> Even as the sun with purple-colored face
> Had ta'en his last leave of the weeping morn,
> Rose-cheeked Adonis hied him to the chase;
> Hunting he loved, but love he laughed to scorn. (1–4)

He begins and ends the poem hostile to love. Despite the fact that Venus plucks him from his horse, Adonis, "the tender boy" (32), "blushed and pouted in a dull disdain, / With leaden appetite, unapt to toy" (33–34). "Toy" is used in the erotic sense of amorous trifling. Venus also calls him "coy" (96), which means modest, but also inaccessible: Adonis is the "flint-hearted boy" (95).

Venus employs an elaborate battery of erotic arguments, including the doctrine of use, which is familiar from the *Sonnets*. Beauty may be precious and valuable in itself, but it must be used as an attractive lure for love, which will be drawn by the desire to beget children. Natural gifts should be put to use, not stored up like money that earns interest ("use" or "usufruct"). This is a much-repeated argument in early Shakespeare, and Venus phrases it in familiar imagery:

> "Torches are made to light, jewels to wear,
> Dainties to taste, fresh beauty for the use,
> Herbs for their smell, and sappy plants to bear.
> Things growing to themselves are growth's abuse.
> Seeds spring from seeds, and beauty breedeth beauty.
> Thou wast begot; to get it is thy duty." (163–68)

Of course, Venus is hardly thinking of begetting children with Adonis, but only of amorous activity. She continues with persuasions right out of the *Sonnets*:

> "By law of nature thou art bound to breed,
> That thine may live when thou thyself art dead;
>   And so in spite of death thou dost survive,
>   In that thy likeness still is left alive." (171–74)

In other words, children provide a kind of immortality and a barrier against oblivion.

Adonis is unimpressed with Venus's traditional arguments, and he asserts forcefully that he is too young and immature to be bothered with love:

> "I know not love," quoth he, "nor will not know it,
> Unless it be a boar, and then I chase it.
> 'Tis much to borrow, and I will not owe it:
> My love to love is love but to disgrace it;
>   For I have heard it is a life in death,
>   That laughs and weeps, and all but with a breath." (409–14)

Love is histrionic and woeful and Adonis is not ready for it. Throughout this energetic verse epyllion, or "little epic," there are grotesque and comic touches, like Adonis's preference for hunting the boar over making love: "and then I chase it," he says of the boar, as if the reaction were automatic for someone who is at heart a hunter. Venus, of course, is always satirized for her ever-ready lustfulness: "By this the lovesick queen began to sweat" (175).

Adonis supplies images from nature to support his coyness: "Who plucks the bud before one leaf put forth?" (416). An even more persuasive image is related to the lustful horses that Venus has unleashed:

> "The colt that's backed and burdened being young
> Loseth his pride, and never waxeth strong." (419–20)

There is wordplay on "pride," meaning erectile power. Finally, Adonis shows himself as merely a petulant adolescent:

> "You hurt my hand with wringing; let us part,
> And leave this idle theme, this bootless chat;
> Remove your siege from my unyielding heart;
> To love's alarms it will not ope the gate.
>   Dismiss your vows, your feignèd tears, your flatt'ry,
>   For where a heart is hard they make no batt'ry."
>
> (421–26)

Shakespeare must have enjoyed writing such an amusing, titillating poem, with the boy Adonis talking back so unself-consciously to Venus, the goddess of love, as if she were his mother, and calling her extended seduction speech mere "bootless chat."

Adonis never tires of his argument from nature, which implies that he is not yet ready for love but might be at some unspecified time in the future. He is just trying to escape from the clutches of the rapacious Venus:

> "Fair queen," quoth he, "if any love you owe me,
> Measure my strangeness with my unripe years.
> Before I know myself, seek not to know me:
> No fisher but the ungrown fry forbears;
> The mellow plum doth fall, the green sticks fast,
> Or being early plucked is sour to taste." (523–28)

The gist of the example of the green plum is something like "Ripeness is all." The orations on either side of the love debate are self-serving and highly conventional, what Adonis later calls "your idle over-handled theme" (770).

In his final speech in the poem, he claims that he is not really an enemy of love but only of lust. This is an ingenious way to escape from Venus's specious persuasions: "Call it not love, for Love to heaven is fled / Since sweating Lust on earth usurped his name" (793–94). This is a facile but false distinction, since love is expressed through the body, as John Donne puts it so well in "The Exstasie": "Loves mysteries in soules doe grow, / But yet the body is his booke."[3] "Sweating Lust" is linked with the sweating "Lovesick queen" (175).

As we have seen, *Venus and Adonis* and the *Sonnets* share many assumptions about love, especially the doctrine of use. Most of the sonnets are addressed to a disdainful but beautiful youth like Adonis, who scorns love and the begetting of children—in other words, putting his beauty to use. The youth seems to be imprisoned in love of himself and his own beauty, like Narcissus. He is cold and scorns the love of another. The natural promptings of nature have no effect on him and he doesn't seek to fulfill himself in sexual union. He doesn't feel any moral or religious obligation to be fruitful and multiply.

All of these themes are powerfully expressed in Sonnet 94, "They that have pow'r to hurt."[4] The subject of the poem is someone who has the ability to move others but is himself "as stone, / Unmovèd, cold, and to temptation slow." Most people are only "stewards of their excellence"; in other words, they possess excellent qualities only in stewardship or guardianship, and they are required by the law of nature to put these qualities to use in relation to other people. But the subject of this sonnet and those like him "husband nature's riches from expense." "They are the lords and owners of their faces," keeping their physical beauty only for themselves, not sharing it with others. All these familiar arguments lead to the couplet conclusion:

> For sweetest things turn sourest by their deeds;
> Lilies that fester smell far worse than weeds.

The lily, like the rose, is one of the noblest flowers, but when it rots, it stinks far worse than a common weed.

Self-love is the theme of many of the early sonnets, especially the self-adoration of someone who is beautiful. Sonnet 4 begins with the essential question: "Unthrifty loveliness, why doest thou spend / Upon thyself thy beauty's legacy?" Beauty is understood metaphorically to be a kind of money, which should not be hoarded up as a miser does, but spent freely and generously. Physical beauty is a gift of nature, and "Nature's bequest gives nothing but doth lend, / And being frank she lends to those are free." Therefore it is a sin to be a "niggard" (the opposite of "free") and not to spend this wealth. To love and to beget offspring is one of the principal ways of cashing in on nature's gift. It is the opposite of "having traffic with thyself alone." The couplet conclusion is a warning against an unprofitable and loveless life:

> Thy unused beauty must be tombed with thee,
> Which, usèd, lives th' executor to be.

In his early comedies Shakespeare often uses the scoffer at love as an easy mark for Cupid's arrows, who will soon fall hopelessly in love and repent his former disdain. Valentine in *The Two Gentlemen of Verona* is a good example. When the play opens, the young and carefree Valentine is about to travel abroad, and he has only compassion for his friend Proteus, who is unable to accompany him because he is in love with Julia. Proteus is a prisoner of love: "affection chains thy tender days / To the sweet glances of thy honored love" (1.1.3–4). Valentine speaks of his friend with measured contempt: "living dully sluggardized at home, / Wear out thy youth with shapeless idleness" (7–8). "Sluggardized" is an amusing

Shakespearean coinage to indicate Valentine's sense of superiority to a friend made a lazy sluggard by love.

Valentine continues to condemn love in his witty discourse, and he draws on the same imagery as Adonis:

> To be in love—where scorn is bought with groans,
> Coy looks with heartsore sighs, one fading moment's mirth
> With twenty watchful, weary, tedious nights;
> If haply won, perhaps a hapless gain;
> If lost, why then a grievous labor won;
> However, but a folly bought with wit,
> Or else a wit by folly vanquishèd. (29–35)

As part of their almost automatic male bonding, Proteus agrees with his friend. "He after honor hunts, I after love" (63), says Proteus in a context in which honor is clearly superior. The effects of love are all negative:

> Thou, Julia, thou hast metamorphized me,
> Made me neglect my studies, lose my time,
> War with good counsel, set the world at nought,
> Made wit with musing weak, heart sick with thought. (66–69)

Proteus is clear about the troubles of love, but he cannot help himself.

By act 2, scene 1, Valentine in Milan is already profoundly in love with Silvia, and in scene 4 he is ready to steal her away and get married. Love moves with celerity in these early comedies. The now doting Valentine confesses to Proteus how Love has attacked him for his former disdain:

> I have done penance for contemning Love,
> Whose high imperious thoughts have punished me
> With bitter fasts, with penitential groans,
> With nightly tears, and daily heartsore sighs; '
> For, in revenge of my contempt of love,
> Love hath chased sleep from my enthrallèd eyes,
> And made them watchers of mine own heart's sorrow. (128–34)

We have again (cf. 2.1.16–31) a detailed catalogue of all the conventional signs of love melancholy, but here they are represented as Love's revenge, his "correction" (137) to the wayward and careless Valentine. It is all very formal, and Valentine's imagined grief is mitigated by his ready wit: "Now can I break my fast, dine, sup, and sleep / Upon the very naked name of love" (140–41).

Not only Valentine is excessively in love with Silvia. Proteus confesses to us in a soliloquy that he is in love with her too:

> Even as one heat another heat expels,
> Or as one nail by strength drives out another,
> So the remembrance of my former love
> Is by a newer object quite forgotten. (191–94)

This resembles in its suddenness *A Midsummer Night's Dream*, where the love objects are chemically switched. Proteus is willing to use any skullduggery to win Silvia.

Love's Labor's Lost begins with a comic premise similar to that of *The Two Gentlemen of Verona*: that the four young lords, under the leadership of the King of Navarre, will forswear love and the company of women for three long years and live in a monastic community devoted to improving the mind. These propositions are highly misogynistic and are also seen to be impossible right from the opening scene of the play. Berowne subscribes but, as he complains in his first speech:

> O, these are barren tasks, too hard to keep,
> Not to see ladies, study, fast, not sleep! (1.1.47–48)

Berowne signs the contract more out of fellowship with his male companions than from any prospect of success. He assures them that what they are doing goes against nature:

> Necessity will make us all forsworn
> Three thousand times within this three years' space:
> For every man with his affects [=passions] is born,
> Not by might mast'red, but by special grace. (148–51)

The "affects" go into effect almost immediately, and all of the lords fall hopelessly in love. At the end of the play, the women take their revenge by inflicting penances on their overproud male suitors. As Berowne says, "Our wooing doth not end like an old play; / Jack hath not Jill" (5.2.875–76). But Jack will have Jill after a year's delay, in which the lords will be schooled to correct their absurd notions of love and women. The ending is witty and didactic, with the women acting as the moral instructors of the men.

The Shakespearean character most like Adonis is surely Bertram in *All's Well That Ends Well*. Both are young, perhaps late adolescent, males who disdain love and women. They are both overly enamored of male ideals and extremely untutored in the ways of the world. Bertram's choice of the foolish and bombastic Parolles as his bosom companion and confidant is already a comment on his lack of sophistication. When the King forbids Bertram, his ward, from going to the wars, his reaction is petulant and misogynistic:

> I shall stay here the forehorse to a smock,
> Creaking my shoes on the plain masonry,
> Till honor be bought up, and no sword worn
> But one to dance with! (2.1.30–33)

Bertram's contempt for the amenities of civil life is equivalent to a distaste for women. When Helena chooses him for her husband as a reward for curing the King, Bertram is filled with boyish disdain and contempt, mixed with pure snobbery: "She had her breeding at my father's charge: / A poor physician's daughter for my wife!" (2.3.115–16). Although the King coerces him to marry Helena, he vows never to consummate the union:

> O my Parolles, they have married me!
> I'll to the Tuscan wars and never bed her. (275–76)

Parolles adds the necessary verbal flourishes that the plain-speaking Bertram is incapable of:

> He wears his honor in a box unseen,
> That hugs his kicky-wicky here at home,
> Spending his manly marrow in her arms,
> Which should sustain the bound and high curvet
> Of Mars's fiery steed. (282–86)

"Manly marrow" is a choice euphemism for seminal fluid, which can be spent either dishonorably in the marriage bed or honorably in battle. There is no middle ground. "Kicky-wicky" is an amusing anglicism that

Shakespeare uses only this once. It translates *quelque chose*, which means literally "something" in French, but the slang reference is to a woman's genitalia. Bertram clearly has learned his contempt for women from his mentor Parolles.

Bertram takes great pains to send Helena home without the rites of marriage—not even a good-bye kiss, for which she entreats him so humbly. His mother calls him a "rash and unbridled boy" (3.2.29) and takes up Helena's cause. But Bertram is determined to flee his wife and even sets up a riddling oracle that seems impossible for Helena ever to fulfill (3.2.58–62)—but, of course, in the end she does. Even then, however, when every improbable circumstance is satisfied, Bertram is still coy and wary of leaping into his loving wife's arms. To the King he shows his obedience by saying coldly:

> If she, my liege, can make me know this clearly,
> I'll love her dearly, ever, ever dearly. (5.3.315–16)

This legalistic declaration is hardly wholehearted, yet everyone rushes to the happy ending of comedy. The last words of the play are the King's justification of the title:

> All yet seems well, and if it end so meet,
> The bitter past, more welcome is the sweet. (333–34)

There is no time left to work out the problems of this acknowledged problem play.[5]

Another problem play, *Measure for Measure*, is concerned with the difficulties of Duke Vincentio. He absents himself from Vienna to observe the workings of his kingdom and declares himself an enemy of love almost from the beginning. As he explains to Friar Thomas, he is definitely not going into hiding to conceal a love affair:

> No, holy father; throw away that thought;
> Believe not the dribbling dart of love
> Can pierce a complete bosom. (1.3.1–3)

Cupid's arrow, which is so piercing elsewhere, is here reduced to a mere "dribbling dart," like a penis afflicted with a sexually transmitted disease. A "complete bosom" suggests one that is perfect and self-sufficient, as if it were covered by armor. Hamlet describes the Ghost as appearing "in complete steel" (*Hamlet* 1.4.52). In other words, the Duke has armed himself against love.

His grand project against fornication in Vienna, from which he retires leaving Angelo as hatchetman in his place, is also directed against love-making and sex. Its first victim is Claudio, who will be put to death for getting Juliet with child, although they are legally married by a pre-contract. The newly enforced laws against fornication are cruel and misapplied in this case; Claudio is hardly guilty of "lechery" (1.2.142) in any except the narrowest legal sense.

Lucio, who is called "a fantastic" in the cast list that precedes the play, is a puzzling character. He is the one person whom the Duke cannot forgive at the end, and Vincentio's anger gives us some insight into the fact that Lucio's comments strike home. In his conversation with the Duke in disguise in act 3, scene 2, Lucio paints a different picture from anything we see or hear in the play: "He had some feeling of the sport; he knew the service, and that instructed him to mercy" (121–23). The Duke protests vigorously: "I never heard the absent Duke much detected for women; he was not inclined that way" (124–25). This sounds like a declaration that Vincentio is gay, but there is nothing else in the play to support this. It seems to mean only that "the dribbling dart of love" (1.3.2) cannot really pierce the Duke's armored bosom. But Lucio is not be dissuaded, and he continues with slangy vigor: "Who, not the Duke? Yes, your beggar of fifty, and his use was to put a ducat in her clack-dish [=beggar's bowl]" (3.2.128–29). There is no stopping Lucio, but in the context of the play there is something in his calumniations that allies the Duke with Angelo.

Self-lovers are linked with the enemies of love on the simple premise that self-love precludes the ability to love someone else. Malvolio in *Twelfth Night* is the most notorious example. His name is an allegory for "bad will," just as Benvolio in *Romeo and Juliet* signifies "good will." The fact that Malvolio is steward in Countess Olivia's noble household puts him in an ambiguous position because, however important his function, he is still a servant, as Sir Toby is at pains to remind him: "Art any more than a steward?" (2.3.113–14). His exalted opinion of himself and his innate snobbishness lay the basis for the plot against him. He looks with disdain at all those whom he deems beneath him and with an insolent toadyishness at all those above him. Feste, the Clown, is someone whom he especially resents, particularly for his favor with Olivia. When he says haughtily, "I marvel your ladyship takes delight in such a barren rascal" (1.5.82–83), Olivia corrects him with a moral observation:

O, you are sick of self-love, Malvolio, and taste with a distempered appetite. To be generous, guiltless, and of free disposition, is to take those things for birdbolts [=blunt arrows] that you deem cannon bullets. (90–93)

This is already a key to the plot against Malvolio, which plays on his tendency to be overly literal and to hyperbolize—all related to his own excessive self-esteem.

It is clear that Malvolio is incapable of love. The ingenious practical joke played against him depends upon his secret belief that he is above his station in life, and he is not surprised that a person as exalted as his mistress Olivia should fall in love with him. Thus, what the world sees as misalliance is really only a gift of the gods to those they favor: "There is example for't. The Lady of the Strachy married the yeoman of the wardrobe" (2.5. 39–40). We will probably never know who the historical Lady of the Strachy was, but her example buoys up Malvolio, although he is hardly of so high a station as "yeoman of the wardrobe." The basic goal of his social climbing is "To be Count Malvolio" (35), and he says this well before he finds the love letter supposedly from his mistress. His whole conception of what it means to be Count Malvolio and Olivia's husband has nothing whatsoever to do with love but only with personal advancement and social ceremony.

When Malvolio does find the letter, it is not surprising that he falls into amazingly crude and vulgar sexual wordplay. That is part of the fun for the onlookers who wrote the letter. Thus Malvolio is made to say:

By my life, this is my lady's hand. These be her very C's, her U's, and her T's; and thus makes she her great P's. (87–89)

"C-U-T" is an obscene reference to the female genitalia, and "her great P's" is obviously scatalogical. Of course, there is no C or P in the superscription of the letter. There are two allusions to Lucrece. The first is to Olivia's wax seal, which presumably has a figure of Lucrece: "By your leave, wax"—Malvolio breaks open the seal as if it were Olivia's maidenhead—"Soft, and the impressure her Lucrece, with which she uses to seal" (94–95).

The other reference is from the poem in the letter: "But silence, like a Lucrece knife, / With bloodless stroke my heart doth gore" (107–8). The net effect of these allusions is to cast Malvolio in the role of Tarquin, who cruelly ravages Lucrece in Shakespeare's poem. Tarquin is manly, bold, impassioned—totally unlike Malvolio but also an obvious enemy of love. The letter gives Malvolio specific instructions on how to play the lover and how to woo Olivia: wear yellow stockings, go cross-gartered, smile continuously in her presence—all things that in reality will appall and astound her. It's obvious that Malvolio, like Angelo in *Measure for Measure*, hasn't a clue about the nature of love or love-making.

Of course, when Malvolio does appear in the guise of a lover to Olivia, she thinks with good reason that he has gone mad. Before he shows himself, she is made to say: "Where's Malvolio? He is sad and civil, / And suits well for a servant with my fortunes" (3.4.4–5). "Sad" means not just melancholy but sober, grave, and serious, and "civil" refers to someone who conforms to the rules and customs of civil life, in other words, well-governed, well-mannered, and dignified. Just the opposite Malvolio suddenly appears, and his first words are the frivolous: "Sweet lady, ho, ho!" (16). He keeps quoting with a leer from Olivia's supposed letter, until his mistress has no doubt that he has lost his wits. She says, "Wilt thou go to bed, Malvolio?" (30), meaning until his mad fit goes away, but the steward understands this as a sexual invitation: "To bed? Ay, sweetheart, and I'll come to thee" (31–32).

Unlike all other lovers in Shakespeare, especially in the comedies, Malvolio doesn't press on in his wooing. He doesn't seize sexual opportunities as we expect him to, but thinks only of social advancement. His tedious and insistent quotations from the letter convince Olivia that "This is very midsummer madness" (58). His soliloquy that follows shows that he understands nothing about love and certainly has no idea what a ridiculous impression he is making. There is nothing in the soliloquy at all about love, only a mean and vulgar sense of triumph: "I have limed her; but it is Jove's doing, and Jove make me thankful" (78–79). The fowler catches birds by spreading sticky bird-lime on the twigs, and Malvolio feels that he has likewise ensnared the helpless Olivia.

In the context of *Twelfth Night*, Malvolio's self-love is related to the self-love of both Olivia and Duke Orsino early in the play. It is odd and contrary to expectations that Olivia is preparing to mourn her dead brother for seven years. There is something wrong too in the Duke's wooing, which opens the play with an almost parodic encomium of love and its irresistible powers:

> If music be the food of love, play on,
> Give me excess of it, that, surfeiting,
> The appetite may sicken, and so die. (1.1.1–3)

This seems to be echoed in Cleopatra's languorous, but rather affected, lines that begin the scene in her palace: "Give me some music: music, moody food / Of us that trade in love" (*Antony and Cleopatra* 2.5.1–2). Is Cleopatra a "trader in love," like Pandarus in *Troilus and Cressida*, who, in his Epilogue, addresses the audience as "Good traders in the flesh" (5.10.46) and "Brethren and sisters of the hold-door trade" (51)? As many critics have pointed out, the Duke seems to be in love with Love rather than with Olivia, or, to put it more bluntly, in love with himself as a lover.[6]

Orsino uses the familiar example of Actaeon in Ovid, transformed into a stag for pursuing Diana, then torn to pieces by his own hounds. The Duke speaks with a kind of polished eloquence that shows him more interested in the shaping of Ovidian poetry than in the person of Olivia:

> O, when mine eyes did see Olivia first,
> Methought she purged the air of pestilence.
> That instant was I turned into a hart,
> And my desires, like fell and cruel hounds,
> E'er since pursue me. (1.1.20–24)

Both the Duke and Olivia are eventually cured of their self-love, but it takes a real effort for the Duke to become a lover, and we are never convinced of the authenticity of his passion. His last lines in the play are:

> Cesario, come—
> For so you shall be while you are a man,
> But when in other habits you are seen,
> Orsino's mistress and his fancy's queen. (5.1.387–90)

The Duke doesn't seem to have any pressing need to instantly convert Cesario into Viola, not even for him to change out of his male "habits," or clothes. Orsino's expressions of love seem merely ceremonial, or at least not much affected by gender.

Romeo and Juliet makes a useful transition from the comedies to the tragedies. Mercutio, for example, is a familiar figure from the comedies in his role as a scoffer at love. He is bluff, hearty, open, and wittily obscene about love, which is not an appropriate manly occupation but something one slips into against one's will.

In act 1, scene 4 he is already making fun of his good friend Romeo, who has the misfortune to be hopelessly in love with Rosaline, but is now on his way to the Capulets' ball. Romeo complains about love in typical images:

> Is love a tender thing? It is too rough,
> Too rude, too boist'rous, and it pricks like thorn. (25–26)

Mercutio is quick with a bawdy reply meant to puncture Romeo's infatuation:

> If love be rough with you, be rough with love;
> Prick love for pricking, and you beat love down. (27–28)

Between Mercutio and the Nurse, *Romeo and Juliet* has one of the largest sexual vocabularies in Shakespeare.[7]

The bawdy punning of Mercutio explodes when he and Benvolio are looking for Romeo after he has left the Capulets' ball. Mercutio tries to conjure up the absent Romeo: "Romeo! Humors! Madman! Passion! Lover!" (2.1.7). This is both extravagantly affectionate for a good friend and wildly satirical of the powers of love to metamorphose an ordinary, decent person. Mercutio conjures by Venus and her son Cupid:

> Cry but "ay, me!" pronounce but "love" and "dove";
> Speak to my gossip Venus one fair word,
> One nickname for her purblind son and heir,
> Young Abraham Cupid. . . . (10–13)

Mercutio is making fun of the clichés in the sonnet literature—such as the rhyme of "love" and "dove"—before he warms to his subject and describes various attractive parts of Rosaline's body, including her "quivering thigh, / And the demesnes that there adjacent lie" (19–20). Of course, Mercutio doesn't yet know that Romeo has shifted his affection to Juliet.

Basically, Mercutio can only imagine love in sexual terms, through which he makes allowance for Romeo's frailty. Mercutio's final speech in this scene is a wild fantasy on sexual intercourse:

> If love be blind, love cannot hit the mark.
> Now will he sit under a medlar tree
> And wish his mistress were that kind of fruit

As maids call medlars when they laugh alone.
O, Romeo, that she were, O that she were
An open *et cetera*, thou a pop'rin pear!   (33–38)

We don't need any elaborate discussion to understand the intent of this passage. "Hit" is a sexual metaphor from archery (cf. *Love's Labor's Lost* 4.1.119ff.), which resembles contemporary slang "to hit on" someone. The medlar tree produces a fruit that is only edible when extremely ripe, like the loquat or persimmon, and the fruit was thought to resemble the female genitalia. A "pop'rin" pear is technically a pear from Poperinghe in Belgium, but there is obvious wordplay on "pop her in"—the pear is shaped like the male genitalia. This speech seems much closer to Mercutio's bawdy instincts than the Queen Mab oration (1.4).

His jesting about love is persistent in the earlier part of the play. He is certainly never shown in love, and he satirizes not only Romeo as lover but also many of the stylistic and narrative conventions of the Petrarchan tradition. When Romeo enters in act 2, scene 4, Mercutio is ready to debunk all of the renowned heroines of love:

Now is he for the numbers [=verses] that Petrarch flowed in. Laura, to this lady, was a kitchen wench (marry, she had a better love to berhyme her), Dido a dowdy, Cleopatra a gypsy, Helen and Hero hildings [=good-for-nothings] and harlots, Thisbe a gray eye or so, but not to the purpose.   (40–46)

This sets off a wit combat between Mercutio and Romeo full of puns, wordplay, and sexual innuendo, very much in the spirit of Shakespeare's early comedies.

With this manly banter, Mercutio thinks that he has talked Romeo out of his love melancholy:

Why, is not this better now than groaning for love? Now art thou sociable, now art thou Romeo; now art thou what thou art, by art as well as by nature. For this driveling love is like a great natural that runs lolling up and down to hide his bauble in a hole.

(92–97)

Love is imagined as Cupid the idiot boy, running up and down with his tongue hanging out and seeking to put his fool's scepter in a hole—with obvious bawdy implications. Mercutio is a good friend but he can never be Romeo's love counselor. He and the Nurse are in the play as foils to Romeo and Juliet.

In the tragedies it is axiomatic that the villains are enemies of love, who work to frustrate it and lead the lovers to their doom. By definition, the villains are always lusty and never in love. This is evident in Shakespeare's first tragedy, *Titus Andronicus*. Aaron, the Moor, is a model for Iago, although in *Othello* the Moor is the protagonist. In his first speech in the play, Aaron deploys a high style that parodies Marlowe's *Tamburlaine*. He is proud of his erotic powers because he holds Tamora, the captured Queen of the Goths, "fettered in amorous chains" (2.1.15). He will "wanton with this queen, / This goddess, this Semiramis, this nymph" (21–22). "Wanton" means to toy amorously, to dally, but Aaron puts more emphasis on his power to rule Tamora than on his sexual conquest.

In act 2, scene 3, Tamora enters the forest alone with Aaron and prepares him for a sexual encounter that comes right out of Vergil's *Aeneid*:

> such as was supposed
> The wandering prince and Dido once enjoyed,
> When with a happy storm they were surprised
> And curtained with a counsel-keeping cave. . . .   (21–24)

But Aaron is not enticed to be "each wreathèd in the other's arms" (25). He has more important work to do:

> Madam, though Venus govern your desires,
> Saturn is dominator over mine. . . .   (30–31)

He protests that he shows "no venereal signs" (37) because he is intent on his plots and his revenge against Titus Andronicus:

> Vengeance is in my heart, death in my hand,
> Blood and revenge are hammering in my head.   (38–39)

Love is not relevant for Aaron, and even his lust is subordinated to revenge.

In counseling the foolish sons of Tamora, Chiron and Demetrius, in how to consummate their love for Lavinia by rape and dismemberment, Aaron shows himself to be a clever and ingenious plotter. He simplifies the quarrel between Chiron and Demetrius by getting to its grossly sexual foundation: "Why then, it seems, some certain snatch or so / Would serve your turns" (2.1.95–96). "Snatch" is a vulgar word for the female genitalia, as it still is today, and "serve your turn" is a familiar euphemism for sexual intercourse. Aaron is alert to sexual punning. When Demetrius says: "Aaron, thou hast hit it" (97), meaning "you have understood our purposes," Aaron replies: "Would you had hit it too, / Then should not we be tired with this ado" (97–98).

Titus Andronicus is conscious of its relation to *The Rape of Lucrece* (or perhaps vice versa) because the two works are close to each other in time of composition, language, and conception. Thus Aaron says, "Lucrece was not more chaste / Than this Lavinia" (108–9), and he advises Chiron and Demetrius to "revel in Lavinia's treasury" (131). "Treasure" is a sexualized word, as in Tarquin's debate with himself before he rapes Lucrece:

"Desire my pilot is, beauty my prize;
Then who fears sinking where such treasure lies?"
(*The Rape of Lucrece* 279–80)

Everything is simplified when Lavinia and Lucrece become sexual objects rather than people to be loved.

Iago is the most powerful and most eloquent antagonist of love in all of Shakespeare. At the end of act 1, scene 3 of *Othello*, after Othello addresses the Venetian Senate and tells how Desdemona came to love him, and after Desdemona appears and confirms her love for the Moor and her desire to accompany him to Cyprus, Iago and Roderigo enter to undo all the noble sentiments. To Iago there is no such thing as love, merely lust. Virtue doesn't exist; nor does any other abstract moral entity: "'Tis in ourselves that we are thus, or thus. Our bodies are our gardens, to the which our wills are gardeners" (314–16). Love is only "a sect or scion," an offshoot, of "our raging motions, our carnal stings or unbitted lusts" (325–26). It is purely physiological, "merely a lust of the blood and a permission of the will" (330–31). Iago lectures Roderigo, as he will later lecture Othello, on the nature and origins of the passions. Desdemona is a typical Venetian lady, who lets "heaven see the pranks / They dare not show their husbands" (3.3.202–3). Being young and lusty, "It cannot be long that Desdemona should continue her love to the Moor" (1.3.338–39).

Iago argues from what he perceives as physical realities, thinking no doubt of the basic *commedia dell'arte* plot of the old man (the pantalone) who marries a young wife. Cuckoldry is the natural resolution of this familiar plot device. He represents Othello's love for Desdemona vulgarly in terms of food, which is a familiar metaphor in plays such as *Troilus and Cressida* and *Antony and Cleopatra*. Sexual desire is an appetite:

> The food that to him now is as luscious as locusts shall be to him·
> shortly as bitter as coloquintida. She must change for youth; when
> she is sated with his body, she will find the errors of her choice.
> (1.3.344–48)

"Locusts" are a sweet fruit like that of the carob tree or honey locust, and "coloquintida," or colocynth, is a small, bitter apple used as a purgative. Iago seems familiar with the technical vocabulary of Renaissance herbals. Earlier in this scene, Desdemona said nobly, "I saw Othello's visage in his mind" (247), which Iago now reverses to "when she is sated with his body." "Sated" is a word associated with digestion—satiety produces a surfeit.

Iago in his guise of manly bluffness is also naturally misogynistic. In act 2, scene 1, when he arrives in Cyprus with Desdemona, Emilia, and Roderigo, his courtly banter with the women draws on familiar, antifeminine discourse. For one of the rare moments in the play, he is fully at ease and witty. His wife Emilia is represented as a shrew or scold, who lacks woman's primary virtue of silence. To Cassio he says of her:

> Sir, would she give you so much of her lips
> As of her tongue she oft bestows on me,
> You would have enough. (100–2)

Iago then goes on expansively to offer general observations about women:

> You are pictures out of door,
> Bells in your parlors, wildcats in your kitchen,
> Saints in your injuries, devils being offended,
> Players in your housewifery, and housewives in your beds. (108–11)

In other words, women are skillful in deceptive appearances: ferocious to avenge an injury, wildcats in the kitchen, and, presumably, choosy about dispensing sexual favors in bed. The fear of women's powers, especially their sexual power, is evident in Iago's ingenious couplet that follows:

> Nay, it is true, or else I am a Turk:
> You rise to play, and go to bed to work. (113–14)

It is in bed that women can easily overpower men. There are a whole series of witty couplets in this scene, anticipating Othello's arrival in Cyprus. This is one side of Iago that is easily forgotten in the play: that, like the clown or jester—especially someone like Touchstone in *Twelfth Night*—he can entertain an audience with the wordplay and conventional jests of antifeminine satire.

Act 2, scene 1, which follows, also ends in a practical discourse, like a pep talk, between Iago and Roderigo, concluding with Iago's soliloquy. It is interesting that Shakespeare repeats the format of the previous scene (1.3) in order to develop and intensify its themes. Again, Iago reduces love to sex and speaks vulgarly of appetite as governing the relations of Othello and Desdemona:

> Her eye must be fed. And what delight shall she have to look on the devil? When the blood is made dull with the act of sport, there should be a game to inflame it and give satiety a fresh appetite, loveliness in favor, sympathy in years, manners, and beauties; all which the Moor is defective in. Now for want of these required conveniences, her delicate tenderness will find itself abused, begin to heave the gorge, disrelish and abhor the Moor.   (223–32)

The passage is highly physiological. Blood carries the sexual impulse, and appetite is represented as both satiated and heaving the gorge, or vomiting. Love enters through the eye, and Desdemona's "eye must be fed"— a grotesque, synesthetic image. Like Aaron in *Titus Andronicus*, Iago is a master of the disgusting, physical detail. This passage matches Iago's earlier aside in this scene, when he first sees Cassio and Desdemona: "Yet again your fingers to your lips? Would they were clyster pipes for your sake!" (174–75). Clyster pipes are enema tubes.

Not only is Iago an enemy of love, but he also displays a random, casual sexuality that trivializes it. As an impulse, love is perilous. He assumes that Roderigo loves Desdemona, but it is convenient for him to believe that Cassio also loves her. While he is on this tack, he says surprisingly:

> Now I do love her too;
> Not out of absolute lust, though peradventure
> I stand accountant for as great a sin,
> But partly led to diet my revenge,
> For that I do suspect the lusty Moor

Hath leaped into my seat; the thought whereof
Doth, like a poisonous mineral, gnaw my inwards;
And nothing can or shall content my soul
Till I am evened with him wife for wife. (291–99)

There is nothing in the play to suggest that Iago's "inwards," or innards, are gnawed by jealousy or that he thinks the Moor is "lusty"—he implies just the opposite, that the Moor is almost impotent. Later in the soliloquy he drops another undeveloped suspicion: "I fear Cassio with my nightcap too" (307). Iago is displacing his own "absolute lust," which he finds difficult to acknowledge, onto others. Does he really love and lust for Desdemona, or is this just his fantasy image of himself as sexually powerful? All of Iago's potential sexuality is left undeveloped by Shakespeare in the plot of *Othello*.

Richard, Duke of Gloucester, later Richard III, is a villain much in the style of Aaron and Iago. Richard's physical deformity adds a special twist, since he is ugly and unlovable, often compared to animals, especially the hedgehog. His basic premise is already clearly articulated in a long soliloquy in the middle of *Henry VI, Part Three*:

Why, Love forswore me in my mother's womb;
And, for I should not deal in her soft laws,
She did corrupt frail Nature with some bribe,
To shrink mine arm up like a withered shrub;
To make an envious mountain on my back,
Where sits deformity to mock my body;
To shape my legs of an unequal size;
To disproportion me in every part,
Like to a chaos, or an unlicked bear-whelp
That carries no impression like the dam.
And am I then a man to be beloved? (3.2.153–63)

Richard equates his congenital exclusion from Love with his own contempt for it, personified as a baleful deity that "did corrupt frail Nature with some bribe." Therefore he rejects his first proposition: "I'll make my heaven in a lady's lap . . . And witch sweet ladies with my words and looks" (148, 150). Since that is either impossible or improbable, then "I'll make my heaven to dream upon the crown" (168). His ambition, like that of Marlowe's Tamburlaine, to "Be round impalèd with a glorious crown" (171), has a distinctly erotic cast.

Richard seems to remember this speech from *3 Henry VI* in the soliloquy that opens *Richard III*. He goes to great lengths to "descant on mine own deformity" (1.1.27), as if he needs compulsively to prove by physical details how Love has abandoned him at birth:

> I, that am not shaped for sportive tricks
> Nor made to court an amorous looking glass;
> I, that am rudely stamped, and want love's majesty
> To strut before a wanton ambling nymph. . . . . (14–17)

Richard is pathologically preoccupied with his deformity, as if it offers him a legitimate substitute for sexual satisfactions. He concludes this part of his soliloquy with firm, non sequitur logic:

> And therefore, since I cannot prove a lover
> To entertain these fair well-spoken days,
> I am determinèd to prove a villain. (28–30)

A lover or a villain are not proper alternatives, but both have comparable erotic attractions for Richard.

It is not surprising that the next scene finds him wooing Lady Anne, the daughter of Warwick and the widow of Henry's son Edward, whom Richard has murdered. It is a tribute to Richard's extraordinary histrionic skill that he can also feign being a lover. He wins Anne by astounding her and puzzling her with his own outrageous inscrutability. He uses the conventional flattery of a Petrarchan suitor:

> Your beauty, that did haunt me in my sleep
> To undertake the death of all the world,
> So I might live one hour in your sweet bosom. (1.2.122–24)

Richard taunts her to kill him with his own sword, which he is so sure she cannot do that he urges her on after her first refusal:

> This hand, which for thy love did kill thy love,
> Shall for thy love kill a far truer love.
> To both their deaths shalt thou be accessory. (189–91)

The word "love" is sprinkled abundantly throughout Richard's discourse, so that Anne doesn't know what to think: "I would I knew thy heart"

(192). But Richard, like Iago, does not wear his heart upon his "sleeve / For daws to peck at; I am not what I am" (*Othello* 1.1.61–62).

Richard's soliloquy at the end of act 1, scene 2 heaps abundant scorn on Anne for being so easily duped by his wooing. This is Richard at his sardonic best, and he is already hinting at her murder: "I'll have her, but I will not keep her long" (229). Anne's consent is a proof of Richard's misogynistic views. There is a disingenuous "Ha!" (238) to express his own astonishment, which is like Iago's "Ha" that begins his undoing of Othello, "Ha! I like not that" (*Othello* 3.3.35) after the conversation of Cassio and Desdemona. Richard sentimentally invokes the person of Edward, Anne's husband, whom he murdered at Tewkesbury:

> A sweeter and a lovelier gentleman,
> Framed in the prodigality of nature,
> Young, valiant, wise, and, no doubt, right royal,
> The spacious world cannot again afford.   (242–45)

Anne is contemptible because she takes Richard for her new husband. She abases her eyes

> On me, whose all not equals Edward's moi'ty [=half]?
> On me, that halts and am misshapen thus?   (249–50)

Richard is boastfully proud of his seductive powers.

The end of the soliloquy repeats a theme that runs throughout the play: that Richard is not repulsive at all, but wondrously attractive to women. He is ironically mistaken in his conviction that he is ugly and monstrous:

> Upon my life, she finds, although I cannot,
> Myself to be a marv'lous proper man.
> I'll be at charges for a looking glass
> And entertain a score or two of tailors
> To study fashions to adorn my body.   (253–57)

The point is repeated in the triumphant couplet conclusion:

> Shine out, fair sun, till I have bought a glass
> That I may see my shadow as I pass.   (262–63)

All of this has practical implications for the staging of Richard as a dramatic character. He must be fastidiously costumed, in such a way as to exaggerate his obvious deformities. He must be shown to be extremely sexual and manly, fully macho like Aaron and Iago. He feels superior to women because he thinks them stupid and governed primarily by lust. Since he doesn't acknowledge the existence of love, he fears women's sexual powers and sexual attraction, which he steels himself to avoid and to annihilate when they appear. When he sees the procession of ghosts in act 5, scene 3, Richard is moved, for the first time in the play, to some understanding of his spiritual desiccation:

> I shall despair. There is no creature loves me;
> And if I die, no soul will pity me. (201–2)

These sentiments appear again, with greater intensity and with fuller development, in *Macbeth*.

Edmund in *King Lear* is not as fully developed as either Richard III or Iago, yet he too is cold, self-seeking, and incapable of love. Already in act 4, scene 2, Goneril is attaching herself to him and disengaging from her husband, Albany. She gives him a gift, perhaps a gold chain, to show her favor, accompanied by a kiss:

> Wear this; spare speech;
> Decline your head. This kiss, if it durst speak,
> Would stretch thy spirits up into the air:
> Conceive, and fare thee well. (21–24)

Edmund says only: "Yours in the ranks of death" (25), committing himself to nothing, yet Goneril is full of sexual exuberance:

> O, the difference of man and man!
> To thee a woman's services are due:
> My fool usurps my body. (26–28)

There is a folk tradition that bastard sons are especially virile and outspoken, as is the bastard Faulconbridge in *King John*. In her love letter to Edmund in act 4, scene 6, Goneril solicits him to kill her husband (266ff.).

Regan is also angling for Edmund's love in act 5, scene 1. She is jealous that he has found his way to Goneril's "forfended place" (11), that he has been "conjunct / And bosomed with her" (12–13)—all sexual euphemisms. Regan seems to be in awe of Edmund's sexual power. She is right in thinking that he is duplicitous, as is apparent in Edmund's soliloquy at the end of the scene. He shows himself incapable of loving either sister, and he speaks in the coldly threatening style of Richard III:

> To both these sisters have I sworn my love;
> Each jealous of the other, as the stung
> Are of the adder. Which of them shall I take?
> Both? One? Or neither? Neither can be enjoyed,
> If both remain alive. . . .   (55–59)

Edmund conceives of himself as the adder, a poisonous snake that has never been supposed to have feelings or a conscience.

In the final scene of the play, Albany speaks of his wife Goneril as "This gilded serpent" (5.3.85), and bars Regan's claim to Edmund because he is contracted to marry Goneril. But she has already poisoned her sister Regan, who is sick at this point and whose death will be announced at the end of the scene. Goneril has also stabbed herself, and her death is reported by a Gentleman, who enters *with a bloody knife* (223 s.d.). Edmund says only: "I was contracted to them both: all three / Now marry in an instant" (230–31).

But when *"The bodies of Goneril and Regan are brought in"* (240 s.d.), Edmund has one of the most remarkable lines about love in all of Shakespeare:

> Yet Edmund was beloved:
> The one the other poisoned for my sake,
> And after slew herself.   (241–43)

The dying Edmund is astonished by this mortal proof that he "was beloved." He seems pleased by the fatal demonstration that Goneril and Regan have made on his behalf. I think the line is extraordinary because Edmund has been totally separated from love throughout the play. He never loved his brother Edgar, whom he conspires against in act 1, scene 2, and he turns his father Gloucester over to Cornwall and Regan in act 3, scene 7 for their savage vengeance. Despite his empty professions, he is incapable of loving either Goneril or Regan and actually plans to dispose of both of them. That's why it is so astounding that Edmund sees the double deaths of Goneril and Regan as one final, desired verification that he is capable of being loved.

This leads immediately to a sense of regeneration in him: "I pant for life: some good I mean to do, / Despite of mine own nature" (245–46). And he sends to rescue Lear and Cordelia from the writ he has issued on their lives. Of course, this is momentary and inconsequential, since Cordelia is already dead and Lear has not far to go. Edmund's recognition that he is lovable fits, ironically, with other expressions of love at the end of the play.

The enemies of love in Shakespeare range from narcissistic young men like Adonis and Bertram to deep-dyed villains like Aaron, Iago, Richard III, and Edmund. The scoffers and disdainers of love need to fear that Venus and Cupid will take their revenge, as they do in the comedies. In *Love's Labor's Lost*, all four of the lords who swear to see no women and follow monastic ideals are quickly forsworn. Self-love also blocks love for another, most notably in the case of Malvolio in *Twelfth Night*. Shakespeare's villains are more deeply misogynistic because they believe that love as such does not exist, only lust. Iago, for example, comes closest to the diabolical in his denial of the possibility of love. This has implications that go far beyond the sexual.

CHAPTER SIX

GENDER
Definitions

Gender plays a significant role in the understanding of love.[1] Since the society represented in Shakespeare's works was overwhelmingly patriarchal, the role of women is circumscribed almost by definition. What it means to be a man or a woman is a social and historical construction rather than an innate set of masculine or feminine traits. Playing against assumed and conventional gender roles in the theater are many cross-gender parts, for example, boys playing women, who then disguise themselves as boys to win (or win back) their lovers. There is a lively dramatic interest in the conflict between gender expectations and the performance of gender in specific roles. Stephen Orgel's recent book is, in fact, called *Impersonations: The Performance of Gender in Shakespeare's England* (1996).

We may begin with a curious example from *King Lear*. In act 5, scene 3, Edmund has taken Lear and Cordelia prisoner. It is clear that he means to kill them, because after they exit guarded, he speaks to a captain:

Come hither, captain; hark.
Take thou this note: go follow them to prison:
One step I have advanced thee; if thou dost
As this instructs thee, thou dost make thy way
To noble fortunes. (27–31)

Edmund tries to persuade the captain in terms of male, military values:

Know thou this, that men
Are as the time is: to be tender-minded
Does not become a sword: thy great employment
Will not bear question; either say thou'lt do 't,
Or thrive by other means. (31–35)

This is a familiar kind of speech soliciting a political assassination, as we may see in the history plays like *Richard II* and *King John*, or in *Macbeth*. The statement, "men / Are as the time is" seems vague but implies that a man in these difficult times must be macho and heroic and respond to immediate exigencies rather than to abstract moral principles. There is a clear admonition that "tender-mindedness" does not become a soldier. Edmund never says what he wants, but it is clear from the context that killing is involved. The captain, like a good soldier, has to answer yes or no at once, without reflection. He is told explicitly that "thy great employment / Will not bear question."

He responds as we expect: "I'll do 't, my lord" (35). Edmund is pleased and doesn't waste words on the moral issue; he is unusually terse:

About it; and write happy when th' hast done.
Mark; I say, instantly, and carry it so
As I have set it down. (36–38)

In other words, do it quickly and efficiently and follow my instructions to the letter. A good soldier knows how to obey and carry out orders exactly. The captain's last words in this scene, however, go beyond the call of duty and express male sentiments that are astounding, even for a Shakespearean assassin:

I cannot draw a cart, nor eat dried oats;
If it be man's work, I'll do 't. (39–40)

The captain asserts his manhood, and "man's work" is specifically identified with murder. This is before the captain even knows what his specific mission is.

There is an element of surprise in this short scene in *King Lear*, partly because of the originality of the definition of "man's work" in contrast with the functions of a horse. But the gender sentiments are not at all unusual in Shakespeare. Murderers who act on orders of their king are all represented as doing what is appropriate for a loyal soldier. The murder is a necessary proof of manliness and unswerving, unquestioning devotion. In *King John*, for example, the King enlists Hubert to dispose of Arthur, his nephew but rival to his son for the succession. Hubert understands at once what King John is driving at:

> Good Hubert, Hubert, Hubert, throw thine eye
> On yon young boy; I'll tell thee what, my friend,
> He is a very serpent in my way,
> And wheresoe'er this foot of mine doth tread
> He lies before me: dost thou understand me?
> Thou art his keeper. (3.2.69–74)

Hubert doesn't hesitate to agree: "And I'll keep him so / That he shall not offend your Majesty" (74–75). As is usual in these cases, the King promises vague rewards: "Well, I'll not say what I intend for thee: / Remember" (78–79). Hubert doesn't ultimately get rid of Arthur, but he fully intends to, and he comes to visit Arthur with his executioners ready.

In *Richard II*, there is no direct conversation between Bolingbroke (now Henry IV) and Sir Pierce Exton, the murderer, but Exton quotes Bolingbroke in act 5, scene 4:

> Didst thou not mark the King, what words he spake?
> "Have I no friend will rid me of this living fear?" (1–2)

Again, Exton makes his manly command from the King very plain:

> And speaking it, he wishtly looked on me,
> As who should say, "I would thou wert the man
> That would divorce this terror from my heart"—
> Meaning the King at Pomfret. Come, let's go:
> I am the King's friend, and will rid his foe. (7–11)

The two murderers whom Macbeth summons to kill Banquo and his son, Fleance, use words similar to the Captain's in *King Lear*. Act 3, scene 1 presents a long conversation between Macbeth and the murderers, in which Macbeth speaks of Banquo as their enemy as well as his. He asks pointedly:

> Are you so gospeled,
> To pray for this good man and for his issue,
> Whose heavy hand hath bowed you to the grave
> And beggared yours for ever?   (88–91)

The First Murderer answers tersely: "We are men, my liege" (91), meaning, of course, that they will act as such and do the murders that the King commands.

But Macbeth insists on further clarification of the word "men"—"Ay, in the catalogue ye go for men" (92), or fit the general category, just as dogs are of all different types with varying qualities. In this extended conversation, Macbeth wants them to declare some special fealty:

> Now if you have a station in the file,
> Not i' th' worst rank of manhood, say 't,
> And I will put that business in your bosoms
> Whose execution takes your enemy off,
> Grapples you to the heart and love of us,
> Who wear our health but sickly in his life,
> Which in his death were perfect.   (102–8)

Again, the expression of manliness is the consent to murder, which also proves love for and devotion to the commander. The murderers vie with each other to convince Macbeth of their aptitude and enthusiasm for the tasks ahead.

Gender issues lie at the heart of *Macbeth*.[2] Before he enters his own castle in act 1, scene 5, Lady Macbeth reads a letter from her husband and more or less predicts the course of the action. She understands only too well Macbeth's hesitations, especially in their formal and ceremonial nature: "wouldst not play false, / And yet wouldst wrongly win" (22–23). She is convinced that she must take an active and manly role if her husband is to become king:

> Hie thee hither,
> That I may pour my spirits in thine ear,

And chastise with the valor of my tongue
All that impedes thee from the golden round
Which fate and metaphysical aid doth seem
To have thee crowned withal.   (26–31)

The martial "spirits" that Lady Macbeth is speaking of are connected with the "valor"—a military word—of her tongue.

This speech leads directly to her next speech, which is an appropriate response to the exigencies of the moment. As Edmund said to the Captain in *King Lear*, "Know thou this, that men / Are as the time is" (5.3.31–32). To Lady Macbeth, the murder of Duncan is already a *fait accompli*, and she calls upon demons, devils, powers of night and blackness to enter her body and unsex her:

Come, you spirits
That tend on mortal thoughts, unsex me here,
And fill me, from the crown to the toe, top-full
Of direst cruelty! Make thick my blood,
Stop up th' access and passage to remorse [=compassion],
That no compunctious visitings of nature
Shake my fell purpose, nor keep peace between
Th' effect and it!   (1.5.41–48)

The passage is surprisingly physiological in that it draws so specifically on the conventional gender qualities of men and women. In order for Lady Macbeth to be successful in the conversion of her husband, she can no longer be a sensitive, caring woman. Her blood, which carries feelings, needs to be thick, and she must cut off any tender emotions of sympathy and compassion. Already in this early scene, before she even sees her husband, we understand that her conception of manliness is frighteningly constricted.

Her rejection of all feminine qualities is also specific and disturbing: "Come to my woman's breasts, / And take my milk for gall, you murd'ring ministers" (48–49). This is still part of her invocation of demonic spirits. Witches were thought to have the power to turn mother's milk sour or bitter or dry it up entirely. She also calls on the powers of hell, as if she herself were going to commit the murder of Duncan and not her husband:

Come, thick night,
And pall thee in the dunnest smoke of hell,

That my keen knife see not the wound it makes,
Nor heaven peep through the blanket of the dark,
To cry "Hold, hold!"   (51–55)

She imagines herself holding the "keen knife" at the very moment that
Macbeth enters.

In act 1, scene 7, Lady Macbeth expostulates with her husband "To be
the same in thine own act and valor / As thou art in desire" (40–41). He
protests, "I dare do all that may become a man; / Who dares do more is
none" (46–47). This opens the question of what it means to be a man,
and what are the limits of "all that may become a man." What lies
beyond? Lady Macbeth thinks she knows:

When you durst do it, then you were a man;
And to be more than what you were, you would
Be so much more the man.   (49–51)

To "do it" has obvious sexual connotations here and elsewhere in the
play. Sex and murder have a strong link well before the Marquis de Sade
and the *120 Days of Sodom* and Roman Polanski's film version of *Macbeth*
(1971). Macbeth now needs to prove himself a man in the eyes of his
wife and according to conventional expectations of masculinity and
valor.

It is significant that at this point in the domestic argument Lady Macbeth reverts to the unsexing images of act 1, scene 5, only this time they
are more deadly and antifeminine. She offers proofs of how manly she
would be if she were Macbeth and how totally she would reject a womanly role:

I have given suck, and know
How tender 'tis to love the babe that milks me:
I would, while it was smiling in my face,
Have plucked my nipple from his boneless gums,
And dashed the brains out, had I so sworn as you
Have done to this.   (54–59)

This ferocious statement seems finally to persuade Macbeth.

It is interesting that Lady Macbeth says, "I have given suck," although
there is no evidence of any of her children in the play. Macduff, in fact,
says later about Macbeth (and presumably also about Lady Macbeth), "He

has no children" (4.3.216). Is actual infanticide the ultimate proof of Lady Macbeth's manliness? Portia, in *Julius Caesar*, claims that she has given herself "a voluntary wound / Here in the thigh" (2.1.300–1) as a "strong proof of my constancy" (299). Macbeth applauds his wife's courage and fortitude:

> Bring forth men-children only;
> For thy undaunted mettle should compose
> Nothing but males.   (1.5.72–74)

He is, for the moment, fully converted to manly values such as killing the King.

The manliness theme appears once more in act 3, scene 4, after the murder of Banquo. The Ghost of Banquo, who comes to sit in Macbeth's place at the banquet, abashes Macbeth and renders him incapable of social interaction. Lady Macbeth is strikingly unsympathetic; she asks accusingly, "Are you a man?" (59). Gender definitions lie at the heart of her judgments:

> O, these flaws and starts,
> Impostors to true fear, would well become
> A woman's story at a winter's fire,
> Authorized by her grandam.   (64–67)

In other words, Macbeth, seeing Banquo's Ghost, is acting like a lily-livered woman. He is, in his wife's words, "quite unmanned in folly" (74). Macbeth protests, but ineffectually: "What man dare, I dare" (100). He cannot stand up to the "horrible shadow! / Unreal mock'ry" (107–8) of the Ghost. Once it exits, Macbeth says confidentially, "I am a man again" (109). This is all quite different from Hamlet's fearless encounter with the Ghost of his father, which may indeed be a diabolic apparition.

There are two additional references to manliness in *Macbeth*. At the end of act 4, scene 3, when Macduff and Malcolm have their armies ready to attack Macbeth—he "Is ripe for shaking" (238)—Malcolm says as a sign that everything is ready, "This time goes manly" (235). This is an odd use of the word "manly," which presumably describes all of the positive martial qualities of a man.

At the end of the play, Ross delivers a eulogy for Young Siward, who has died nobly in battle, slain by Macbeth:

> Your son, my lord, has paid a soldier's debt:
> He only lived but till he was a man;
> The which no sooner had his prowess confirmed
> In the unshrinking station where he fought,
> But like a man he died.   (5.8.39–43)

"Like a man" is a simile of a general, laudatory nature. No specific qualities need be specified.

This resembles Antony's funeral eulogy for the dead Brutus in *Julius Caesar*, who "was the noblest Roman of them all" (5.5.68):

> His life was gentle, and the elements
> So mixed in him that Nature might stand up
> And say to all the world, "This was a man!"   (73–75)

"Man" in this context seems an abbreviated form of the word "Roman." Brutus has all the positive qualities—again, there is no need to enumerate them—that characterize a Roman man. *Julius Caesar* is dedicated, in part, to indicating what these moral and temperamental qualities are.

The gender theme in *Coriolanus* echoes many of the concerns of *Macbeth,* and in fact, Lady Macbeth and Volumnia, the mother of Coriolanus, were often played by the same actress. Mrs. Siddons made her name in both roles in the late eighteenth and early nineteenth centuries.[3] Like Lady Macbeth, Volumnia rejects a woman's part, which is associated with peace, in favor of a male role and the values of war. Thus, love is downgraded in the play in preference to honor, which is thoroughly steeped in a martial context. Some of the images in which this is expressed are startling in their savagery. When Virgilia, Coriolanus's wife, shrinks in horror at the idea of blood, Volumnia upbraids her:

> Away, you fool! It more becomes a man
> Than gilt his trophy. The breasts of Hecuba,
> When she did suckle Hector, looked not lovelier
> Than Hector's forehead when it spit forth blood
> At Grecian sword.   (1.3.42–46)

Blood vs. mother's milk echoes Lady Macbeth's image of plucking her nipple from the gums of the babe that milks her and dashing its brains out (*Macbeth* 1.7.54–58).

The whole of act 1, scene 3 in *Coriolanus* sets the woman's values of

Virgilia against the martial values of her mother-in-law. The scene is strikingly domestic from the opening stage direction: "*Enter Volumnia and Virgilia, mother and wife to Marcius. They set them down on two low stools, and sew.*" Woman's work defines the setting, but Volumnia in her first speech makes it immediately clear that honor is vastly superior to sexual love:

> If my son were my husband, I should freelier rejoice in that absence wherein he won honor than in the embracements of his bed where he would show most love. (2–5)

Volumnia's imagination is alarmingly incestuous, going so far as to suppose "If my son were my husband." She has programmed her son's career for him as if he needed to represent her manly ideals. Her long first speech is full of traditional assumptions about male superiority. She is proud of having sent her son "To a cruel war" (14–15) and of the fact that he returned with military honors ("bound with oak"):

> I tell thee, daughter, I sprang not more in joy at first hearing he was a man-child than now in first seeing he had proved himself a man. (16–18)

Virgilia's human concerns are irrelevant: "But had he died in the business, madam, how then?" (19–20). Marcius's mother answers decisively in praise of a noble death in battle:

> had I a dozen sons, each in my love alike, and none less dear than thine and my good Marcius, I had rather had eleven die nobly for their country than one voluptuously surfeit out of action. (23–27)

It is just a step from here to Marlowe's *Tamburlaine, Part II*, where Tamburlaine stabs his son Calyphas, who "voluptuously surfeits out of action" (act 4, scene 1).[4] We remember that Titus, in *Titus Andronicus*, stabs his son Mutius in the first scene because of some slight he imagines to martial honor. He also stabs his raped and mutilated daughter Lavinia in the final scene to rescue her from the stain to her honor and the honor of her family.

Throughout *Coriolanus*, manliness is praised as a virtue superior to mere love, and therefore woman's qualities associated with peace and civil life are downrated. Anything lyric and poetic is feminine and therefore not desirable. Probably the most striking image in the play is in Volumnia's politic speech to her son about how to win over the plebeians to vote for him as counsel. She lays out the histrionic role he must play: "Now humble as the ripest mulberry / That will not hold the handling" (3.2.79–80). This lyrical image of the dead-ripe mulberry is used pejoratively to characterize a hypocritical role. Coriolanus understands clearly that his mother wants to unsex him and convert him into a shameful and ridiculous feminine figure:

> Away, my disposition, and possess me
> Some harlot's spirit! My throat of war be turned,
> Which quired with my drum, into a pipe
> Small as an eunuch or the virgin voice
> That babies lulls asleep! (3.2.111–15)

The "virgin voice" is not the "throat of war," and Coriolanus is ashamed of himself for yielding to his mother's duplicitous counsel.

Theatrical imagery is used effectively in this play to express ideas of hypocritical role-playing. Cominius, Coriolanus's general, for example, describes him at sixteen fighting against Tarquin. Again, there is a gender contrast between the youth, with "his Amazonian chin" (that is, beardless, like that of an Amazon—one of the mythological Greek female warriors associated with the Scythians), driving "The bristled lips before him" (2.2.92–93). Cominius praises him for playing the man at such an early age:

> In that day's feats,
> When he might act the woman in the scene,
> He proved best man i' th' field. (96–98)

Since boys whose voices had not yet changed played all the women's parts in the Elizabethan theater, Marcius could well have acted "the woman in the scene," but instead he acted heroically beyond all other men on the field of battle. The speech continues with a recital of Marcius's manly accomplishments:

> His sword, death's stamp,
> Where it did mark, it took; from face to foot
> He was a thing of blood, whose every motion
> Was timed with dying cries. (108–11)

All these deeds are summed up by Menenius's comment: "Worthy man!" (123).

Queen Margaret in the *Henry VI* plays is another manlike woman on the model of Lady Macbeth and Volumnia. In *3 Henry VI*, after Clifford has killed Rutland, the son of Richard, Duke of York, Margaret savagely taunts York, her captive. She stages him on a molehill with a paper crown on his head and gives him a napkin dipped in Rutland's blood to wipe his tears. Her orders are to murder him slowly: "take time to do him dead" (1.4.108). York's response is not to plead for his life, but to launch an elaborate gender argument against Margaret, who is not acting the way a woman is supposed to:

> She-wolf of France, but worse than wolves of France,
> Whose tongue more poisons than the adder's tooth!
> How ill-beseeming is it in thy sex
> To triumph like an Amazonian trull
> Upon their woes whom fortune captivates! (111–15)

York is preoccupied with Margaret's violation of expected female norms:

> O tiger's heart wrapped in a woman's hide!
> How couldst thou drain the lifeblood of the child,
> To bid the father wipe his eyes withal,
> And yet be seen to bear a woman's face?
> Women are soft, mild, pitiful, and flexible;
> Thou stern, obdurate, flinty, rough, remorseless. (137–42)

"Tiger's heart wrapped in a woman's hide" is the famous line parodied by Robert Greene in his attack on Shakespeare in *A Groatsworth of Wit* (1592): "*Tygers hart wrapt in a Players hide*."[5] This echoes Lavinia's plea to the sons of Tamora in *Titus Andronicus*:

> When did the tiger's young ones teach the dam?
> O, do not learn [=teach] her wrath; she taught it thee.
> The milk thou suck'st from her did turn to marble;
> Even at thy teat thou hadst thy tyranny. (2.3.142–45)

Tamora, Queen of the Goths, is a savage woman whose ferocity is symbolized by the tiger, especially the Hyrcanian tiger, represented in Aeneas's tale to Dido in *Hamlet* by "'The rugged Pyrrhus, like th' Hyrcanian beast'" (2.2.461).

York's gender typology of men and women repeats a familiar stereotype in Shakespeare and other Elizabethan writers. Women are passive, full of feeling, compassionate, tender, quick to weep, whereas men are active, creatures of will, given to strong and decisive impulses. The *Henry VI* plays share the gender assumptions of *Titus Andronicus* and *The Rape of Lucrece*, all of which were written within a few years of each other. In *The Rape of Lucrece* we learn that

> men have marble, women waxen minds,
> And therefore are they formed as marble will;
> The weak oppressed, th' impression of strange kinds
> Is formed in them by force, by fraud, or skill.
> Then call them not the authors of their ill,
> No more than wax shall be accounted evil
> Wherein is stamped the semblance of a devil.   (1240–46)

Although Lucrece is clearly raped against her will, an elaborate apology is offered in the poem to absolve her of guilt. Since women have waxen minds, they passively absorb impressions, like the wax on which a seal ring is pressed, and are therefore not responsible for the ills that befall them.

Women are naively honest and open, whereas men are dissemblers, as the couplet of the next stanza indicates:

> Though men can cover crimes with bold stern looks,
> Poor women's faces are their own faults' books.   (1252–53)

Women are passive and waxen, "weak-made" (1260), which makes them easy targets for "men's abuses" (1259). Shakespeare goes to what seems unnecessary lengths to apologize for Lucrece's rape in terms of familiar gender traits.

Hippolyta, the Queen of the Amazons, appears in two plays of Shakespeare: *A Midsummer Night's Dream* and *The Two Noble Kinsmen*. Both open with her imminent marriage to Theseus, Duke of Athens. The mythological background of Theseus and Hippolyta is lightly touched on but doesn't figure importantly in the action. In *A Midsummer Night's Dream*, the wedding, which will take place in four days, is set in a martial context. The Duke says:

> Hippolyta, I wooed thee with my sword,
> And won thy love, doing thee injuries;

But I will wed thee in another key,
With pomp, with triumph, and with reveling. (1.1.16–19)

We learn from Plutarch's "Life of Theseus," in Sir Thomas North's translation, that Theseus subdued the Amazons and captured Hippolyta for his
wife (Antiopa in some accounts).[6] In Titania and Oberon's domestic quarrel, we hear about their amours with Theseus and Hippolyta. Titania says:

> the bouncing [=swaggering] Amazon,
> Your buskined mistress and your warrior love,
> To Theseus must be wedded, and you come
> To give their bed joy and prosperity. (2.1.70–73)

The buskin (*cothurnus*) was a high hunter's boot, also worn by actors in
Greek and Roman tragedy. Oberon reminds Titania of "thy love to Theseus" (76), which completes the intermingling of the King and Queen of
the Fairies with Theseus and Hippolyta. Their roles are sometimes doubled on stage.

The Two Noble Kinsmen also begins with the marriage of Theseus and
Hippolyta, which is interrupted by the "*three Queens in black*" (1.1.24 s.d.)
and never brought to conclusion (as it is in *A Midsummer Night's Dream*).
We learn more about Hippolyta the Amazon in this play, especially from
the petition of the Second Queen, who begins her speech with an
account of Hippolyta's warlike deeds:

> Most dreaded Amazonian, that hast slain
> The scythe-tusked boar, that with thy arm as strong
> As it is white, wast near to make the male
> To thy sex captive. (1.1.78–81)

But Theseus subdued her with both force and affection, in the same
measure as she subdued him:

> Whom now I know hast much more power on him
> Than ever he had on thee, who ow'st his strength
> And his love too, who is a servant for
> The tenor of thy speech. (87–90)

This is a very different Theseus from the character in *A Midsummer
Night's Dream*.

In act 1, scene 3, Hippolyta once again represents herself to Pirithous, the noble friend of Theseus, as a savage, ferocious warrior:

We have been soldiers, and we cannot weep
When our friends don their helms, or put to sea,
Or tell of babes broached on the lance, or women
That have sod [=boiled] their infants in—and after eat them—
The brine they wept at killing 'em.   (18–22)

Hippolyta is no pussycat even compared to Othello, with his exotic adventures among the Cannibals, the Anthropophagi, "and men whose heads / Grew beneath their shoulders" (*Othello* 1.3.143–44). In the Amazon figure there is a mingling of male and female gender values.

The most persistent sign of femaleness in Shakespeare is tears. That tears are womanish is axiomatic; men who cry are acting like women, and they generally apologize for their emotional outbursts. When Laertes learns that his sister is drowned, his immediate reaction is to make one of the worst puns in the play:

Too much of water hast thou, poor Ophelia,
And therefore I forbid my tears; but yet
It is our trick; nature her custom holds,
Let shame say what it will: when these are gone,
The woman will be out.   (*Hamlet* 4.7.185–89)

Laertes is ashamed to be yielding to "nature," and to be acting like a woman, but it will soon be over and his mourning will be quenched by revenge. He has already sworn to murder Hamlet by poison and by the unbated rapier.

In his first soliloquy, Hamlet is preoccupied with the false tears his mother has shed for her dead husband:

frailty, thy name is woman—
A little month, or ere those shoes were old
With which she followed my poor father's body
Like Niobe, all tears, why she, even she . . . married with my uncle. . . .
                                                                              (1.2.146–51)

The weeping Niobe, whose twelve (or fourteen) children were all slain by Apollo and Artemis, Leto's offspring, is a stock type of bereavement.

Gertrude weeps crocodile tears for her dead husband, soon to be replaced by his brother:

> Within a month,
> Ere yet the salt of most unrighteous tears
> Had left the flushing in her gallèd eyes,
> She married. (153–56)

Othello attributes "Unrighteous tears" to Desdemona, when he strikes her in the presence of Lodovico:

> O devil, devil!
> If that the earth could teem with woman's tears,
> Each drop she falls would prove a crocodile. (*Othello* 4.1.244–46)

Tears are seemingly fruitful, but Desdemona's would generate monsters.

The crocodile's tears were already proverbial in Shakespeare's time (see Tilley C831), and they were shed either to mourn hypocritically over a victim or to allure unsuspecting prey, as in a telling passage in *2 Henry VI*. The Queen is speaking of Richard, Duke of Gloucester's ability to manipulate King Henry:

> Gloucester's show
> Beguiles him as the mournful crocodile
> With sorrow snares relenting passengers,
> Or as the snake, rolled in a flow'ring bank,
> With shining checkered slough, doth sting a child
> That for the beauty thinks it excellent. (3.1.225–30)

So womanish tears are suspicious as a way to trick a credulous victim.

In *Romeo and Juliet*, when Romeo learns of his banishment for killing Tybalt, his grief transforms him from a man to a womanish creature. His gender transformation is the subject of Friar Lawrence's scorn, supported by the Nurse. The Friar points him out to her: "There on the ground, with his own tears made drunk" (3.3.83). Romeo is wallowing in tears as a form of self-indulgent grief, which leads to his attempt to stab himself. The Friar prevents him with righteous indignation:

> Art thou a man? Thy form cries out thou art;
> Thy tears are womanish, thy wild acts denote

The unreasonable fury of a beast.
Unseemly woman in a seeming man!
And ill-beseeming beast in seeming both! (109–13)

The Friar is disturbed by Romeo's desperate, unreasonable, androgynous state, "Unseemly woman in a seeming man." It is "unseemly," or indecorous, for a man to weep; to imitate a woman is to surrender manly integrity.

When Juliet weeps, however, it is only appropriate. Her mother supposes that her tears are for the dead Tybalt:

Evermore weeping for your cousin's death?
What, wilt thou wash him from his grave with tears? (3.5.70–71)

When she informs her daughter that she must marry Paris "early next Thursday morn" (113), Juliet's tears are again mistaken by her father, who thinks it quite normal that his daughter should be weeping for her dead cousin. Capulet plays garruously with the figure of tears:

How now? A conduit, girl? What, still in tears?
Evermore show'ring? In one little body
Thou counterfeits a bark, a sea, a wind:
For still thy eyes, which I may call the sea,
Do ebb and flow with tears; the bark thy body is,
Sailing in this salt flood; the winds, thy sighs,
Who, raging with thy tears and they with them,
Without a sudden calm will overset
Thy tempest-tossèd body. (130–38)

Capulet speaks in the elaborate, conceited style of *Richard II*, a play probably from 1595, the same year as *Romeo and Juliet*. Richard plays fancifully on the power of tears to dig him a grave:

Or shall we play the wantons with our woes
And make some pretty match with shedding tears,
As thus, to drop them still upon one place,
Till they have fretted us a pair of graves
Within the earth; and, therein laid, "there lies
Two kinsmen digged their graves with weeping eyes."
                    (*Richard II* 3.3.163–68)

Like Romeo, Richard is unmanly in his grief and his tears are womanish.

The gender issue of tears is nowhere more decisively expressed than in the climax of *Coriolanus*, where Aufidius uses the image of tears to destroy his seemingly invincible antagonist. He and his conspirators attack Coriolanus for his effeminate submission to his mother and family in act 5, scene 3, when he yields to their entreaties to spare Rome. Although tears are never shed in this scene, Aufidius uses them as an image of compassion and unmanly surrender of the Volscian cause. He brings Coriolanus down deliberately by harping on tears and provoking him to blind rage. The basic case is that he has betrayed the Volscians:

> At a few drops of women's rheum [=tears], which are
> As cheap as lies, he sold the blood and labor
> Of our great action. Therefore shall he die. (5.6.46–48)

When Coriolanus enters, Aufidius accuses him as a traitor:

> You lords and heads o' th' state, perfidiously
> He has betrayed your business and given up,
> For certain drops of salt, your city Rome,
> I say "your city," to his wife and mother . . . at his nurse's tears
> He whined and roared away your victory;
> That pages blushed at him, and men of heart
> Looked wond'ring each at others. (91–94, 97–100)

Of course, Coriolanus's action is represented as offensive to "men of heart."

When Coriolanus calls upon Mars, Aufidius has the final, stunning insult: "Name not the god, thou boy of tears!" (101). There are two insults here: Coriolanus is called "boy" rather than man, and he is represented as a sniveling, unheroic, mama's boy of womanish "tears." The defiant Coriolanus says exactly what Aufidius needs to provoke his death:

> If you have writ your annals true, 'tis there,
> That, like an eagle in a dovecote, I
> Fluttered your Volscians in Corioles.
> Alone I did it. "Boy"? (114–17)

"An eagle in a dovecote" is the opposite of a "boy of tears," but Coriolanus conveniently instigates his own slaughter by Aufidius's trusted conspirators, rather than taking the offensive. This is like Hector's death in *Troilus and Cressida*.

Marriage defines gender roles in specific ways. What is interesting in Shakespeare is how male and female characters seem to play against conventional expectations. It is as if Shakespeare is determined to set up a counterpoint between what is expected and what actually occurs, so that characters have latitude to move in and out of preconceived stereotypes. In *Julius Caesar*, for example, Portia surprises us. She wants to go beyond what is required of the good and obedient wife, who serves her husband's interests. The play offers us a rare glimpse at the idea of a companionate marriage.

In act 2, scene 1, Portia wants to know why her husband has separated himself from her: "Y'have ungently, Brutus, / Stole from my bed" (237–38). Notice that she says "my bed" and not "your bed" or "our bed." She wants to know the secret that is tormenting him: "Make me acquainted with your cause of grief" (256). Brutus demurs, but Portia presses on by declaring the rights of a Roman wife to share in the secrets of her husband:

> No, my Brutus;
> You have some sick offense within your mind,
> Which by the right and virtue of my place
> I ought to know of. (267–70)

In Elizabethan books on marriage and family life, it was hardly the role of an Elizabethan wife to share equally in the personal experience of her husband; this was rather meant for her husband's male friend or confidant.[7] But Portia insists that the marriage vow—"that great vow / Which did incorporate and make us one" (272–73)—makes it imperative that Brutus "unfold" his perturbations to her, "your self, your half" (274).

Portia develops this idea of the companionate marriage as a gender ideology:

> Within the bond of marriage, tell me, Brutus,
> Is it excepted I should know no secrets
> That appertain to you? Am I your self
> But, as it were, in sort or limitation,

>   To keep with you at meals, comfort your bed,
>   And talk to you sometimes? (280–85)

Portia defines what an Elizabethan husband would expect of a good wife, but her argument is leading somewhere else, as is apparent in her next question, "Dwell I but in the suburbs / Of your good pleasure?" (285–86). The "suburbs" are strongly associated with prostitutes, and there is an obvious pun on "pleasure." Brutus is not represented as a sensual man, as Antony is, so that Portia's conclusion is doubly emphatic: "If it be no more, / Portia is Brutus' harlot, not his wife" (286–87).

Brutus is shocked out of his complacency and reassures his wife with one of the most lyrical speeches in the play:

>   You are my true and honorable wife,
>   As dear to me as are the ruddy drops
>   That visit my sad heart. (288–90)

This comes as close to defining what a Roman gentleman means by love as any statement in Shakespeare. It is homely—"ruddy" drops, not red— and the blood is personified as a visitor to Brutus's serious and grave ("sad") heart.

This declaration sets off a flood of assertions by Portia that she is a certain kind of Roman female:

>   I grant I am a woman; but withal
>   A woman that Lord Brutus took to wife.
>   I grant I am a woman; but withal
>   A woman well reputed, Cato's daughter.
>   Think you I am no stronger than my sex,
>   Being so fathered and so husbanded? (292–97)

Portia can claim to be more than a conventional woman, derived as she is from Marcus Cato, who committed suicide to avoid capture, and married to such a moral exemplar as Brutus. To prove her fortitude and moral fiber, she imitates heroic Roman warriors like Coriolanus:

>   I have made strong proof of my constancy,
>   Giving myself a voluntary wound
>   Here in the thigh; can I bear that with patience,
>   And not my husband's secrets? (299–302)

Presumably, "Here in the thigh" is demonstrative. With this gesture she wins Brutus over completely: "O ye gods, / Render me worthy of this noble wife!" (302–3).

The consequences of Brutus's confiding in his wife are disastrous. It is already apparent in act 2, scene 4 that Portia's fortitude is weakening and that she is falling back on a typical female trepidation:

> I have a man's mind, but a woman's might.
> How hard it is for women to keep counsel! (8–9)

She is perturbed and disoriented by the secrets Brutus has revealed to her. The point of this scene is to show Portia's "constancy" wavering, and to prepare for her eventual death by swallowing live coals (4.3). In her final speech in act 2, scene 4, she deplores her feminine weakness: "Ay me, how weak a thing / The heart of woman is!" (39–40).

The scene with Brutus and Portia is almost directly inverted in act 2, scene 3 of *1 Henry IV* between Hotspur and his wife Kate. Like Brutus, Hotspur is a sworn conspirator, and his wife remarks on his perturbation:

> For what offense have I this fortnight been
> A banished woman from my Harry's bed? (39–40)

Kate speaks frankly of her marriage rights, which have been surrendered by her husband "To thick-eyed musing and cursed melancholy" (47). Like Portia, she demands to share in her husband's secrets:

> Some heavy business hath my lord in hand,
> And I must know it, else he loves me not. (64–65)

The point is that Hotspur does love his wife and therefore will tell her nothing, as in their punning dialogue:

LADY   What is it carries you away?
HOTSPUR   Why, my horse, my love—my horse! (77–78)

This charming love scene turns on conventional gender expectations. Kate threatens her husband: "In faith, I'll break thy little finger, Harry, and if thou wilt not tell me all things true" (87–89). Presumably, Kate is holding his finger when she says this. But Hotspur answers with typical male bravado, making a clear distinction between male and female values:

Away, away, you trifler! Love? I love thee not;
I care not for thee, Kate. This is no world
To play with mammets and to tilt with lips.
We must have bloody noses and cracked crowns. (90–93)

Hotspur seems to reject the romantic images of civil life that define his
world. "Mammets" is a variant of "maumets," derived from Mahomet, a
false god or idol, extended metaphorically to the doll or puppet a child
plays with. In the world of action, people do not engage in mock tour-
naments where they tilt with lips.

Hotspur has an equally romantic image of the heroic world of political affairs, from which women are excluded. When he is "a-horseback, I
will swear / I love thee infinitely" (101–2), but Kate is a woman and
therefore Hotspur will not confide in her:

> constant you are—
> But yet a woman; and for secrecy,
> No lady closer—for I well believe
> Thou wilt not utter what thou dost not know. (108–11)

"Constancy" is Portia's word—her "voluntary wound / Here in the
thigh" is a "strong proof" of it (*Julius Caesar* 2.1.299–301). Hotspur
rejects all radical ideas of a companionate marriage.

The sharp distinction between what is appropriate for a man and for
a woman lies at the heart of *Antony and Cleopatra*. From the Roman
point of view, Antony has lost his manhood in Egypt, and his efffemina-
tion expresses his tragic loss of command. There is a blurring or inversion of male and female roles that can only lead to Antony's destruction.
Shakespeare is alert to the gender markers in Plutarch, for example, when
Cleopatra boasts of an exchange of male and female roles:

> Ere the ninth hour, I drunk him to his bed;
> Then put my tires [=headdresses] and mantles on him whilst
> I wore his sword Philippan. (2.5.21–23)

Antony's sword is named after the battle of Philippi, which occurs in
Julius Caesar, and in which Antony defeats Brutus and Cassius.

Enobarbus is emphatic about separating the world of men from the
world of women, and in act 3, scene 7 he clearly indicates to Cleopatra
why Antony will be defeated in the forthcoming Battle of Actium. If

Cleopatra insists on appearing in the battle, Antony will be lost, as Enobarbus explains wittily in his aside:

> If we should serve with horse and mares together,
> The horse were merely [=absolutely] lost; the mares would bear
> A soldier and his horse. (7–9)

Enobarbus has nothing against women, as attested by his magnificent
oration on how Cleopatra first met Mark Antony on the river Cydnus
(2.2.197ff.), but women and men operate in different and separate
spheres.

He tells Cleopatra explicitly what he has already said in an aside:

> Your presence needs must puzzle Antony;
> Take from his heart, take from his brain, from's time,
> What should not then be spared. He is already
> Traduced for levity; and 'tis said in Rome
> That Photinus an eunuch and your maids
> Manage this war. (3.7.10–15)

As a woman, Cleopatra does not belong in the battle. Later in the scene,
Canidius sums up Antony's fateful predicament: "so our leader's led, /
And we are women's men" (69–70). "Women's men" signifies the cor-
ruption of manhood on which the tragedy is based.

After the Battle of Actium has been lost, with Antony fleeing after the
ships of Cleopatra, there is a moment of truth between Enobarbus and
Cleopatra. She asks him, "What shall we do, Enobarbus?" and he answers
curtly, "Think, and die" (3.13.1)—in other words, grow melancholy
through thought, which will bring on your death. But Enobarbus blames
only Antony for what has happened:

>   that would make his will
> Lord of his reason. What though you fled
> From that great face of war, whose several ranges
> Frighted each other? Why should he follow?
> The itch of his affection should not then
> Have nicked his captainship. (3–8)

As a woman, Cleopatra is not expected to behave heroically in war, but
Antony is, and like Tarquin in *The Rape of Lucrece*, he makes his will lord

of his reason. Will is associated with desire and sexual appetite, as in the puns in Sonnet 135: "Whoever hath her wish, thou hast thy *Will*." Antony's capacity to lead is imagined as a sword, which his passion has nicked.

The relationship of Antony and Cleopatra violates assumed gender norms, which is what makes it so exciting and so certain to end tragically. In the comedies, gender norms are sometimes stated in a form that seems almost caricatural, but these statements don't seem to have much bearing on how characters actually behave. In the marriage debate in *The Comedy of Errors*, it is the unwed Luciana who lectures her sister, Adriana, on the nature of men:

> A man is master of his liberty.
> Time is their master, and when they see time,
> They'll go or come; if so, be patient, sister. (2.1.7–9)

But Adriana asks some embarrassing questions: "Why should their liberty than ours be more?" (10). Luciana then launches her didactic explanation (in couplets) of why, according to the law of nature, man is the "bridle" (14) of woman's will:

> The beasts, the fishes, and the wingèd fowls
> Are their males' subject, and at their controls;
> Man, more divine, the master of all these,
> Lord of the wide world and wild wat'ry seas,
> Indued with intellectual sense and souls,
> Of more preeminence than fish and fowls,
> Are masters to their females, and their lords;
> Then let your will attend on their accords. (18–25)

This is a textbook explanation of male preeminence in the scheme of things, to which Adriana retorts cleverly, "This servitude makes you to keep unwed" (26). In other words, this is orthodox doctrine of gender relations, but does not refer to what really happens. Luciana declares further: "Ere I learn love, I'll practice to obey" (29), and preaches patience to her sister: "Till he come home again, I would forbear" (31). But Adriana will have none of this official gender ideology:

> So thou, that hast no unkind mate to grieve thee,
> With urging helpless patience would relieve me. (38–39)

But in the next scene, Adriana with her supposed husband (who is actually his twin brother, Antipholus of Syracuse), takes the opposite tack and enunciates conventional ideas about male superiority. She woos, in couplets, the wrong Antipholus to take up his rightful role as her husband:

> Come, I will fasten on this sleeve of thine:
> Thou art an elm, my husband, I a vine,
> Whose weakness, married to thy stronger state,
> Makes me with thy strength to communicate. (2.2.174–77)

The figure of the vine and the elm is biblical as well as proverbial (see Tilley V61), as in Titania's enamored concern for Bottom:

> Sleep thou, and I will wind thee in my arms . . .
> So doth the woodbine the sweet honeysuckle
> Gentle entwist; the female ivy so
> Enrings the barky fingers of the elm.
> (*A Midsummer Night's Dream* 4.1.43–47)

Ivy is female because it needs the male elm for support. The winding of the ivy and its tendrils is envisioned as a tender, loving act.

Some of this thinking surely lies behind the action in *The Taming of the Shrew*, which turns on traditional gender distinctions. Throughout the play Kate is called "intolerable curst / And shrewd and froward" (1.2.88–89), all of which more or less means that she does not have the proper character traits of a woman. The play is presented as a theatrical case study of how to tame a shrew; Tranio says that Petruchio maintains a "taming school" (4.2.54). The didactic aspect of the play is obvious as Petruchio seeks to recondition Kate in Pavlovian style, especially in the scenes in his country house (4.1 and 3).

In some sense Petruchio is influenced by his own powerful educational ideas. Does Kate finally figure out how to tame Petruchio and to go him one better in his gender expectations? This is a teasing question, but it is clear by the end of act 4, scene 5 that Kate knows how to play the right role according to society's expectations. She understands the gender game. She is willing to say anything to indulge her husband's fantasy:

> Forward, I say, since we have come so far,
> And be it moon or sun or what you please.

And if you please to call it a rush-candle,
Henceforth I vow it shall be so for me.   (4.5.12–15)

Hortensio says, aside, "Petruchio, go thy ways. The field is won" (23), but
it is not clear whether it has been won by Petruchio or by Kate. She is no
longer "intolerable curst / And shrewd and froward" (1.2.88–89); rather,
she is now sophisticated, clever, and gamesome.

To understand the role of gender in Shakespeare's plays it is important
to grasp conventional Elizabethan ideas and expectations of what men
and women are supposed to be like. Shakespeare plays heterodox ideas of
gender off against the stereotypes of the audience. The fact that his characters work against type generates theatrical interest; in this way, gender
can be used to titillate the spectators. Since women's roles were played by
boy actors, there is a built-in source of titillation, especially in the comedies. If we can free ourselves for the moment of modern gender ideas,
The Taming of the Shrew, for example, offers a good place to examine the
performance of gender against received ideas. Petruchio and Kate may
well enact a relation different from what we expect between a shrewish
woman and a fortune-hunting man, or even different from what they
expected at the beginning of the play.

CHAPTER SEVEN

HOMOEROTIC
Discourses

The issues of the homoerotic in Shakespeare are hopelessly entwined in academic controversy. Everything seems to come back to the unanswerable question of Shakespeare's own sexual orientation. It is necessary to separate homoerotic discourses in Shakespeare's work from biographical speculation. The whole topic is distorted by ahistorical, polemical positions. Contemporary terms such as "homosexuality," "lesbianism," and "bisexuality" have no direct reference to the sexual ideologies of the late sixteenth and early seventeenth centuries, and euphemisms such as "male friendship" or "female friendship" do not provide successful substitutions. There are obvious homoerotic, same-sex discourses in Shakespeare's works that are an important aspect of the theme of love. In Marlowe the homoerotic references are so direct and so overt that critics do not hesitate to speak of Marlowe as a homosexual writer.[1] The same is not true for Shakespeare. Perhaps this is because he is so impersonal an author that his works reveal little about his life, which is not the case with Marlowe and Jonson, for example, who seem eager to project constructed images of their lives in their works.

Let us begin with a late play, *The Two Noble Kinsmen*, which is generally thought to be a collaboration between Shakespeare and John Fletcher.[2] Same-sex discourse, both male and female, is so obvious in this play that it offers a model with which to compare earlier and less overt relationships. But what is significant is that old-fashioned heterosexual discourse, as in the early comedies, is freely mingled with homoerotic discourse. One doesn't exclude the other, and I think this is also true of many other Shakespearean plays. Various sexualities, including a strong strain of self-love and chastity, exist comfortably side by side without contradicting one another.

The most heterosexual creature in the play is the Jailer's Daughter, who falls in love at first sight with Palamon, her father's noble prisoner. She knows that she is "base" (2.3.2), or of low birth, but she cannot resist her sexual promptings: "What pushes are we wenches driven to / When fifteen once has found us!" (6–7). Her love is distinctly sexual: "What should I do to make him know I love him, / For I would fain enjoy him?" (29–30). She resolves to free him from prison. Like Ophelia in *Hamlet*, on whom she is modeled, the Jailer's Daughter soon goes mad from unrequited love, and her lyrical, broken discourse is full of sexual innuendo: "O for a prick now like a nightingale, / To put my breast against!" (3.4.25–26).

The cure for her love melancholy is announced confidently by the Doctor: the Wooer should pretend to be Palamon and make love to her. In act 5, scene 2, the cure becomes specifically sexual. The Doctor tells the Wooer, "And when your fit comes, fit her home, and presently" (11), which is followed by even more explicit counsel:

> Please her appetite
> And do it home: it cures her *ipso facto*
> The melancholy humor that infects her. (35–37)

The Doctor's practical advice proves to be remarkably successful in returning the Jailer's Daughter to sanity.

The play begins with the marriage of Theseus and Hippolyta, which is also the overarching action of *A Midsummer Night's Dream*. What is interesting is that Hippolyta talks so sympathetically of the noble love between Theseus and his friend Pirithous, who shares with him the joy of manly exercises and warlike peril. Hippolyta has a grand homoerotic speech outlining the exploits of her husband and his dearest friend:

> They two have cabined
> In many as dangerous as poor a corner,
> Peril and want contending. They have skiffed
> Torrents whose roaring tyranny and power
> I' th' least of these was dreadful; and they have
> Fought out together where Death's self was lodged,
> Yet Fate hath brought them off. Their knot of love,
> Tied, weaved, entangled, with so true, so long,
> And with a finger of so deep a cunning,
> May be outworn, never undone. (1.3.35–44)

The point is that the "knot of love" binding Theseus and Pirithous does not at all weaken the knot of love binding Theseus and Hippolyta in marriage.

Similarly, Palamon and Arcite are presented as the two noble kinsmen, both nephews to Creon, King of Thebes. When they are captured by Theseus and imprisoned in act 2, scene 1, their discourse is full of homoerotic terms expressing their love and devotion for each other. Arcite begins by acknowledging that their youth will wither in prison and they will never be able to marry:

> The sweet embraces of a loving wife,
> Loaden with kisses, armed with thousand Cupids,
> Shall never clasp our necks, no issue know us. (89–91)

They have only each other.

Arcite goes on to find a secret blessing in their imprisoned state:

> And here being thus together,
> We are an endless mine to one another;
> We are one another's wife, ever begetting
> New births of love. (137–40)

These are among the most overtly homoerotic declarations in Shakespeare, and Arcite goes even further to argue that "Were we at liberty, / A wife might part us lawfully" (147–48). Palamon answers that his cousin Arcite has made him "almost wanton / With my captivity" (155–56).

"Wanton" is a word with strong sexual connotations. But a few lines further, as soon as Palamon sees Emilia in the garden below, the homoerotic discourse comes to an abrupt end. Both men fall in love instantaneously, and their love for each other is forgotten.

Palamon proclaims his primacy because he saw Emilia first, but Arcite declares a specifically sexual intention, which distinguishes his love from his cousin's:

> I will not as you do, to worship her,
> As she is heavenly and a blessèd goddess:
> I love her as a woman, to enjoy her.
> So both may love. (2.1.222–25)

Arcite thinks that Palamon betrays the assumptions of "a noble kinsman" to love Emilia alone without sharing her with his friend. Issues of homoerotic and heterosexual identity become blurred in this scene. Palamon's love discourse is extravagant, and he goes so far as to transform gender roles:

> Were I at liberty, I would do things
> Of such a virtuous greatness that this lady,
> This blushing virgin, should take manhood to her
> And seek to ravish me. (317–20)

What "things / Of such a virtuous greatness" does Palamon have in mind to provoke a rape on Emilia's part? The sexual is strangely confounded with the ethical.

We learn later, when Arcite comes to succor his cousin, who has escaped from prison with the aid of the Jailer's Daughter, that both of the noble kinsmen were at one time lusty heterosexual lovers. When Arcite gives him wine, Palamon pledges his cousin "to the wenches / We have known in our days" (3.3.28–29). Palamon reminds him specifically of "The Lord Steward's daughter" (29): "She met him in an arbor: / What did she there, coz? Play o' th' virginals?" (33–34). The virginals were a small keyboard instrument, like a spinet, popular with young women, but here used with a sexual implication that Palamon drives home with his next remark. Arcite's coy "Something she did, sir," is completed by Palamon's "Made her groan a month for't; / Or two, or three or ten" (35–36). Arcite parries with "The Marshal's sister" (36), Palamon's girlfriend:

> A pretty brown wench 'tis. There was a time
> When young men went a-hunting—and a wood,
> And a broad beech, and thereby hangs a tale. (39–41)

The proverbial phrase, "and thereby hangs a tale" (see Tilley T48), is completed by the understood obscene reference of the Clown in *Othello*: "Marry, sir, by many a wind instrument that I know" (3.1.10–11), which is like our vulgar expression "a piece of tail."

Emilia, of whom Palamon and Arcite are both enamored at first sight, is a good example of the mingling of seemingly contradictory sexual discourses. In act 2, scene 1, Emilia and her waiting-gentlewoman have the sort of witty, bantering conversation of heroines in Shakespeare's early comedies. They speak mostly about flowers and their conventional symbolism, beginning with the narcissus. Emilia observes that the garden "has a world of pleasures in't" (177), but Narcissus—both the flower and the "fair boy"—was "but a fool / To love himself: were there not maids enough?" (179–80). And further, "were they all hard-hearted?" (181). Emilia cautions her woman against too much kindness, because "Men are mad things" (185). Emilia is "wanton" (206) and "wondrous merry-hearted" (210); she "could laugh now," which innocent phrase her woman completes with obvious innuendo: "I could lie down, I am sure" (211). "Laugh and lie down" is the title of a lost play of Shakespeare's time, and it was a frequently used proverbial tag (see Tilley L92).

But earlier in act 1, scene 3, Emilia responds to Hippolyta's account of the noble friendship of Theseus and Pirithous with an even more touching homoerotic discourse about her childhood friend Flavina, when they were both eleven. It is like Leontes' account of his boyhood friendship with Polixenes in *The Winter's Tale*, but also elegiac because Flavina has long since died.

Emilia distinguishes between the love of Pirithous and Theseus and her innocent involvement with Flavina. The two men's love

> is more maturely seasoned,
> More buckled with strong judgment, and their needs
> The one of th' other may be said to water
> Their intertangled roots of love. (56–59)

But she and Flavina "were things innocent" (60), who loved spontaneously,

like the elements
That know not what, nor why, yet do effect
Rare issues by their operance. (61–63)

Emilia celebrates an idyllic, preadolescent sexuality:

the flow'r that I would pluck
And put between my breasts, O then but beginning
To swell about the blossom, she would long
Till she had such another, and commit it
To the like innocent cradle, where phoenix-like
They died in perfume. . . . (66–71)

They follow each other in adornment, clothes, and music without any conscious intention, all of which proves "That the true love 'tween maid and maid may be / More than in sex dividual" (81–82).

Emilia's affirmations would seem to make the love banter of the garden scene (2.1) problematical, but they do not contradict each other. Hippolyta draws the obvious conclusion: "That you shall never, like the maid Flavina, / Love any that's called man" (84–85). Emilia agrees: "I am sure I shall not" (85). But Hippolyta demurs, even though Emilia has "said enough to shake me from the arm / Of the all-noble Theseus" (92–93). Hippolyta, the Queen of the Amazons, will vie with Pirithous for the "high throne" (96) of Theseus's heart. She doesn't really believe that Emilia's homoerotic discourse excludes her from heterosexual love. She speaks of Emilia's confession as "a sickly appetite / That loathes even as it longs" (89–90). So the issue still remains open.[3]

Later in the play, Emilia has a long soliloquy before the pictures of Arcite and Palamon, praising their beauty in conventional terms but unable to choose between them. There is a curious comparison of Arcite to Ganymede, the youth beloved of Jupiter, but also an Elizabethan slang term for a sodomite:

Here Love himself sits smiling:
Just such another wanton Ganymede
Set Jove a-fire with and enforced the god
Snatch up the goodly boy and set him by him,
A shining constellation. (4.2.14–18)

The opening scene of Marlowe's Dido play shows us Jove dandling Ganymede in a frivolous and wanton manner.[4] It is interesting that this is how Emilia conceives of Arcite. Palamon's charms too are rather vague and ornamental. Emilia concludes her important soliloquy with childlike indecision:

> What a mere child is Fancy,
> That having two fair gawds of equal sweetness
> Cannot distinguish, but must cry for both! (52–54)

It doesn't bode well for the future love life of either Palamon or Arcite that they are represented by their beloved as "two fair gawds of equal sweetness." A "gawd" (or "gaud") is a toy or trifle, something trivial and of little value that a child plays with (see *OED*, substantive 2, #2).

The upshot of all this indeterminacy comes in act 5, scene 1, when the knights pray at the altars of Mars and Venus, and Emilia, following them, prays at the altar of Diana, the goddess of chastity and virginity. Emilia stands as Diana's "priest," "humbled 'fore thine altar" (142–43). She is "bride-habited, / But maiden-hearted" (150–51). She must have one of the two knights as her husbands, "but I / Am guiltless of election" (153–54).

At the end of the scene, the *"silver hind,"* (136 s.d.), or female red deer, symbol of virginity and sacred to Diana that Emilia has brought with her, *"vanishes under the altar, and in the place ascends a rose tree, having one rose upon it"* (162 s.d.). Emilia's interpretation is surprising in a sacred and solemn scene about her marriage choice:

> but one rose.
> If well inspired, this battle shall confound
> Both these brave knights, and I a virgin flow'r
> Must grow alone, unplucked. (165–68)

As if by wish-fulfillment, *"Here is heard a sudden twang of instruments, and the rose falls from the tree"* (168 s.d.). Emilia shows no enthusiasm for her imminent marriage, and her prayer to Diana seems to affirm her earlier assertion "That the true love 'tween maid and maid may be / More than in sex dividual" (1.3.81–82).

Emilia's sexual ambiguities only reproduce a familiar pairing between young girls from Shakespeare's early comedies. These relationships, although entirely innocent, are conducted in a gushing emotional language. In *A Midsummer Night's Dream*, Helena, who is suddenly beloved by both Lysander and Demetrius, doesn't believe in her good luck, brought on (unbeknownst to her) by the mischievousness of Puck. She suspects a plot against her in which her school friend Hermia is involved. Helena reminds her of their passionate attachment:

> Is all the counsel that we two have shared,
> The sister's vows, the hours that we have spent,
> When we have chid the hasty-footed time
> For parting us—O, is all forgot?
> All school days friendship, childhood innocence?   (3.2.198–202)

Helena uses the erotic language of conventional lovers, even drawing on the familiar Platonic conceit of the union of the two lovers in a single transcendent soul:

> We, Hermia, like two artificial gods,
> Have with our needles created both one flower,
> Both on one sampler, sitting on one cushion,
> Both warbling of one song, both in one key;
> As if our hands, our sides, voices, and minds,
> Had been incorporate. So we grew together,
> Like to a double cherry, seeming parted,
> But yet an union in partition;
> Two lovely berries molded on one stem;
> So, with two seeming bodies, but one heart;
> Two of the first, like coats in heraldry,
> Due but to one, and crownèd with one crest.   (203–14)

The gods are "artificial" in the sense of artful, skilled in the arts, especially needlework and music. The image of the lovers being "incorporate" has spiritual as well as physical connotations. In its Latin sense, the word means being made into one body. Their two bodies are only "seeming," since they share "one heart." It is interesting how easily and how fluidly Helena slips into homoerotic discourse.

The same is also true for Rosalind and Celia in *As You Like It*, where their passionate girlhood friendship is a preparation for their heterosexual unions. When Rosalind is banished from Duke Senior's court, her cousin Celia cannot bear to part with her, but insists on accompanying her to the Forest of Arden. Celia uses ordinary lovers' language to describe their relation:

> We still have slept together,
> Rose at an instant, learned, played, eat together;
> And wheresoe'er we went, like Juno's swans,
> Still we went coupled and inseparable. (1.3.71–74)

The language is sexual but the thoughts are not. Celia goes on to argue, as an excuse for fleeing court together, the union of lovers:

> Rosalind lacks then the love
> Which teacheth thee that thou and I am one.
> Shall we be sund'red, shall we part, sweet girl?
> No, let my father seek another heir. (94–97)

In most productions of the play, Celia is shown to be petulantly jealous of Rosalind's love for Orlando.

Rosalind, in her male disguise, assumes caricatural male attributes:

> A gallant curtle-ax upon my thigh,
> A boar-spear in my hand; and, in my heart
> Lie there what hidden woman's fear there will,
> We'll have a swashing and a martial outside,
> As many other mannish cowards have
> That do outface it with their semblances. (115–20)

A boar-spear is what Adonis carries in *Venus and Adonis*. As Ganymede, Rosalind will have exaggeratedly male qualities, as if she were conscious of the need to play the part of a man to the hilt, because she isn't a man. But, of course, the irony is that Rosalind was played by a boy actor.

Male homoerotic discourse is much more common in Shakespeare and in Elizabethan/Jacobean literature than female because friendship, especially male friendship, was conventionally taken to be of higher spiritual value than heterosexual love. The word "love" was used indiscriminately to describe all degrees of affection, including quite casual relations among strangers or near-strangers. *The Two Gentlemen of Verona*, an early comedy, anticipates *The Two Noble Kinsmen*, a late romance, in its theme of the noble friends as rivals in love. But the ending of *The Two Gentlemen of Verona* is almost parodic as the noble friend, Valentine, graciously offers Silvia to his dastardly comrade, Proteus, who was just about to rape her. Luckily, Julia, Proteus's old flame, intervenes just in time. The homoerotic moral of the story is summed up in Valentine's couplet:

> And, that my love may appear plain and free,
> All that was mine in Silvia I give thee.   (5.4.82–83)

This proves that Valentine's love for his friend is far greater than his love for Silvia, who is disposed of as if she were a chattel. But the dramatic action works against Valentine's generosity and the play ends with the expected pairings.

In *Twelfth Night*, the sea captain Antonio is strikingly attracted to Sebastian, the twin brother of Viola, whom he saves from shipwreck.[5] His concern for Sebastian when they first appear in act 2, scene 1 seems to go beyond mere graciousness. He wants to accompany Sebastian to Orsino's court, even though as a proscribed outlaw he is in great danger of being apprehended there. There is something excessive in Antonio's affections, as when he says to Sebastian, "If you will not murder me for my love"—that is, kill me by parting from me—"let me be your servant" (37–38). Sebastian refuses and speaks in a rather odd and stilted way in this scene, presumably from grief about his sister, whom he thinks drowned. Antonio's soliloquy after Sebastian exits is in the romantic style of erotic discourse:

> But come what may, I do adore thee so
> That danger shall seem sport, and I will go.   (47–48)

Antonio plans to go to Orsino's court despite his own peril. The word "adore" is strong here and different in intensity from the familiar word "love."

When we next see Sebastian in act 3, scene 3, Antonio has overtaken him and makes elaborate excuses for protecting his younger companion:

> I could not stay behind you. My desire
> (More sharp than filèd steel) did spur me forth;
> And not all love to see you (though so much
> As might have drawn one to a longer voyage)
> But jealousy what might befall your travel,
> Being skilless in these parts.   (4–9)

Again, "desire" is a strong word, intensified by being called "More sharp than filèd steel." Antonio is full of "jealousy," or anxiety, about Sebastian and therefore his "willing love" is spurred on "by these arguments of fear" (11–12). He is solicitous about his young charge; before he leaves he establishes that they will stay at the Elephant and that he will order their meals. To cap it all, he insists that Sebastian take his purse:

> Haply your eye shall light upon some toy
> You have desire to purchase, and your store
> I think is not for idle markets, sir. (44–46)

The purse is intended not for necessities, but for the purchase of whatever trifles strike Sebastian's fancy.

This purse, of course, has unforeseen consequences. When Antonio is arrested in the next scene, he asks Viola, Sebastian's twin (in male disguise as Cesario), for it back. Antonio's grief for what he thinks is Sebastian's perfidy is expressed in the overwrought emotional style of homoerotic discourse:

> This youth that you see here
> I snatched one half out of the jaws of death;
> Relieved him with such sanctity of love,
> And to his image, which methought did promise
> Most venerable worth, did I devotion. (3.4.371–75)

Antonio speaks in the rhetoric of a lover, doing devotion to his beloved's image, which is part of the ceremonies demanded by the sanctity of love.

This rhetoric is reinforced by Antonio's speech in the last scene of the play, when he appears as a prisoner before the Duke. He still mistakes Viola for Sebastian and upbraids her bitterly:

> That most ingrateful boy there by your side
> From the rude sea's enraged and foamy mouth
> Did I redeem. A wrack past hope he was.
> His life I gave him, and did thereto add
> My love without retention or restraint,
> All his in dedication. For his sake
> Did I expose myself (pure [=purely] for his love)
> Into the danger of this adverse town. (5.1.77–84)

Antonio's solicitude can be seen from his own exaggerated watching over Sebastian:

for three months before,
No int'rim, not a minute's vacancy,
Both day and night did we keep company. (94–96)

One doesn't need to literalize what Antonio is saying to understand the homoerotic thrust of his statements. Once Sebastian appears, all of Antonio's bitterness evaporates in wonder: "How have you made division of yourself?" (222).

Twelfth Night, like many of Shakespeare's comedies, delights in disguises, gender transformations, and other surprises, like Viola's wooing of Duke Orsino in male disguise as Cesario. When the Duke finally takes Viola/Cesario's hand, presumably in marriage, he seems to be in no hurry to see his beloved "in thy woman's weeds" (5.1.273). Viola soliloquizes on the dangers of the love game at the end of act 2, scene 2, when she fears that Olivia is in love with her in her male disguise: "Poor lady, she were better love a dream" (26). This means, here and elsewhere (as, for example, in Phebe's falling in love with Rosalind in *As You Like It*), that same-sex relations are absolutely ruled out, yet the characters delight in homoerotic games with their appropriate discourse. Viola weighs her alternatives:

As I am man [i.e., as Cesario],
My state is desperate for my master's love.
As I am woman (now alas the day!),
What thriftless sighs shall poor Olivia breathe? (36–39)

Luckily, the comic heroine doesn't have to cope with the resolution of these conflicts:

O Time, thou must untangle this, not I;
It is too hard a knot for me t' untie. (40–41)

This is a characteristic comic stance of completely avoiding any of the implications of the double, especially the sexual double.

Antonio in *The Merchant of Venice* has certain resemblances to Antonio in *Twelfth Night*, as an older man who acts as protector of a younger man, but there the comparison ends. In the theatrical tradition, Antonio has often been portrayed as a homosexual dismayed that his good friend Bassanio is going to marry Portia. This is a facile solution to Antonio's ingrained sadness, because there is no homoerotic discourse in the play to support this motivation.[6] Antonio is presumably the merchant of Venice, and he opens the play with a strange declaration of melancholy:

> In sooth I know not why I am so sad.
> It wearies me, you say it wearies you;
> But how I caught it, found it, or came by it,
> What stuff 'tis made of, whereof it is born,
> I am to learn;
> And such a want-wit sadness makes of me
> That I have much ado to know myself. (1.1.1–7)

We never learn the reason for Antonio's sorrow, but it seems to continue to the end, since he accepts his death at Shylock's hands with Christian and martyrlike forbearance. This puzzle is unacceptable to theater people, who are great motive hunters; Shakespeare's work contains so much overt homoerotic discourse that there seems no need to supply it as the key to deliberate ambiguity.

There is a striking insistence on the homoerotic in *Coriolanus*, but this imagery is connected with fundamental issues in the play. Everything associated with love and amorousness is subordinated to the values of war and manliness. Heterosexual impulses are unmistakably identified with civil life, whereas masculinity, honor, and bravery are all involved with an inverted epithalamial imagery, which is expressed in sometimes surprising, homoerotic declarations.

Volumnia, the mother of Coriolanus, sets the tone for the inversion of traditional love imagery in her first speeches in act 1, scene 3. Marcius picks up his mother's images when he approaches his general, Cominius, mantled in his own blood:

> O, let me clip [=embrace] ye
> In arms as sound as when I wooed; in heart
> As merry as when our nuptial day was done,
> And tapers burned to bedward! (1.6.29–32)

It is clear that Marcius places a higher value on deeds of honor in battle than on deeds of love on the wedding night. This is a familiar discourse in the play.

When Coriolanus deserts Rome and appears *"in mean apparel, dis-*

guised and muffled" (4.4. s.d.) at the house of his former antagonist, Aufidius greets him with a curious epithalamial image:

> Know thou first,
> I loved the maid I married; never man
> Sighed truer breath. But that I see thee here,
> Thou noble thing, more dances my rapt heart
> Than when I first my wedded mistress saw
> Bestride my threshold. (4.5.117–22)

Thoughts of manliness and heroic enterprise obviously turn Aufidius on, but there is nothing in the play that specifically identifies him as a homosexual. His homoerotic discourse is an expected part of manly, heroic imagery. The report of the Third Servingman confirms what Aufidius himself says, that Coriolanus has become a venerated object of devotion:

> Our general himself makes a mistress of him; sanctifies himself with's hand [i.e., treats his hand as if it were a holy relic], and turns up the white o' th' eye to his discourse. (204–6)

This enthusiasm is soon converted to a murderous and envious passion to destroy Coriolanus. If there is a homoerotic component to this rage, it is not expressed in the language of the play.

The cult of male virtues and martial honor in *Coriolanus* has some relation to Adonis in Shakespeare's *Venus and Adonis*. The young Adonis is a sworn enemy of love, offered so rapaciously by the sweating Venus. She describes him in androgynous terms:

> "Thrice fairer than myself," thus she began,
> "The field's chief flower, sweet above compare,
> Stain to all nymphs, more lovely than a man,
> More white and red than doves or roses are." (7–10)

In other words, Adonis shares in the attributes of feminine beauty because he is "more lovely than a man." He is "the tender boy," who "blushed and pouted in a dull disdain, / With leaden appetite, unapt to toy" (32–34). He is a beautiful youth unready for love. Venus accuses him, "Thou art no man, though of a man's complexion" (215).

The upshot is that the boar is represented in homoerotic terms as

Adonis's proper lover because he is a fitting masculine antagonist. Thus Venus thinks of the boar's wound as Adonis's broken virginity:

> the wide wound that the boar had trenched
> In his soft flank, whose wonted lily white
> With purple tears that his wound wept was drenched.   (1052–54)

A later stanza is more overtly sexual:

> "'Tis true, 'tis true! thus was Adonis slain:
> He ran upon the boar with his sharp spear,
> Who did not whet his teeth at him again,
> But by a kiss thought to persuade him there;
>   And nuzzling in his flank, the loving swine
>   Sheathed unaware the tusk in his soft groin."   (1111–16)

The language of penetration is specifically erotic—"kiss," "nuzzling," "soft groin"—but this is not surprising in a verse epyllion meant to titillate its readers. Obviously the homoerotic is just as exciting as the heterosexual.

The homoerotic discourse of Shakespeare's girls in *The Two Noble Kinsmen*, *A Midsummer Night's Dream*, and *Twelfth Night* is echoed in the account of Leontes and Polixenes as boys in *The Winter's Tale*. The whole subject of Leontes' jealousy is buried in psychological complexities about heterosexual love, but the description of Leontes and Polixenes' boyhood is simplified and idyllic. As children they manage to escape not only from the taint of Original Sin but also from the ravages of Time. It looks as if Leontes' insane jealousy comes out of the strains and anxieties of heterosexuality. It was all much simpler when he was "boy eternal."

Shakespeare's most overtly homoerotic play is *Troilus and Cressida*,[7] which is probably also his most intensely sexual play. Thersites, a foulmouthed, satirical rogue, calls Patroclus "Achilles male varlet" (5.1.15) and translates the epithet as "his masculine whore" (17). This makes Achilles and Patroclus the only specifically homosexual characters in Shakespeare. We learn from Ulysses' report early in the play that Achilles and Patroclus spend their time lying about idly in their tent mocking the designs of the Greek leaders. Patroclus

> Upon a lazy bed the livelong day
> Breaks scurril jests,

And with ridiculous and silly action
(Which, slanderer, he imitation calls)
He pageants us. (1.3.147–51)

As audience, "The large Achilles, on his pressed bed lolling, / From his deep chest laughs out a loud applause" (162–63). Achilles' idleness and his enacting a clownish and outrageous role plays into the hands of Ulysses.

Even Patroclus chides Achilles on his inactivity:

A woman impudent and mannish grown
Is not more loathed than an effeminate man
In time of action. (3.3.217–19)

But he also acknowledges that their amorous activity is a bar to manly deeds and heroic endeavor:

They think my little stomach to the war
And your great love to me restrains you thus.
Sweet, rouse yourself; and the weak wanton Cupid
Shall from your neck unloose his amorous fold
And, like a dewdrop from the lion's mane,
Be shook to air. (220–25)

This speech more or less confirms Thersites' charge that Patroclus is Achilles' "masculine whore," but it places little value on "weak wanton Cupid."

We also learn that Achilles is in love with Polyxena, as Ulysses tells us: "'Tis known, Achilles, that you are in love / With one of Priam's daughters" (192–93). Ulysses is never at a loss for moral apothegms:

And better would it fit Achilles much
To throw down Hector than Polyxena. (207–8)

Not much is made in the play of Achilles' relation to Polyxena, although that is one of the reasons alleged for his refusal to fight the Trojans. When Cressida arrives in the Greek camp, Achilles shows himself perfectly sociable in offering her a kiss: "I'll take that winter from your lips, fair lady" (4.5.24).

Achilles' relation to Hector is more disturbing. He is preoccupied with Hector, who fills his thoughts in an obsessive way not unlike the fascination of Aufidius with Coriolanus. This is more sharply homoerotic than Achilles' relation to Patroclus. In act 4, scene 5, Achilles gazes on Hector's body with rapt attention, like a voyeur: "I will the second time, / As I would buy thee, view thee limb by limb" (236–37). The gracious Hector is made uneasy by the intensity of this look: "Why dost thou so oppress me with thine eye?" (240). But Achilles answers with murderous fascination:

> Tell me, you heavens, in which part of his body
> Shall I destroy him, whether there, or there, or there?
> That I may give the local wound a name,
> And make distinct the very breach whereout
> Hector's great spirit flew. Answer me, heavens! (241–45)

Hector can only reply with common-sense astonishment: "It would discredit the blessed gods, proud man, / To answer such a question" (246–47).

By the end of act 5, scene 5, Achilles is pursuing Hector with monomaniacal rage:

> Where is this Hector?
> Come, come, thou boy-queller, show thy face;
> Know what it is to meet Achilles angry.
> Hector, where's Hector? I will none but Hector. (44–47)

It is not surprising that Achilles plots with his Myrmidons to slaughter him:

> Empale him with your weapons round about;
> In fellest manner execute your arms. (5.7.5–6)

In his wild frenzy Achilles violates honor at every point, and he doesn't even engage Hector himself, but has his band of Myrmidons strike him down. Achilles' couplets at the end of act 5, scene 8 are frightening in their savagery:

> My half-supped sword, that frankly would have fed,
> Pleased with this dainty bait, thus goes to bed. (19–20)

The imagery has a menacing, homoerotic tone, as if Achilles' sword, personified, has not only penetrated Hector's body but also cannibalisticly fed upon him—"this dainty bait."

The most extensive body of homoerotic discourse is in Shakespeare's *Sonnets*.[8] The first 126 of the 154 poems are addressed to a young man and frankly use the conventions of noble male friendship. The issues are complicated by the fact that the last sonnets, addressed to a woman (the "Dark Lady"), are among the most sexual poems that Shakespeare ever wrote. Another disturbing element is the fact that the Noble Friend appears to have been seduced by the poet's own mistress. There are endless biographical inferences that have been drawn from the *Sonnets* and applied to the putative life of Shakespeare, but these deductions tend to be contradictory and cancel each other out.

In many of the early sonnets, the poet praises his friend's physical beauty, which, according to Platonic doctrine, is the root cause of love. But the praise is fairly general and makes no attempt at particular characterization:

> Shall I compare thee to a summer's day?
> Thou art more lovely and more temperate.
> Rough winds do shake the darling buds of May,
> And summer's lease hath all too short a date.   (#18)

The idea is repeated many times that the sonnets offer a way of defying time and preserving his love's beauty:

> For such a time do I now fortify
> Against confounding Age's cruel knife,
> That he shall never cut from memory
> My sweet love's beauty, though my lover's life.
> His beauty shall in these black lines be seen,
> And they shall live, and he in them still green.   (#63)

A variation of the same idea is that his lover's beauty was given to be used, specifically in propagating children, who will, like the sonnets themselves, preserve this beauty for posterity.

The later sonnets have darker hints that the young man is not only beautiful but also disdainful, cold, and narcissistic: "Who, moving others, are themselves as stone" (#94). Sonnet 94 expresses this eloquently:

The summer's flow'r is to the summer sweet,
Though to itself it only live and die;
But if that flow'r with base infection meet,
The basest weed outbraves his dignity:
    For sweetest things turn sourest by their deeds;
    Lilies that fester smell far worse than weeds.

The homoerotic sonnets have a clear basis in physical desire, but the sexual element is muted. Sonnet 57 begins:

Being your slave, what should I do but tend
Upon the hours and times of your desire?
I have no precious time at all to spend,
Nor services to do till you require.

"Services" is often used in Shakespeare in a sexual sense, although here it seems neutral. The sonnet ends with a teasing couplet:

So true a fool is love that in your will,
Though you do anything, he thinks no ill.

There is a pun on will as desire and Will as Shakespeare's first name (compare the multiple puns on "Will" in Sonnet 135). "Desire" is also a theme in Sonnet 45:

The other two, slight air and purging fire,
Are both with thee, wherever I abide;
The first my thought, the other my desire,
These present-absent with swift motion slide.

Desire as a "purging fire" is a typical Petrarchan image.

It is interesting that the heterosexual sonnets are much more specifically physical than the homoerotic ones. Sonnet 151, for example, plays shamelessly on the penis and tumescence:

My soul doth tell my body that he may
Triumph in love; flesh stays no farther reason,
But, rising at thy name, doth point out thee,
As his triumphant prize. Proud of this pride,
He is contented thy poor drudge to be,
To stand in thy affairs, fall by thy side.

There are puns galore on erection ("reason," "rising," "proud," "stand"). Sonnet 129 is specifically about the expenditure of semen ("Th' expense of spirit") and the brittle glory of orgasm.

Both the homoerotic and the heterosexual sonnets speak about love and sexual expression. The bittersweet conclusion of Sonnet 129, for example, is not necessarily restricted to either same-sex or opposite-sex lovemaking:

> A bliss in proof, and proved, a very woe,
> Before, a joy proposed; behind, a dream.
> All this the world well knows, yet none knows well
> To shun the heaven that leads men to this hell.

Shakespeare seems to explore a large gamut of possibilities in love without presenting a polemical argument for the love between men, the love between women, or the love between men and women. Love can be glorious or bitter and disappointing (or some inexplicable combination of these extremes) from whatever perspective you look at it.

Sonnet 20 presents most explicitly the gender problems of homoerotic discourse. The loved one was created by Nature as a woman in all respects except one, but this raises profound ambiguities:

> A woman's face, with Nature's own hand painted,
> Hast thou, the master mistress of my passion;
> A woman's gentle heart, but not acquainted
> With shifting change, as is false women's fashion;
> An eye more bright than theirs, less false in rolling,
> Gilding the object whereupon it gazeth;
> A man in hue all hues in his controlling,
> Which steals men's eyes and women's souls amazeth.

There is witty punning on masculine-feminine categories, as in "master mistress," but no easy resolution. The final quatrain and couplet propose an unworkable compromise:

> And for a woman wert thou first created,
> Till Nature as she wrought thee fell a-doting,
> And by addition me of thee defeated,
> By adding one thing to my purpose nothing.
> But since she pricked thee out for women's pleasure,
> Mine be thy love, and thy love's use their treasure.

What Nature adds in her dotage is a prick (made explicit by the clown-like pun in the next to the last line of the couplet). It is puzzling in an explicitly homoerotic sonnet why this "one thing" (a penis) is, for the "purpose" of the lover, said to be "nothing." The concluding couplet expresses a theme familiar from the abundant homoerotic references in Shakespeare. There is a difference between love as a spiritual entity and love as a sexual entity for "pleasure" and "use." This is a diplomatic and Solomonic division, but unconvincing.

The homoerotic discourses in Shakespeare present a puzzling and much-controverted topic. There is no firm and polarizing distinction between homoerotic and heterosexual impulses in regard to love, so that the contemporary categories of homosexual, bisexual, lesbian, and heterosexual desire aren't really relevant to Shakespeare and early modern literature. In Ovid's *Metamorphoses*, for example, a whole series of male figures are represented in homoerotic terms—Ganymede, Narcissus, and Hermaphroditus are just a few.[9] Male beauty is almost necessarily described in feminine terms in both Ovid and Shakespeare. There is a much more fluid link between homoerotic and heterosexual discourse in Shakespeare than we would acknowledge at the end of the twentieth century. He moves freely between homoerotic and heterosexual love without any hesitation or fear of contradiction.

CHAPTER EIGHT

& LUST: SEXUAL WIT

All love in Shakespeare expresses itself sexually, but there is an important distinction between love and lust. Lust is a product of desire and appetite and is often associated with imagery of food, eating, and animals. The fulfillment of lust may be connected with violence or rape, as in *The Rape of Lucrece*, in which the sexual assault is an expression of power and control over an innocent, unprotected, and defenseless woman. Shakespeare echoes a familiar Renaissance misogyny, where women are seen in the Old Testament context of Eve and Original Sin. Especially in the tragedies, the anxiety about women's sexual powers is overwhelming. Men seem to be trying to protect themselves from being destroyed by women.

Sonnet 129, "Th' expense of spirit in a waste of shame," is a good example of how problematic and paradoxical sex is in Shakespeare.[1] The first line refers to the expenditure of "spirit," or semen, which in popular physiology was thought to be carried by the blood, and seminal emissions, like sighing, that were supposed to shorten one's life. In either sense it is a shameful waste, but there may also be a pun on "waste" (as the waist of the body). Lust is represented as a violent, deceitful, and impulsive enterprise:

> perjured, murd'rous, bloody, full of blame,
> Savage, extreme, rude, cruel, not to trust;
> Enjoyed no sooner but despisèd straight;
> Past reason hunted, and no sooner had,
> Past reason hated as a swallowed bait
> On purpose laid to make the taker mad.

Lust runs directly contrary to reason, and its pleasures are momentary and transient:

> A bliss in proof, and proved, a very woe,
> Before, a joy proposed; behind, a dream.

The couplet conclusion sums up the irreconcilable opposites of lust:

> All this the world well knows, yet none knows well
> To shun the heaven that leads men to this hell.

This is one of the most dramatic sonnets, without any easy and neat solution proposed in the final couplet. Lust always brings with it madness, bad dreams, and a living hell. Yet why is the sexual impulse described as "a joy proposed" and "A bliss in proof," offering a sudden, disappearing glimpse of heaven?

Some of the troubling issues of Sonnet 129 are worked out in the character of Tarquin in *The Rape of Lucrece*. The first stanza already identifies him as "Lust-breathèd Tarquin," who

> lurks to aspire
> And girdle with embracing flames the waist
> Of Collatine's fair love, Lucrece the chaste. (5–7)

Here is the same implied "waste-waist" pun as in Sonnet 129. Tarquin reasons with himself very much in the sonnet's conflicted imagery of lust as momentary pleasure and lasting woe:

"What win I if I gain the thing I seek?
A dream, a breath, a froth of fleeting joy.
Who buys a minute's mirth to wail a week?
Or sells eternity to get a toy?
For one sweet grape who will the vine destroy?" (211–15)

Both Lucrece and Tarquin are endlessly didactic, especially at moments of psychological stress.

The rape of Lucrece produces predictable remorse in Tarquin. Lust is represented in the imagery of animals and food and appetite:

Look as the full-fed hound or gorgèd hawk,
Unapt for tender smell or speedy flight,
Make slow pursuit, or altogether balk
The prey wherein by nature they delight,
So surfeit-taking Tarquin fares this night:
His taste delicious, in digestion souring,
Devours his will, that lived by foul devouring. (694–700)

A surfeit is a cloying excess of food or drink that produces indigestion; thus lust is specifically connected with overindulgence and its physiological effects. Surfeit is purged by heaving the gorge, or vomiting, an image that continues the conceit in the next stanza:

Drunken Desire must vomit his receipt
Ere he can see his own abomination. (703–4)

Tarquin progresses from Drunken Desire to Feeble Desire, and the next stanza shows him in the guilty state of satisfied lust:

And then with lank and lean discolored cheek,
With heavy eye, knit brow, and strengthless pace,
Feeble Desire, all recreant, poor, and meek,
Like to a bankrout beggar wails his case.
The flesh being proud, Desire doth fight with Grace,
For there it revels; and when that decays,
The guilty rebel for remission prays. (708–14)

"The flesh being proud" is a euphemism for male erection, but the whole stanza bewails detumescence in its physiological symptoms: "heavy eye, knit brow, and strengthless pace." These are signs of love melancholy.[2]

Love and lust are also dichotomized throughout *Venus and Adonis*, Shakespeare's high-spirited verse epyllion, but here the aggressor is Venus, the goddess of love. The poem is wittily erotic, with a strong sense of play befitting the gods. From the first stanza we know that the lovesick Venus has chosen the beautiful boy, Adonis, as her amorous prey:

> Sick-thoughted Venus makes amain unto him,
> And like a bold-faced suitor 'gins to woo him.   (5–6)

The love-play is expressed in the familiar imagery of food and appetite. Venus promises:

> "And yet not cloy thy lips with loathed satiety,
> But rather famish them amid their plenty,
> Making them red and pale with fresh variety:
> Ten kisses short as one, one long as twenty."   (19–22)

Cleopatra, in *Antony and Cleopatra*, is like the Venus of the poem, at least as Enobarbus describes her:

> Age cannot wither her, nor custom stale
> Her infinite variety: other women cloy
> The appetites they feed, but she makes hungry
> Where most she satisfies.   (2.2.241–44)

To "cloy" the appetite and so produce a surfeit is a sure sign of erotic failure. "Infinite variety" is the rhyming opposite of cloying satiety.

It is obvious that the aging Venus is promising more than she can sexually deliver, which may be one reason why the nubile Adonis is coy. She plucks him from his horse, but her efforts are fruitless in the conflict between lust and indifference. The tender boy

> blushed and pouted in a dull disdain,
> With leaden appetite, unapt to toy;
> She red and hot as coals of glowing fire,
> He red for shame, but frosty in desire.   (33–36)

Throughout the poem, heat and fire represent passion. "Toy" is a familiar erotic word meaning to dally amorously, to wanton. "Toy" as a noun is a trifle one takes a fancy to, a thing of little intrinsic worth, a bauble, a gaud. Thus love-play is immediately devalued.

Venus the love goddess is represented in mock-epic terms as a rapacious and hungry eagle:

> Even as the empty eagle, sharp by fast,
> Tires with her beak on feathers, flesh, and bone,
> Shaking her wings, devouring all in haste,
> Till either gorge be stuffed or prey be gone—
> Even so she kissed his brow, his cheek, his chin,
> And where she ends she doth anew begin. (55–60)

Tender love has nothing to do with this violent image of a predator and its prey, and again, sexual activity is represented in terms of appetite.

One familiar erotic conceit is that the lover's body is in itself something edible. This involves some pleasant pictorial euphemisms for sexual activity. Thus Venus proposes to Adonis:

> "I'll be a park, and thou shalt be my deer:
> Feed where thou wilt, on mountain or in dale;
> Graze on my lips; and if those hills be dry,
> Stray lower, where the pleasant fountains lie." (231–34)

In this topographical extension of the human body, desire is pastoralized, as if it were a harmless, innocent occupation before the Fall:

> "Within this limit is relief enough,
> Sweet bottom-grass, and high delightful plain,
> Round rising hillocks, brakes obscure and rough,
> To shelter thee from tempest and from rain.
> Then be my deer since I am such a park;
> No dog shall rouse thee though a thousand bark." (235–40)

One wouldn't want to literalize "Sweet bottom-grass" and "brakes obscure and rough." They are a harmonious part of an erotic promise of pleasure—"A bliss in proof," in the words of Sonnet 129.

The erotic park in *Venus and Adonis* is like Dromio of Syracuse's bawdy inventory of Nell (or Luce), the kitchen maid, "I could find out countries in her" (*The Comedy of Errors* 3.2.116–17). Of course, "countries" may in itself be a sexual word—an imagined noun (or adjectival) form of "cunt"—as in Hamlet's leering remark to Ophelia: "Do you think I meant country matters?" (*Hamlet* 3.2.119). Dromio's countries are part of a standard joke in which he finds Ireland, by its bogs, in her buttocks, and France in her forehead, "making war against her heir" (127) because venereal disease (the "French disease") causes the hair to fall out. As for Belgium, or the Netherlands, Dromio protests that "I did not look so low" (143). This may be tedious but it provides a typical clown's routine in the early comedies.

In *Venus and Adonis*, the amorous play of the horses is meant to suggest to Adonis the spontaneous workings of desire. "Adonis' trampling courser" (261), who breaks his rein to be with the "breeding jennet, lusty, young, and proud" (260), serves as a sexual analogue for his master. The erotic scene is in a lyrical high style, but the frequent references to "His ears up-pricked" (271) and the "pricking spur" (285) suffice to make the point. The noble courser is richly anthropomorphized:

> His eye, which scornfully glisters like fire,
> Shows his hot courage and his high desire. (275–76)

This scene strongly enacts Venus's seductive purposes, but in a comic mode. The details of sexual arousal in the horses are applicable to the human condition:

> Then, like a melancholy malcontent,
> He vails his tail, that, like a falling plume,
> Cool shadow to his melting buttock lent;
> He stamps, and bites the poor flies in his fume.
>> His love, perceiving how he was enraged,
>> Grew kinder, and his fury was assuaged. (313–18)

No gross descriptions, but "melting buttock" is suggestive.

Venus is quick to moralize on this natural example of the horses:

>> "Thy palfrey, as he should,
> Welcomes the warm approach of sweet desire.
> Affection is a coal that must be cooled;
> Else, suffered, it will set the heart on fire." (385–88)

Desire is conventionally represented as a flame that must be put out by appropriate means before it sets "the heart on fire." Adonis is unresponsive to Venus's love rhetoric about the horses, so she knows she has to be more direct:

> "Who sees his true-love in her naked bed,
> Teaching the sheets a whiter hue than white,
> But, when his glutton eye so full hath fed,
> His other agents aim at like delight?
>   Who is so faint that dares not be so bold
>   To touch the fire, the weather being cold?" (397–402)

This is one of the most sexual stanzas in the poem, although the language is polite and lofty, especially in phrases such as "His other agents." The first line is a choice example of the rhetorical figure of hendiadys,[3] which offers a way to compact adjective and substantive. Thus, "her naked bed" is the bed in which "his true-love" lies naked, as is obvious from the next line. Venus makes it plain that it is necessary "To touch the fire," or at least play with fire.

Before Adonis departs on his fatal boar hunt, he delivers some concluding stanzas on Love and "sweating Lust" (794). He speaks with all the personified gravity of *The Rape of Lucrece*, and in his farewell to Venus, he has suddenly become a spokesman for traditional moral values:

> "Love comforteth like sunshine after rain,
> But Lust's effect is tempest after sun.
> Love's gentle spring doth always fresh remain;
> Lust's winter comes ere summer half be done.
>   Love surfeits not, Lust like a glutton dies;
>   Love is all truth, Lust full of forgèd lies." (799–804)

This didactic stanza sums up truisms about Love and Lust, but it is not the most charming in the poem.

There is a surprising amount of bawdy in Shakespeare, although not as much as some fanciful lexicographers, like Frankie Rubinstein, would claim.[4] Everything depends on the dramatic context rather than on the possible dictionary meanings and etymological roots of the words. There are some unexpected double entendres and sexual innuendoes in highly charged contexts, such as the scenes between Angelo and Isabella in *Measure for Measure* (especially 2.2 and 4), in which neither character has the slightest intention to speak bawdy. Standard sexual puns and wordplay are associated with the clowns in the comedies, who are in the plays for their witty, entertainment value and have no essential bearing on the action. The clowns provide a symmetrical contrast with their overblown, romantic masters and mistresses and balance the lyrical expression of deeply felt love and the more homely utterances of lower-class characters, who see love in a more practical sense, as inextricably connected with sex and lust.

As Touchstone says so memorably to Audrey, his goatherd bride, in *As You Like It*, "Come, sweet Audrey. / We must be married, or we must live in bawdry" (3.3.92–93). Earlier, Touchstone tells Rosalind about his love affair with Jane Smile, the milkmaid:

> I remember the kissing of her batler [=wooden paddle used in washing], and the cow's dugs that her pretty chopt [=chapped] hands had milked; and I remember the wooing of a peascod [=peapod] instead of her, from whom I took two cods, and giving her them again, said with weeping tears, "Wear these for my sake." (2.4.46–51)

"Cods" is a familiar term for testicles, but even the lovelorn Rosalind applauds the clown's joke: "Thou speak'st wiser than thou art ware of" (55). But Touchstone is a pretty subtle fellow, an artificial and not a natural fool, who is keenly aware of how much he can get away with in conversation with his betters. He is not so careful in talk with his social equals.

The sexual jesting of clowns and servants occurs everywhere in Shakespeare and is almost an assumed part of class relations in the comedies. In *The Two Gentlemen of Verona*, for example, the servants of the two gentlemen, Speed and Launce, have a witty scene (2.5) to themselves to discuss their masters' love affairs. When Speed, the servant of Valentine, asks Launce, the servant of Proteus, how matters stand between Proteus and Julia, Launce replies wittily in a kind of sexual proverb: "Marry, thus: when it stands well with him, it stands well with her" (20–21). "Stands" is a sexual euphemism for erection. Speed professes not to comprehend, so Launce continues the sexual wordplay with his staff, which is endowed with phallic meaning:

LAUNCE   Look thee, I'll but lean, and my staff understands me.
SPEED   It stands under thee, indeed.
LAUNCE   Why, stand-under and under-stand is all one. (26–29)

This is not exactly subtle, but it is a familiar pun in Shakespeare, as in the Induction to *The Taming of the Shrew*, where the metamorphosed drunk, Christopher Sly, has sexual designs on the Page disguised as his wife, who absents herself from his bed for fear of rekindling his supposed madness. The Page says: "I hope this reason stands for my excuse," and Sly answers: "Ay, it stands so that I may hardly tarry so long" (Ind. 2.124–25). Sly's penis "stands so"—is so erect—that it can hardly hold out for "a night or two," as the Page suggests. There is another familiar phallic pun on erection in the word "reason," which was a homophone of "raising," as in Sonnet 151, "Love is too young to know what conscience is." Here is a network of sexual puns on "reason," "raising," and "stand," ending in the explicit couplet:

> No want of conscience hold it that I call
> Her "love" for whose dear love I rise and fall.

Sexual puns and wordplay are part of the high-spirited love game in comedy. *Love's Labor's Lost* devotes a good deal of time to them, as if it were natural for lovers to engage in verbal games. Shakespeare is imitating the witty, courtly style of John Lyly,[5] which is expressed in rhetorical flourishes. This imitation is also, in many places, parody, especially in such fantastics as Don Armado, the Spaniard, and Holofernes, the schoolmaster. Don Armado's affected love letter to Jaquenetta, a country wench, sets off Rosaline, Boyet, and Costard the clown in a glorious wit combat. The talk begins with references to horns as the sign of the cuckold, but Boyet, the old lord who attends on the Princess of France, switches the conversation to women: "But she herself is hit lower. Have I hit her now?" (4.1.119–20). "Hit" is a sexual metaphor from archery, and nowhere in Shakespeare is it elaborated so fully and so explicitly as in this scene. Rosaline drives the point home by singing a bit from an old dance song or catch: "Thou canst not hit it, hit it, hit it, / Thou canst not hit it, my good man" (127–28). Boyet supplies the answering lines: "And [=if] I cannot, cannot, cannot, / And I cannot, another can" (129–30).

As if this were not explicit enough, Maria, another lady attending on the Princess of France, continues the wordplay: "A mark marvelous well shot, for they both did hit it!" (132). A mark is the target that an archer aims at, whose sexual sense Boyet exuberantly picks up and makes even more plain:

> A mark! O, mark but that mark! A mark, says my lady!
> Let the mark have a prick in 't, to mete [=aim] at if it may be.
> (133–34)

There are a few more punning sequences on "hit the clout" (136), or nail in the middle of the target, and "cleaving the pin," or striking the center of the target—all with obvious sexual double entendre—until Maria calls a halt to the bawdy talk: "Come, come, you talk greasily; your lips grow foul" (139). Except for Costard, these are all upper-class speakers, who aim for a certain elegance in their broad sexual allusions.

The language lesson in *Henry V* (3.4) is also an elegant, spicy scene with upper-class speakers: Katherine, the daughter of the King and Queen of France, and Alice, her waiting-gentlewoman. The scene is unusual because it is in French, but Shakespeare must have counted on his audience to more or less understand it, especially the sexual puns. The bawdy is slipped in surreptitiously, as the disingenuous Katherine is amazed that the English language has dirty words in it, especially when they are pronounced as if they were French. The whole scene adds a farcical dimension to this heroic history play. The sexual sequence begins with Katherine's question, "Comment appelez-vous le col?" (31) ("What do you call the neck?"). Alice, who has a broadly gallicized pronunciation of English, says: "De nick, madame" (32). "Nick" is part of a familiar group of words like "breach," "case," "cut," etc. that refer to the vulva. The next word is "le menton" (33), or chin, which Katherine pronounces as "sin" before she repeats the whole sequence.

The next two words are the most explicit and cap off the English lesson. Katherine asks: "Comment appelez-vous le pied et la robe?" (48–49) ("What do you call the foot and the gown?"). Alice answers in her inimitable pronunciation: "Le foot, madame; et le count" (50). "Count" is a French pronunciation of "gown," but Katherine is scandalized:

Le foot et le count! O Seigneur Dieu! Ils sont les mots de son mauvais, corruptible, gros, et impudique, et non pour les dames d'honneur d'user: je ne voudrais prononcer ces mots devant les seigneurs de France pour tout le monde. Foh, le foot et le count!

(51–59)

(The foot and the count [=gown]! O dear God! They are bad words, wicked, gross, and indecent, and not for women of honor to use. I don't want to pronounce these words before the lords of France for the whole world. Foh, the foot and the count.)

"Foot" is a form of the French *foutre*, to fuck, as in Pistol's "A foutra for the world and worldlings base!" (*2 Henry IV* 5.3.100), presumably accompanied by an obscene gesture like the sign of the fig or biting the thumbnail. Alice's "count" is an attempt to say the English word "gown," but Katherine hears it as the French word "con" or cunt. Compare the wordplay on "count" in *Henry VIII*, when the worldly-wise Old Lady speaks to the young Anne Bullen about marrying the King: "I would not be a young count in your way, / For more than blushing comes to" (2.3.41–42).

There is further sexual play in the language of King Henry's wooing of Katherine in act 5, scene 2. Henry wants to appear a plain, bluff soldier, unused to courtly flattery:

> If I could win a lady at leapfrog, or by vaulting into my saddle with my armor on my back, under the correction of bragging be it spoken, I should quickly leap into a wife. (139–43)

"Leap" and "vault" are both euphemisms for the sexual act, as in Benedick's comment on Europa and the bull:

> Bull Jove, sir, had an amiable low,
> And some such strange bull leaped your father's cow
> And got a calf in that same noble feat. (*Much Ado About Nothing* 5.4.48–50)

In *1 Henry IV*, Prince Hal speaks of "leaping houses" (1.2.9), or brothels.

One other odd sexual usage in the wooing scene in *Henry V* is the French word *baiser*, which means to kiss, but seems already to imply its meaning in modern French, to fuck. In this scene, Shakespeare dwells on the word as if it had an off-color connotation. Katherine says: "Les dames et demoiselles pour être baisées devant leur noces, il n'est pas la coutume de France" (5.2.269–71) ("It is not the custom in France for ladies and young girls to be kissed before their marriage"). Henry seems not to understand the simple French: "Madam my interpreter, what says she?" (272), and Alice answers ambiguously, "Dat it is not be de fashon pour le ladies of France—I cannot tell what is 'baiser' en Anglish" (273–74). King Henry, who understands more French than he acknowledges, says, "To kiss" (275) and Alice answers, "Your Majestee entendre bettre que moi" (276).

The sexual line is continued in King Henry's conversation with the Duke of Burgundy, immediately after the wooing. The Duke advises King Henry:

If you would conjure in her, you must make a circle; if conjure up love in her in his true likeness, he must appear naked and blind. Can you blame her then, being a maid yet rosed over with the virgin crimson of modesty, if she deny the appearance of a naked blind boy in her naked seeing self? (305–11)

This passage, in its allusions to the "naked blind boy" Cupid, is self-consciously sexual, as if the Duke needed to insist on a point that King Henry should take for granted. "Circle" (like "ring" and "O") is often used to refer to the female genitalia, as in Mercutio's bawdy conjuring of the absent Romeo:

> 'Twould anger him
> To raise a spirit in his mistress' circle
> Of some strange nature, letting it there stand
> Till she had laid it and conjured it down.   (*Romeo and Juliet* 2.1.23–26)

The innocent-seeming word "circle" is embedded in a context of leering sexuality.

The language lesson in *The Merry Wives of Windsor* (4.1) matches the language lesson in *Henry V* in its deliberate cultivation of verbal innuendo. Here the commentator is Mistress Quickly, revived with Falstaff and his crew from the *Henry IV* plays, who acts as an ignorant, sexual chorus to the Latin lesson given by the Welsh parson, Master Evans, to William, the son of Page. The Latin is simplified phonetically for a popular audience, who themselves would have studied Latin, probably from William Lilly's Latin grammar (1549). Evans, in his inimitable Welsh accent, asks his pupil, "What is the focative case, William?" (48–49). This sets Mistress Quickly off because she hears Parson Evans say "fuckative," and "case" is a frequent slang word for pudendum, on analogy with the Latin *vagina*, which is a scabbard or sheath for a sword. Evans then says that "focative is *caret*" (51), or lacking, but Mistress Quickly hears only familiar dirty words. She answers, "And that's a good root" (52)—both "root" and "carrot" are obvious euphemisms for the penis.

Once Mistress Quickly embarks on her bawdy course there is no stopping her, and this scene is like the jesting between clowns and servants in Shakespeare's early comedies. Evans asks his pupil for the genitive case plural, and William replies dutifully: "*horum, harum, horum*" (58), which Quickly hears as "*whorum, wharum, whorum*." There is a strong suggestion in this scene that Mistress Quickly is illiterate—she certainly has never studied Latin—and that her knowledge of language is purely phonetic. She is scandalized that what is supposed to be high-powered education in Latin turns out to be a miscellaneous collection of dirty words: "Vengeance of Jenny's case! Fie on her! Never name her, child, if she be a whore" (59–60).

Mistress Quickly is justifiably indignant that the schoolmaster should be speaking familiarly of Jenny's case. Jenny (phoneticized from "genitive") is clearly one of the "whorum" that Parson Evans is acquainted with. Quickly upbraids him:

> You do ill to teach the child such words. He teaches him to hick and hack, which they'll do fast enough of themselves, and to call "horum." Fie upon you! (62–65)

The meaning of "hick and hack" is uncertain but it is clearly sexual in context. The lesson finishes with *qui, quae, quod,* "Your *qui*'s, your *quae*'s, and your *quod*'s" (74–75), which are spoken as "keys, case, and cods." "Case" is a repeated sexual pun in this scene, "cods" are testicles, and "keys" may be penises (as the keys that unlock a case).

Probably the bawdiest play, or the play most specifically concerned with sexual activities, is *Pericles,* which has a troubled textual history and is probably not completely by Shakespeare. *Pericles* has among its characters a Pander, a Bawd, and their servant Boult. There are three scenes in a brothel in Mytilene. Commercial lust is set against absolute innocence as Marina, the girl they have purchased from pirates, manages to convert everyone in the brothel, including Lysimachus, the Governor of Mytilene. This is a good play in which to study the abrupt contrasts between love and lust that are an important motif in the late romances.

When act 4, scene 2 opens, the Pander complains that his brothel is "too wenchless" (5), which is an odd word that occurs only once in Shakespeare. Apparently, the trade is destructive not only of whores but also of clients. We learn that "The poor Transylvanian is dead that lay with the little baggage"—"she quickly pooped him; she made him roast meat for worms" (22–25). "Pooped" is probably a Shakespearean coinage meaning "infected with venereal disease," on analogy with the poop or stern of a ship (=vagina), although the word seems close to the American slang meaning of "pooped" as exhausted. The Pander and the Bawd buy Marina from the pirates as an authentic virgin for the extraordinary (but vague) price of "a thousand pieces" (53–54). Then she is instructed specifically in the whore's trade:

you must seem to do that fearfully which you commit willingly; despise profit where you have most gain. To weep that you live as ye do makes pity in your lovers: seldom but that pity begets you a good opinion, and that opinion a mere [=sheer] profit. (122–27)

Sex is represented in terms of food and eating, as it often is in Shakespeare. Boult does not want to miss out on his share of the bargain. He asks his mistress allusively: "if I have bargained for the joint—," and she grants his request: "Thou mayst cut a morsel off the spit" (136–37). Boult is a pleasant, good-hearted bawd's assistant, like Pompey in *Measure for Measure*, but he thinks of Marina only as a commodity—"this piece" (145), as the Bawd calls her, related to the "thousand pieces" (53–54) that were paid for her. Boult is enthusiastic about his work, and he draws on a curious bit of Elizabethan natural history to advertise Marina and her powers to provoke desire: "thunder shall not so awake the beds of eels as my giving out her beauty stirs up the lewdly inclined" (149–51). Marina calls on the virgin goddess Diana (who appears to Pericles in a vision at the end of the play, 5.1.242ff.) to aid her in preserving her maidenhead:

> If fire be hot, knives sharp, or waters deep,
> Untied I still my virgin knot will keep.
> Diana aid my purpose! (4.2.154–56)

This is the same "virgin-knot" that is so important for Prospero's daughter in *The Tempest* (4.1.15).

In act 4, scene 6 Marina triumphs over lust, but disappoints her owners. The Bawd is astounded at her powers:

> She's able to freeze the god Priapus, and undo a whole generation. We must either get her ravished or be rid of her. When she should do for clients her fitment and do me the kindness of our profession, she has me her quirks, her reasons, her master-reasons, her prayers, her knees; that she would make a puritan of the devil, if he should cheapen [=bargain for] a kiss of her. (3–10)

The innocent Marina freezes the hot god of lust, Priapus, and she has the power to convert the devil, if he has the foolish idea of trying to buy a kiss from her. "Fitment" is an odd word, meaning what is fitting and proper, in other words, duty, but Marina has what the Pander calls "her green-sickness" (14), an anemic disorder of young ladies, but here intended to indicate sexual squeamishness. This is what Boult will later call "virginal fencing" (60).

Marina manages to convert Lysimachus, the Governor of Mytilene, and also Boult himself, with her magical preachings. Lust is exposed for what it is by being set against Virtue and Innocence. It is all very allegorical. The Bawd's practical imprecations prove to be useless, as in her directions to Boult: "Use her at thy pleasure. Crack the glass of her virginity, and make the rest malleable" (147–49). Boult answers boldly before he converses with Marina: "And if she were a thornier piece of ground than she is, she shall be ploughed" (150–51). This is like what Agrippa says so admiringly of Cleopatra:

> Royal wench!
> She made great Caesar lay his sword to bed;
> He plowed her, and she cropped. (*Antony and Cleopatra* 2.2.232–34)

The word "plowed" is still used in this enduring sexual sense. Marina dampens Boult's ardor by making him aware of his moral status: "For what thou professest a baboon, could he speak, / Would own a name too dear" (4.6.183–84). This is the ultimate putdown.

The late romances of Shakespeare all have strong sexual themes, but they function allegorically rather than psychologically; in other words, extreme lustfulness is set against extreme virtue and innocence without any middle ground. In *The Winter's Tale*, Leontes' jealousy springs full blown from his imagination and fantasy rather than from any evident psychological causes. It is quite different from Othello's jealousy, which develops bit by bit in relation to Iago's cunning insinuations. Leontes' jealousy does seem to have a foundation in his idyllic, prelapsarian views of his childhood with his friend, Polixenes. As soon as Polixenes agrees to stay on in Sicilia in act 1, scene 2, he recounts his ideal youth:

> We were, fair Queen,
> Two lads that thought there was no more behind
> But such a day tomorrow as today,
> And to be boy eternal. (62–65)

And further:

> We were as twinned lambs, that did frisk i' th' sun,
> And bleat the one at th' other; what we changed [=exchanged]

Was innocence for innocence; we knew not
The doctrine of ill-doing, nor dreamed
That any did. (67–71)

So he and Leontes were in a protected state, apart from postlapsarian Christian theology.

The change in Polixenes and Leontes has been caused by puberty and the development of sexual awareness. This has pulled them roughly out of their ideal and innocent boyhood, as Polixenes explains:

had we pursued that life,
And our weak spirits ne'er been higher reared
With stronger blood, we should have answered heaven
Boldly, "not guilty"; the imposition cleared,
Hereditary ours. (71–75)

"Stronger blood" implies the onset of adult sexuality. In other words, once a boy reaches puberty he is drawn into Original Sin, which is represented here by sexual desire.

Hermione picks up the sexual innuendo immediately: "By this we gather / You have tripped since" (75–76). In her next speech, she makes the hint explicit:

Th' offenses we have made you do we'll answer,
If you first sinned with us, and that with us
You did continue fault, and that you slipped not
With any but with us. (83–85)

"If you first sinned with us" means that the wives first brought sin into the childlike worlds of Polixenes and Leontes by the act of married love.

These speeches about sin and childhood innocence are abbreviated, so that they supply only a sketchy basis for understanding what follows. Leontes moves suddenly into his jealous fit, which is strongly and disgustingly sexual, like Hamlet's imagination of his mother's sexual exploits in the Closet Scene (3.4). Leontes' asides have no immediate motivation: "Too hot, too hot! / To mingle friendship far is mingling bloods" (1.2.108–9). Here is "stronger blood" expressing itself in "mingling bloods," and Leontes puts a neurotic emphasis on physical signs of the workings of the blood, or passion:

But to be paddling palms and pinching fingers,
As now they are, and making practiced smiles
As in a looking glass. . . . (115–17)

Do we actually see Polixenes and Hermione on stage "paddling palms and pinching fingers"? I think not, as Hamlet's feverish imaginings about his mother's sexuality—Claudius "paddling" in Gertrude's neck "with his damned fingers" (*Hamlet* 3.4.186) and pinching wanton on her cheek— are equally a product of fantasy.

Once Leontes starts on his jealous fit, however, it feeds on itself. He is soon telling the good Camillo about erotic events that are unlikely ever to have occurred:

Is whispering nothing?
Is leaning cheek to cheek? Is meeting noses?
Kissing with inside lip? Stopping the career
Of laughter with a sigh (a note infallible
Of breaking honesty)? Horsing foot on foot? (1.2.284–88)

How could Leontes possibly know whether his wife and Polixenes are "kissing with inside lip"? He goes Othello one step further in inflamed imagination, and he acts as his own Iago. Whereas Iago in *Othello* teases with sexual possibilities that develop and expand piece by piece, in *The Winter's Tale* the torrid sexuality comes suddenly, like a storm cloud, and disappears just as fast.

Leontes' jealousy is partly a revulsion against sex, which is equated in *The Winter's Tale* with Original Sin, though he speaks not of illicit sexual encounters but of married love, perfectly licit and encouraged by religious precept. Women, however, end the innocent and sinless state of Leontes and Polixenes; they can no longer be "twinned lambs, that did frisk i' th' sun." There is an almost necessary burden of misogyny that accompanies heterosexual relations in Shakespeare, both in wooing and in marriage. [6] In some way, all men are reenacting Adam's sin.

This is certainly true in *Hamlet*, where Gertrude's hasty marriage to Claudius, the brother of Hamlet's dead father—"but no more like my father / Than I to Hercules" (1.2.152–53)—leads to Hamlet's melancholy and sex nausea. This is the burden of his first soliloquy in act 1, scene 2, before his encounter with the Ghost and before he hears the Ghost's allegations about Claudius. Hamlet is depressed:

> How weary, stale, flat, and unprofitable
> Seem to me all the uses of this world!
> Fie on't, ah, fie, 'tis an unweeded garden
> That grows to seed. Things rank and gross in nature
> Possess it merely [=completely].   (133–37)

One of the "things rank and gross in nature" that possesses Hamlet's garden is Claudius; the word "rank" refers to something that stinks.

But his mother too is corrupted because she has married Claudius in less than two months since the death of her husband. The King is consistently represented by Hamlet as gross and lustful, a "satyr" to his father, who is like "Hyperion" (140), the sun god. A satyr is a mythical creature, half man, half goat, a follower of the drunken Bacchus and the phallic god Priapus. The satyr imagery leads Hamlet to exclaim against his mother's lust: "a beast that wants discourse of reason / Would have mourned longer" (150–51). The accusation of incest is repeated over and over again, coupled with adultery, so that the play begins in an aura of sexual sin. Claudius is, as the Ghost says, "that incestuous, that adulterate beast" (1.5.42). The image of Gertrude is stained by her association with Claudius, and the moral of Hamlet's first soliloquy is powerfully misogynistic: "frailty, thy name is woman" (1.2.146).

In act 1, scene 5, the Ghost is strong in his sexual message: Claudius

> With witchcraft of his wits, with traitorous gifts—
> O wicked wit and gifts, that have the power
> So to seduce!—won to his shameful lust
> The will of my most seeming-virtuous queen.   (43–46)

The Ghost makes it plain that Claudius seduced Gertrude and that lust was an important factor in his own murder. Lust is personified as it is in *The Rape of Lucrece* and *Venus and Adonis*:

> But virtue, as it never will be moved,
> Though lewdness court it in a shape of heaven,
> So lust, though to a radiant angel linked,
> Will sate itself in a celestial bed
> And prey on garbage.   (53–57)

The lust is Gertrude's, who feeds greedily like an animal.

The Ghost reiterates its sexual warning to Hamlet:

> Let not the royal bed of Denmark be
> A couch for luxury and damnèd incest. (82–83)

"Luxury" is Luxuria, one of the seven deadly sins. Again, the Ghost warns against incest. But the Ghost also cautions Hamlet not to "contrive / Against thy mother aught" (85–86). Her own sin will torment her:

> Leave her to heaven
> And to those thorns that in her bosom lodge
> To prick and sting her. (86–88)

This prepares for the Closet Scene, in which Hamlet does not leave his mother to heaven and her own conscience, but needles her with his moral discourse.

In Claudius's only important aside in the play, the pricking of his own conscience is expressed in sexual terms. He is reacting to Polonius's misgivings about placing Ophelia with a prayer book as a decoy for Hamlet:

> We are oft to blame in this,
> 'Tis too much proved, that with devotion's visage
> And pious action we do sugar o'er
> The devil himself. (3.1.46–49)

Claudius is quick to react to the idea of sexual hypocrisy:

> O, 'tis too true.
> How smart a lash that speech doth give my conscience!
> The harlot's cheek, beautied with plast'ring art,
> Is not more ugly to the thing that helps it
> Than is my deed to my most painted word. (49–53)

The mad Lear too, in his exchanges with the blind Gloucester, is preoccupied with false appearances, especially those triggered by sexual hypocrisy:

> Thou rascal beadle, hold thy bloody hand!
> Why dost thou lash that whore? Strip thy own back;
> Thou hotly lusts to use her in that kind
> For which thou whip'st her. (*King Lear* 4.6.162–65)

Claudius's painting image is taken up by Hamlet when he tells Ophelia: "I have heard of your paintings, well enough. God hath given you one face, and you make yourselves another" (3.1.144–46). It is hard to believe, literally, that the fair Ophelia is "beautied with plast'ring art," but Hamlet's mind is shocked beyond recovery with evidence of women's hypocrisy. On the model of his mother, all women are fearful.

When Ophelia goes mad in act 4, scene 5, she sings popular love ballads of bawdy content. The Valentine's Day song is about a maid who is deflowered:

> Then up he rose and donned his clothes
>> And dupped [=opened] the chamber door,
> Let in the maid, that out a maid
>> Never departed more.   (52–55)

Ophelia is preoccupied not only with her dead father, but also with her own burdensome virginity. The next song is also about illicit love outside of marriage:

> Young men will do't if they come to't,
>> By Cock, they are to blame.
> Quoth she, "Before you tumbled me,
>> You promised me to wed."

He answers:

> "So would I 'a done, by yonder sun,
>> An thou hadst not come to my bed."   (60–66)

"Young men" like Hamlet, with their irresistible sexual appetites, prey on Ophelia's mind.

Another aspect of the love discourse in *Hamlet* is the King's relation to Gertrude. In act 4, scene 7, he explains to Laertes why he cannot go to a "public count"(17) with Hamlet:

> the Queen his mother
> Lives almost by his looks, and for myself—
> My virtue or my plague, be it either which—
> She is so conjunctive to my life and soul,
> That, as the star moves not but in his sphere,
> I could not but by her.   (11–16)

Is Claudius sincerely in love with Gertrude, perhaps against his conscious will and interest—"My virtue or my plague"—or is he temporizing with Laertes to win him to his plot? There is no way of knowing, since Claudius is such an ambiguous character.

Later in the scene the King speaks mysteriously about the uncertain and changeable nature of love:

> I know love is begun by time,
> And that I see, in passages of proof,
> Time qualifies the spark and fire of it.
> There lives within the very flame of love
> A kind of wick or snuff that will abate it,
> And nothing is at a like goodness still,
> For goodness, growing to a plurisy,
> Dies in his own too-much. (111–18)

Love is like a candle, whose burning wick consumes it—a traditional image of mortality. Has Claudius's love died in its "own too-much"? We think of Macbeth's despairing "Out, out, brief candle!" (*Macbeth* 5.5.23). Stylistically, Macbeth has some striking resemblances to Claudius, as both have to Bolingbroke, who becomes King Henry IV.

At the end of the play, the King makes little effort to prevent Gertrude from drinking the poisoned wine. He says only, "Gertrude, do not drink" (5.2.291), but she insists: "I will, my lord; I pray you pardon me" (292). The King responds only in the perfunctory aside, "It is the poisoned cup; it is too late" (293). The suggestion here is that love passes, that everything depends upon the critical moment, that the King's own life is more important to him than the Queen's. We recall the chilling conclusion of the King's love speech: "That we would do / We should do when we would" (4.7.118–19).

Troilus and Cressida has many similarities with *Hamlet*, especially in its sense of disillusion and misogyny. Act 5, scene 2, in the Greek camp, with Troilus and Ulysses as observers of Cressida and Diomede, is full of a revulsion at love and a sex nausea that are characteristic of Shakespearean tragedy. The first note in the scene is Troilus's disgust with Cressida, whom he sees whispering to Diomede, her "sweet guardian" (7): "Yea, so familiar!" (8). Ulysses supports him: "She will sing any man at first sight" (9)—in other words, she sightreads music, with bawdy implications. Compare his reaction to Cressida when she first arrives in the Greek camp and kisses everyone in turn: "Her wanton spirits look out / At every joint and motive [=moving part] of her body" (4.5.56–57). He sets her down among "these encounterers" (58): "sluttish spoils of opportunity / And daughters of the game" (62–63). So we know what Ulysses is likely to think in act 5, scene 2, but for Troilus the scene opens fresh wounds. Thersites makes his gross and vulgar comment on Ulysses' quip about sightreading: "And any man may sing her, if he can take her cliff; she's noted" (10–11). There is a pun on "cliff" the musical scale and "cleft" the female pudendum.

The base Thersites functions as an explicit sexual chorus throughout the scene. When Cressida asks, "What would you have me do?" (22), Thersites answers for Diomede to torment Troilus: "A juggling trick—to be secretly open" (23). This is a paradox, but its sexual meaning is plain, and "open" has strong sexual connotations. Thersites is never subtle, but his role here is to voice explicitly what Troilus is thinking:

> How the devil Luxury, with his fat rump and potato finger, tickles these together. Fry, lechery, fry! (53–55)

The potato was a familiar aphrodisiac in Elizabethan herbals, and lechery fries because it burns the bodily humors.

Troilus tries to deny the physical reality of what he sees, especially the presence of Cressida, because if this is really his beloved then her example insults all womankind:

> Let it not be believed for womanhood!
> Think we had mothers; do not give advantage
> To stubborn critics, apt, without a theme,
> For depravation, to square the general sex
> By Cressid's rule. Rather think this not Cressid. (126–30)

Troilus recognizes the contradictions of his reasoning: "O madness of discourse, / That cause sets up with and against itself" (139–40), but the doubleness of Cressida is the only way to explain the lovers' vows earlier in the play. If "Cressid is mine, tied with the bonds of heaven" (151), then

> The bonds of heaven are slipped, dissolved, and loosed,
> And with another knot, five-finger-tied,
> The fractions of her faith, orts of her love,
> The fragments, scraps, the bits, and greasy relics
> Of her o'ereaten faith, are given to Diomed. (153–57)

Love is expressed in terms of food and the disorder and disgust of the dinner table after a meal.

Troilus ends his scene with recollections of the past, which register the degree of his disillusionment with love: "Never did young man fancy / With so eternal and so fixed a soul" (162–63). We have the impression that Troilus is no longer young. The last words in the scene are spoken in soliloquy by Thersites:

> Lechery, lechery; still wars and lechery; nothing else holds
> fashion. A burning devil take them! (192–94)

Thersites is the unofficial chorus of the play, a commentator on the meaning of the Trojan War. He destroys all thoughts of manliness and heroic virtue that Troilus, especially, has laid claim to. In the Trojan Council Scene he postulated that Helen

> is a theme of honor and renown,
> A spur to valiant and magnanimous deeds,
> Whose present courage may beat down our foes
> And fame in time to come canonize us. (2.2.199–202)

Now all is reduced to "Lechery, lechery." In addition, Thersites mentions "A burning devil," presumably venereal disease, which will destroy all the amorous heroes.

The bitter disillusionment with love and sex in *Troilus and Cressida* echoes in *King Lear*, which is not a very sexual play, except for the wild imprecations of the mad Lear in act 4, scene 6. Lear is with the blind Gloucester in this scene, so that his speech denouncing all moral and natural order is directed at him. Lear subscribes to a kind of lawless naturalism, like that of Edmund when he enunciates "Thou, Nature, art my goddess" (1.2.1). All assumptions of civilized society are discarded as Lear takes upon himself the dispensing of justice:

> I pardon that man's life. What was thy cause?
> Adultery?
> Thou shalt not die: die for adultery! No:
> The wren goes to 't, and the small gilded fly
> Does lecher in my sight.
> Let copulation thrive. (4.6.111–16)

Lear uses Edmund as an example:

for Gloucester's bastard son
Was kinder to his father than my daughters
Got 'tween the lawful sheets. (116–18)

Of course, Lear is wrong about Edmund, as the blind Gloucester can witness, but Goneril and Regan offer their own powerful persuasion.

From here on Lear orates furiously against sexual restraint. He invokes the goddess Luxuria: "To 't, luxury, pell-mell! for I lack soldiers" (119). He then goes on to the familiar theme of hypocrisy and false appearances, of which there are many previous examples, but sexual hypocrisy is a new note:

> Behold yond simp'ring dame,
> Whose face between her forks presages snow,
> That minces virtue and does shake the head
> To hear of pleasure's name.
> The fitchew, nor the soilèd horse, goes to 't
> With a more riotous appetite. (120–25)

The "simp'ring dame" is like Regan or Goneril, both of whose lecherous feelings for Edmund are not so carefully concealed. "Pleasure" is sexual pleasure, which is described in animal terms. The fitchew is the polecat, an animal like the weasel, with a disgusting natural smell, which is a familiar image for a prostitute. The "soilèd" horse is an animal put to pasture and hence wanton and sexually eager, like the horses in *Venus and Adonis*. These images perhaps explain why the dame is "simp'ring," or smirking.

Lear ends his speech with a savage denunciation of all women. This is perhaps the most misogynistic speech in all of Shakespeare, but it projects a bitter, diabolic vision in keeping with the tragedy of the play:

> Down from the waist they are Centaurs,
> Though women all above:
> But to the girdle do the gods inherit,
> Beneath is all the fiend's.
> There's hell, there's darkness, there is the sulphurous pit.
> Burning, scalding, stench, consumption; fie, fie, fie!
> pah, pah! Give me an ounce of civet; good apothecary, sweeten
> my imagination. (126–33)

Again, Lear in his sexual nightmare is preoccupied with animals. The mythical Centaurs are lustful, wine-loving creatures, half man and half horse. The "stench" that fills Lear's consciousness resembles Hamlet's disgust with Yorick's skull in the Graveyard Scene: "Dost thou think Alexander looked o' this fashion i' th' earth? . . . And smelt so? Pah!" (*Hamlet* 5.1.199–202). "Pah" seems to be an interjection reserved for something that stinks. It is curious that "civet," the perfume, is made from the musklike, genital secretions of the civet cat, which is close to the fitchew or polecat. The "Burning" and "scalding" are presumably references to the effects of venereal disease.

In Lear's terrifying vision, women are bifold creatures, like the Centaurs, divided at the waist between a rational being above and a lustful, instinctive, sexually voracious animal below. And the animal not only stinks, but it also burns, scalds, and consumes men in the sexual act. The upshot of this imagery is in Lear's recognition of Gloucester:

> I remember thine eyes well enough. Dost thou squiny at me? No,
> do thy worst, blind Cupid; I'll not love. (138–40)

"Blind Cupid" is apparently a familiar painted sign hung up before brothels. At this point in the play, Lear speaks only of lechery and hypocrisy. He is not capable of love until he is reunited with Cordelia and recovers from his madness.

If *Timon of Athens* is "an after vibration" of *King Lear*, as Coleridge called it,[7] it also picks up some of the savagery of Lear's sex nausea in act 4, scene 6. *Timon* is not only misanthropic, but also misogynistic. There is a great deal of talk, especially in the second part of the play, of venereal disease and cuckoldry, both caused by women. Timon doesn't have any mistresses, and the only women in the play are the actors in the Masque of Amazons and the whores Phrynia and Timandra, who accompany Alcibiades when he comes to conquer his native country. The Athenian society of Timon and his friends is the scene of male bonding and conspicuous consumption. There is a macho competition in the acts of generosity, as if the men were trying to outdo each other with their flamboyant gifts. As a Senator says contemptuously:

> If I want gold, steal but a beggar's dog
> And give it Timon—why the dog coins gold. (2.1.5–6)

Everything is expressed in material values, especially money.

Timon presents his Masque of Amazons as an entertainment at a great banquet in act 1, scene 2. Cupid introduces the masque as an allegory of the five senses:

> The five best senses
> Acknowledge thee their patron, and come freely
> To gratulate thy plenteous bosom. (125–27)

The Ladies of the masque enter "*with lutes in their hands, dancing and playing*" (132 s.d.), but they have no speaking parts. We can perhaps infer the content of the masque from what the base, satirical Apemantus says: "What a sweep of vanity comes this way" (134). This seems to attest to the lavishness of the costumes and scenic effects. There is a hint of menace in Apemantus's last comment: "I should fear those that dance before me now / Would one day stamp upon me" (145–46).

At the conclusion of the masque, we have an elaborate stage direction: "*The Lords rise from table, with much adoring of Timon, and to show their loves, each single out an Amazon, and all dance, men with women, a lofty strain or two to the hautboys, and cease*" (147 s.d.). Remember that Amazons are represented as female warriors, who were reputed to cut off their right breasts to improve their aim in archery. Hippolyta, who appears as the bride of Theseus in *A Midsummer Night's Dream* and *The Two Noble Kinsmen*, is the best known Amazon in Shakespeare.

Alcibiades enters in act 4, scene 3, "*with drum and fife, in warlike manner*" (48 s.d.), and he is accompanied by the whores Phrynia and Timandra. He comes right after the banished Timon digs for roots in the woods and finds an unlimited supply of gold. The scene is saturated with disgustingly physical references to venereal disease. Timon speaks like a *momento mori* preacher of mortality, prophesying the end of the world through mankind's corruption. He says to Alcibiades:

> This fell [=fierce, fatal] whore of thine
> Hath in her more destruction than thy sword,
> For all her cherubin look. (62–64)

Phrynia, who is not so articulate as Timon, says simply: "Thy lips rot off" (64), to which Timon retorts:

> I will not kiss thee; then the rot returns
> To thine own lips again. (65–66)

To Timandra, Timon discourses on the same theme of sexual disease:

Be a whore still; they love thee not that use thee.
Give them diseases, leaving with thee their lust.
Make use of thy salt hours. Season the slaves
For tubs and baths; bring down rose-cheeked youth
To the tub-fast and the diet. (84–88)

Timon is specific on the supposed cures for venereal disease: the sweating-tub and hot baths, fasting and special diets.[8]

He implores Alcibiades to take his vengeance on Athens, in lines that recall the mad Lear:

Strike me the counterfeit matron:
It is her habit [=clothes] only that is honest,
Herself's a bawd. Let not the virgin's cheek
Make soft thy trenchant sword: for those milk paps,
That through the window-bars bore at men's eyes,
Are not within the leaf of pity writ. (113–18)

Timon's sexuality is inverted, and he remembers the virgin's breasts, seeming to "bore at men's eyes" through a window, with a horrified nostalgia like Othello's. Timon must try to destroy the world he has lost.

He lavishes gold on Alcibiades' whores, but only if they freely receive his tedious homily. As they say in unison: "More counsel with more money, bounteous Timon" (168). He speaks with authority about the symptoms of venereal disease, as they were understood in Shakespeare's time, and the physical effects of the treatment:

Down with the nose,
Down with it flat, take the bridge quite away
Of him, that his particular to foresee,
Smells from the general weal. Make curled-pate ruffians bald,
And let the unscarred braggarts of the war
Derive some pain from you. Plague all,
That your activity may defeat and quell
The source of all erection. (158–65)

The pox, or French disease, destroys the bridge of the nose and causes the hair to fall out, but Timon's denunciation is directed toward sexuality itself, "The source of all erection." It is an apocalyptic speech, set in a context that has led some older critics to infer that Shakespeare himself must have been suffering from venereal disease in order to write about it so knowingly.[9]

The sex nausea of *Timon of Athens, King Lear, Hamlet,* and *Troilus and Cressida* is very different from the buoyant sexual wit of the comedies, while the transcendent love imagery of *Romeo and Juliet* only reappears in the late romances, especially in *The Winter's Tale.* In general, there is a strong misogynistic current in Shakespeare that develops from a fear of women's sexual power. In Renaissance thinking, this is based on ideas about Eve and the Fall. Sexual desire is an ambiguous motive at best, and it often leads to violence and rape. Romantic love figures importantly in the comedies, although it is usually undercut by clowns and by other figures of lower social status.

Unfortunately, at the conclusion of our project, we are unable to present a single, coherent concept of love in Shakespeare. There is no doubt that he was strongly influenced by ideas about love in Petrarch, which were widely disseminated by writers of sonnets and lyric poems. But Shakespeare is also distinctly anti-Petrarchan in his constant satire of those ideas. Lovers in Shakespeare are supposedly blessed and set apart from ordinary mortals, but they are also often absurdly self-preoccupied and affected. Some of the prevailing Platonic sense of love is certainly present in Shakespeare, but love is not generally conceived as something transcendental that leads upward to a higher enlightenment; rather, it has a strongly physical and sexual basis.

The assumptions about love are radically different in the comedies and in the tragedies. In the comedies, the women lead the love game. They are strikingly intelligent and witty and enjoy role-playing, especially when they are disguised as boys. Shakespeare takes full dramatic advantage of the fact that in the Elizabethan theater all the women's parts were played by boys. He delights in the titillation aroused by transvestite situations. Juliet in *Romeo and Juliet* is very much like the heroines of comedy in her lyric inventiveness and her determination to overcome all obstacles to true love. She moves skillfully from her ecstatic wedding night to her resolution to follow Friar Lawrence's advice about the potion that induces a sleep resembling death.

In the problem comedies, the heroines are already moving into a more constricted role. Helena in *All's Well That Ends Well*, for example, is wonderfully exuberant and a wonder-worker when she cures the King of his fistula, but she is faced with a recalcitrant reality in the person of her husband, Bertram. Cressida in *Troilus and Cressida* is also uncomfortably paired with the romantic and heroic Troilus. In her sexual sophistication and feminine wiles, she is very different from the women of the comedies. In Shakespeare's plays written toward the end of the Elizabethan period, there is a certain fall-off in the idealization of women. Hamlet's mother is a case in point, and Ophelia lacks the positive and confident qualities of earlier heroines.

The women in tragedy are radically different from their counterparts in comedy. Lady Macbeth, for example, strives to unsex herself, to get rid of her womanly characteristics in preparation for the murder of the King. When she first speaks of unsexing, it looks as if she is ready to do the murder herself. Volumnia in *Coriolanus* has already unsexed herself in order to raise her son as a Roman warrior, and Goneril and Regan in *King Lear* have steeped themselves in the malevolence necessary to subjugate their old father. The progression descends to its lowest point in the foul-mouthed, mercenary whores Phrynia and Timandra in *Timon of Athens*.

In Shakespeare's late romances, there is a distinct revival of the positive and lyric qualities of women. Miranda in *The Tempest* is filled with awe and admiration at the prospect of the larger world presented to her, and she falls in love with a lyrical grace that rivals Juliet's. Marina in *Pericles* effects miracles, busily converting all the men in the brothel in Mytilene and awakening her father from his profound and speechless depression. In *The Winter's Tale*, Perdita is goddesslike, especially in the Sheep-shearing Scene. These romances depend upon a sense of renewal and resolution of all difficulties that goes far beyond the earlier comedies. The culmination is in the rebirth of the supposedly dead Hermione as a polychromed statue by Julio Romano in the final scene of *The Winter's Tale*.

Love and lust are generally polar opposites in Shakespeare, and lust is associated with villains. Tarquin provides a powerful example in *The Rape of Lucrece*, where he himself is already aware of the debilitating effects of lust in action. This is certainly a continuing theme in the *Sonnets*, and in *Venus and Adonis*, Adonis lectures the goddess on the abrupt distinctions between Lust and Love. All of Shakespeare's villains are lustful because they believe only in the natural order, according to Edmund's declaration: "Thou Nature, art my goddess." Iago, for example, fantasizes about seducing Desdemona, but he has an extraordinarily limited erotic range because he is so sure that there is no possibility of love in human experience. That is what makes him diabolical and why he sees a "daily beauty" in Cassio's life from which he is forever excluded.

Another aspect of lust is in the sexual wit of clowns, servants, and lower-class characters, who make fun of the romantic pretensions of their betters. The clowns and fools, especially, are given to undercutting their masters' high-flown amorous expressions. But lords and ladies also engage in elaborate sexual badinage as they satirize the earnest absurdities of Petrarchan conventions in such plays as *Love's Labor's Lost*. In *Henry V* the sexual banter of Henry in his wooing of Katherine, the daughter of the King and Queen of France, is meant to prove his hearty humanity and manliness.

The idea of love in Shakespeare depends on prevalent gender conceptions and Elizabethan assumptions about typical masculine and feminine roles. Since theater so much relies on the values of the society in which it is presented, the dramatist has room to play against audience expectations. Thus, independent, witty, and intelligent heroines like Rosalind in *As You Like It* must have provided marriageable young ladies in the audience with a powerful example different from the tracts that their parents were reading. This is certainly a notion that Marc Norman and Tom Stoppard play on in the recent movie, *Shakespeare in Love* (1998). I think there is also an element of social disruption in *The Taming of the Shrew*. The play was written in a context of violently antifeminine shrew literature, but it turns out differently. In Kate, Petruchio may get more than he bargains for. The gender assumptions in an avowedly patriarchal and misogynistic society don't fix the way gender may be used in any particular play.

Shakespeare's attitudes to love tragedy are difficult to establish. On the one hand, true love seems only achievable in death, as in *Antony and Cleopatra*, where the lovers (especially Cleopatra) reach an ecstatic climax in their separation from the vile world. This is definitely a romantic idea.

In *Romeo and Juliet* too, the lovers cannot live on surrounded by feuds and interfamily strife. There may be an inherent problem in love tragedy because the positive energy of love works against any tragic feeling. Only *Othello* arouses such strong pity and fear for the protagonists that it is convincingly tragic. As Othello explains it, he loves "not wisely but too well."

We would understand love in Shakespeare's works better if we knew more about Shakespeare the man. We know much more about the lives of Ben Jonson and Christopher Marlowe, partly through their own efforts at self-advertisement, but Shakespeare remains curiously hidden. His works hardly reveal a consistent subjectivity. Even the *Sonnets*, which seem autobiographical, may be much more traditional in their so-called revelations than we would like to think. The advantage of the absentee author is that such a wide variety of representations about love cannot be narrowed to the ideology of a single, powerful personality. In other words, some aspects of love are inconsistent with others in the total picture, which adds depth and interest. Thus, for example, heterosexual and homoerotic references exist side by side, sometimes in the same play, as in *Troilus and Cressida* and *The Two Noble Kinsmen*, not canceling each other out. This allows for an extraordinarily wide range in Shakespeare for the presentation of love, "the right Promethean fire," as Berowne calls it in *Love's Labor's Lost*.

NOTES

CHAPTER ONE: FALLING IN LOVE: CONVENTIONS

1. See Lu Emily Pearson, *Elizabethan Love Conventions* (Berkeley: University of California Press, 1933), which puts a strong emphasis on Petrarch, especially as he was used by English sonnet writers. See also John Charles Nelson, *Renaissance Theory of Love: The Context of Giordano Bruno's "Eroici furori"* (New York: Columbia University Press, 1958), and Jean H. Hagstrum, *Esteem Enlivened by Desire: The Couple from Homer to Shakespeare* (Chicago: University of Chicago Press, 1992), especially pp. 237–41 on Petrarch. See also Leonard Forster, *The Icy Fire: Five Studies in European Petrarchism* (Cambridge: Cambridge University Press, 1969), esp. chapter 1, "The Petrarchan Manner: An Introduction," which discusses the basic Petrarchan imagery of love.

2. David Lloyd Stevenson's book, *The Love-Game Comedy* (New York: Columbia University Press, 1946), is basic here, especially in its examina-

tion of Renaissance ideas about love. "The novelty of Shakespeare's plays lies, not in the fact that they point out the unreality of romantic conventions, but in the fact that they derive comedy from showing these conventions to be as delightful and necessary as they are illusionary and insubstantial" (p. 8). Arthur Kirsch's book, *Shakespeare and the Experience of Love* (Cambridge: Cambridge University Press, 1981), attempts to use both Christian and Freudian sources to talk about love, in my opinion unsuccessfully.

3. Lawrence Babb deals in detail with the physiological symptoms of falling in love in *The Elizabethan Malady: A Study of Melancholia in English Literature from 1580 to 1642* (East Lansing, Mich.: Michigan State College Press, 1951). In love at first sight, for example, "The procedure apparently was to freeze into statuesque abstraction and to gaze in wide-eyed and speechless wonder at the newly beloved" (p. 172).

4. See the note in the Arden edition of the play, ed. Harold F. Brooks (London: Methuen, 1979).

5. "Dote" and its variant forms are strong words. The definitions in the *OED* point at a physiological cause, as in weakness of mind, mental decay, and the senility and dementia associated with old age. There is an implication that the dotage caused by love has a physical basis, which is one way to relieve the guilt associated with the surrender of manliness. These issues are most fully developed in relation to Antony in *Antony and Cleopatra*.

6. See Jan Kott, *Shakespeare Our Contemporary* (London: Methuen, 1964). In the atmosphere of Goya's grotesques, Kott sees the *Dream* as "the most erotic of Shakespeare's plays" (p. 73), and he reminds us that "Since antiquity and up to the Renaissance the ass was credited with the strongest sexual potency and among all the quadrupeds is supposed to have the longest and hardest phallus" (p. 81).

7. Gender issues in *Twelfth Night* (and other contemporary plays) are richly discussed in the larger context of cross-dressing in Jean E. Howard, "Cross-dressing, The Theatre, and Gender Struggle in Early Modern England," *Shakespeare Quarterly* 39 (1988): 418–40. See also the authoritative discussion in Valerie Traub, *Desire and Anxiety: Circulations of Sexuality in Shakespearean Drama* (London: Routledge, 1992), especially chapter 5, and Stephen Orgel, *Impersonations: The Performance of Gender in Shakespeare's England* (Cambridge: Cambridge University Press, 1996).

8. John Donne, "The Extasie," in *The Elegies and The Songs and Sonnets,* ed. Helen Gardner (Oxford: Clarendon Press, 1965), p. 59.

9. Neal L. Goldstein sets the play in a context of Petrarchism and Florentine neo-Platonism in *"Love's Labor's Lost* and the Renaissance Vision of Love," *Shakespeare Quarterly* 25 (1974): 335–50.

10. Face-painting strictly follows the assumptions about a woman's beauty in early modern England. See Annette Drew-Bear, *Painted Faces on the Renais-*

sance Stage: The Moral Significance of Face-Painting Conventions (Lewisburg, Pa.: Bucknell University Press, 1994), esp. chapter 1. See also Shirley Nelson Garner, "'Let Her Paint an Inch Thick': Painted Ladies in Renaissance Drama and Society," *Renaissance Drama* 20 (1989): 123–39, and Frances E. Dolan, "Taking the Pencil Out of God's Hand: Art, Nature, and the Face-painting Debate in Early Modern England," *Publications of the Modern Language Association* 108 (1993): 224–39.

11. The *OED* defines "conceit" as a substantive, in sense 8, as: "A fanciful, ingenious, or witty notion or expression; now applied disparagingly to a strained or far-fetched turn of thought, figure, etc., an affectation of thought or style."

12. There is a full discussion of love melancholy in Babb, *The Elizabethan Malady*.

13. For a witty discussion of courtly love in all of its branches in the late twelfth century, see Andreas Capellanus, *The Art of Courtly Love*, tr. John Jay Parry (New York: Columbia University Press, 1941).

CHAPTER TWO: LOVE DOCTRINE IN THE COMEDIES

1. See Zvi Jagendorf, *The Happy End of Comedy: Jonson, Molière, and Shakespeare* (Newark: University of Delaware Press, 1984). The first two chapters contain a long, formal discussion of patterns of resolution in comedy.

2. There is an interesting commentary on Donatus's idea of "perturbations" in comedy in the opening chapter, "Shakespeare's New Comedy," of Ruth Nevo, *Comic Transformations in Shakespeare* (London: Methuen, 1980). The phrase attributed to Donatus in Evanthius, *De Fabula*, is that comedy is concerned with the "*incrementum processusque turbarum*," the increase and progression of perturbations (p. 9).

3. See Jonathan Bate, *Shakespeare and Ovid* (Oxford: Clarendon Press, 1993), esp. chapter 1, "Shakespeare and the Renaissance Ovid." See also Christopher Martin, *Policy in Love: Lyric and Public in Ovid, Petrarch and Shakespeare* (Pittsburgh: Duquesne University Press, 1994), although this deals chiefly with Shakespeare's poems.

4. See Stephen Booth, *"King Lear," "Macbeth," Indefinition, and Tragedy* (New Haven: Yale University Press, 1983), appendix 2, "Speculations on Doubling in Shakespeare's Plays," pp. 127–55. See also Arthur Colby Sprague, *The Doubling of Parts in Shakespeare's Plays* (London: The Society for Theatre Research, 1966).

5. See the notes on proper names in the Arden editions of *A Midsummer Night's Dream*, ed. Brooks, and *The Taming of the Shrew*, ed. Brian Morris (London: Methuen, 1981).

6. Blount is quoted from Gregory W. Bredbeck, *Sodomy and Interpretation: Marlowe to Milton* (Ithaca: Cornell University Press, 1991), p. 17. Bruce R. Smith notes that "contemptuous slang words existed only for the supposedly pas-

sive object of male homoerotic desire—'minion,' 'ganymede,' 'ingle'—and not for the desiring subject" ("L[o]cating the sexual subject" in Terence Hawkes, ed., *Alternative Shakespeares*, vol. 2 [London: Routledge, 1996], p. 101). The whole theme is developed in the illuminating essay of Mario Di Gangi, "Queering the Shakespearean Family," *Shakespeare Quarterly* 47 (1996): 269–90. See also his book, *The Homoerotics of Early Modern Drama* (Cambridge: Cambridge University Press, 1997), especially chapter 2, for fuller development. The context of desire and anxiety is theorized in Valerie Traub's book, *Desire and Anxiety*, especially as it relates to homoeroticism. See also Bruce R. Smith's authoritative book, *Homosexual Desire in Shakespeare's England: A Cultural Poetics* (Chicago: University of Chicago Press, 1991). For Ganymede (and related figures) in Renaissance art, see especially James M. Saslow, *Ganymede in the Renaissance: Homosexuality in Art and Society* (New Haven: Yale University Press, 1986). See also Leonard Barkan, *Transuming Passion: Ganymede and the Erotics of Humanism* (Stanford: Stanford University Press, 1991).

7. The love doctrine of *As You Like It* is well established by Kent Talbot Van Den Berg in "Theatrical Fiction and the Reality of Love in *As You Like It*," *Publications of the Modern Language Association* 90 (1975): 885–93. The author puts particular emphasis on the debt to Spenser's *Fowre Hymnes*, especially the poems to love and beauty. See also Valerie Wayne, "Desire and the Differences It Makes," in Valerie Wayne, ed., *The Matter of Difference: Materialist Feminist Criticism of Shakespeare* (Ithaca: Cornell University Press, 1991), pp. 81–114.

8. The topic of optical toys in literature is explored with fascinating detail in Ernest B. Gilman, *The Curious Perspective: Literary and Pictorial Wit in the Seventeenth Century* (New Haven: Yale University Press, 1978).

9. See the note in the Arden edition of *Much Ado About Nothing*, ed. A. R. Humphreys (London: Methuen, 1981), p. 100. "LOVE is blind" is a familiar Elizabethan proverb (see Tilley L506).

10. There is a great deal of physiological detail about Renaissance ideas of blood in Babb, *The Elizabethan Malady*. For example, Babb quotes from Ferrand's *Erotomania* (1640) that sperm is "nothing else but Blood, made White by the Naturall Heat, and an Excrement of the third Digestion" (p. 129). See also Gail Kern Paster, *The Body Embarrassed: Drama and the Disciplines of Shame in Early Modern England* (Ithaca: Cornell University Press, 1993), chapter 2, and Thomas Laqueur, *Making Sex: Body and Gender from the Greeks to Freud* (Cambridge: Harvard University Press, 1990).

11. See the discussion of this play in Margaret Loftus Ranald, *Shakespeare and His Social Context: Essays in Osmotic Knowledge and Literary Interpretation* (New York: AMS Press, 1987), chapter 1, section 2. Ranald is strong on the theme of the education into love, "with the maturing of both Claudio and

Benedick into love-worthiness" (p. 12). She also presents the legal aspects of betrothal and marriage.

12. In *Shakespeare's Comedy of Love* (London: Methuen, 1974), Alexander Leggatt notes the artificiality of the love discourse in *The Two Gentlemen of Verona*: "love is not so much an experience as an announced subject of debate" (p. 29).

13. The conflict between love and friendship is proverbial. See Tilley L549: "When LOVE puts in friendship is gone," who cites the passage from *The Two Gentlemen of Verona* (5.4.53–54). See Ronald A. Sharp, *Friendship and Literature: Spirit and Form* (Durham: Duke University Press, 1986).

14. See, for example, Shirley Nelson Garner's strong, personal argument in *"The Taming of the Shrew*: Inside or Outside of the Joke?" in Maurice Charney, ed., *"Bad" Shakespeare: Revaluations of the Shakespeare Canon* (Madison, N.J.: Fairleigh Dickinson University Press, 1988), pp. 105–19. Garner's point of view is unequivocally stated: "*Taming* is responsive to men's psychological needs, desires, and fantasies at the expense of women. It plays to an audience who shares its patriarchal assumptions: men and also women who internalize patriarchal values. As someone who does not share these values, I find much of the play humorless. Rather than making me laugh, it makes me sad or angry" (p. 117). See also the essay of Peter Berek, "Text, Gender, and Genre in *The Taming of the Shrew*," in the same volume, pp. 91–104. For an account of the historical background see Lisa Jardine, *Still Harping on Daughters: Women and Drama in the Age of Shakespeare*, 2nd ed. (New York: Columbia University Press, 1989), especially chapter 4, "Shrewd or Shrewish? When the Disorderly Woman has her Head."

For an opposing view, with emphasis on game-playing, see John C. Bean, "Comic Structure and the Humanizing of Kate in *The Taming of the Shrew*," in Carolyn Ruth Swift Lenz, Gayle Greene, and Carol Thomas Neely, eds., *The Woman's Part: Feminist Criticism of Shakespeare* (Urbana: University of Illinois Press, 1980), pp. 65–78. See also Coppélia Kahn, *Man's Estate: Masculine Identity in Shakespeare* (Berkeley: University of California Press, 1981), chapter 4. Kahn makes the sensible point that "Unlike other misogynistic shrew literature, this play satirizes not woman herself in the person of the shrew, but the male urge to control woman. Long before Petruchio enters, we are encouraged to doubt the validity of male supremacy" (p. 104). See also Ranald, *Shakespeare and His Social Context*, chapter 4. Leggatt observes that we are always aware that Petruchio "is putting on an act," that he is "seen as a performer" (*Shakespeare's Comedy of Love*, p. 56). Carol Thomas Neely more or less concurs in this positive view of the play; see her *Broken Nuptials in Shakespeare's Plays* (Urbana: University of Illinois Press, 1993; first published in 1985), pp. 28–31 plus notes. For the context of *The Taming of the Shrew*, see the essay of Maureen Quilligan, "Staging Gender: William Shakespeare and Elizabeth Cary," in James Grantham Turner, ed., *Sexuality and Gender in Early Modern Europe: Institutions, Texts, Images* (Cambridge: Cambridge University Press, 1993), pp. 208–32.

15. William C. Carroll has witty observations on "virgin-knot" and related matters in "The Virgin Not: Language and Sexuality in Shakespeare" in Deborah Barker and Ivo Kamps, eds., *Shakespeare and Gender: A History* (London: Verso, 1995), pp. 283–301. First published in *Shakespeare Survey* 46 (1994): 107–20.

CHAPTER THREE: LOVE DOCTRINE IN THE PROBLEM
PLAYS & *HAMLET*

1. See William Witherle Lawrence, *Shakespeare's Problem Comedies*, 2nd ed. (New York: Frederick Ungar, 1960); first published in 1931. F. S. Boas was the first to use the term "problem comedy" in his *Shakspere and his Predecessors* (New York, 1905). There has been much dispute about the problem plays as a group, with serious claims for problematic plays such as *Hamlet* and *Julius Caesar*. The bed trick is used significantly in both *Measure for Measure* and *All's Well That Ends Well*, and they have many other relations to each other. *Troilus and Cressida* is an odd play in the Shakespeare canon, but its difficulties fit well with the sense of disillusion and sex nausea in *Measure for Measure* and *All's Well*. These three plays are central in most accounts of the problem plays.

2. See the discussion in the introduction to *The Problem Plays of Shakespeare* by Ernest Schanzer (New York: Schocken, 1963). *Hamlet* was included in Boas's original list of the problem plays and also in E. M. W. Tillyard, *Shakespeare's Problem Plays* (1951).

3. Philip C. McGuire devotes an entire chapter (pp. 63–96) to "The Final Silences of *Measure for Measure*" in *Speechless Dialect: Shakespeare's Open Silences* (Berkeley: University of California Press, 1985). This is a fascinating, intense, theatrically well-informed argument about the play that McGuire thinks "provides the most challenging and complex example of Shakespeare's use of open silence" (p. 63). See also Harry Berger, Jr., *Making Trifles of Terrors: Redistributing Complicities in Shakespeare* (Stanford: Stanford University Press, 1997), whose very long final chapter is devoted to problems in *Measure for Measure*.

4. See Marliss C. Desens, *The Bed-Trick in English Renaissance Drama: Explorations in Gender, Sexuality, and Power* (Newark: University of Delaware Press, 1994). Desens takes up the bed trick as a story motif in a wide variety of sources. See also the perceptive essay by Janet Adelman, "Bed Tricks: On Marriage as the End of Comedy in *All's Well that Ends Well* and *Measure for Measure*," in Norman N. Holland, Sidney Homan, and Bernard J. Paris, eds., *Shakespeare's Personality* (Berkeley: University of California Press, 1989), pp. 151–74, and Neely, *Broken Nuptials*, chapter 2.

5. See Gayle Greene's carefully articulated reading of the play in "Shakespeare's Cressida: 'A kind of self,'" in Lenz, Greene, and Neely, eds., *The Woman's Part*, pp. 133–49. Another illuminating discussion is in Traub's *Desire and Anxiety*, chapter 3. In Laura Levine's perceptive chapter in *Men in Women's Clothing: Anti-theatricality and Effeminization, 1579–1642* (Cambridge: Cambridge University Press, 1994), she argues that the play develops two contradictory Cressidas: "the play insists on her ultimate unreadability, her unknowability, her openness" (p. 43). *Troilus and Cressida* is complexly discussed in Janet Adelman's essay, " 'This Is and Is Not Cressid': The Characterization of Cressida," in Shirley Nelson Garner, Claire Kahane, and Madelon Sprengnether, eds., *The (M)other Tongue: Essays in Feminist Psychoanalytic Interpretation* (Ithaca: Cornell University Press, 1985), pp. 119–41.

6. Valerie Traub writes energetically about Hamlet's sexual nausea set against a background of male fears of the chaos associated with the sexual act and the uncontrollability of women's sexuality in "Jewels, Statues, and Corpses: Containment of Female Erotic Power in Shakespeare's Plays," in Barker and Kamps, eds., *Shakespeare and Gender*, pp. 120–41. First published in *Shakespeare Studies* 21 (1988): 215–40. This is chapter 1 of Traub's book, *Desire and Anxiety*.

7. See Maurice Charney, "Shakespeare's *Hamlet* in the Context of the Hebrew Bible," *JTD: Journal of Theatre and Drama* 2 (1996): 93–100. Using the Hebrew Bible in the Geneva translation, the article concentrates on incest. See also Jason P. Rosenblatt, "Aspects of the Incest Problem in *Hamlet*," *Shakespeare Quarterly* 29 (1978): 349–64.

CHAPTER FOUR: LOVE DOCTRINE IN THE TRAGEDIES

1. Roger Stilling writes very well on *Romeo and Juliet* as a love tragedy, but his book, *Love and Death in Renaissance Tragedy* (Baton Rouge: Louisiana State University Press, 1976), is mostly devoted to non-Shakespearean examples. The most important study of the mingling of comedy and tragedy in Shakespeare is Susan Snyder, *The Comic Matrix of Shakespeare's Tragedies: Romeo and Juliet, Hamlet, Othello, and King Lear* (Princeton: Princeton University Press, 1979). In her introduction and first chapter, Snyder offers a valuable account of contemporary genre notions, especially about comedy. Neely in *Broken Nuptials* is preoccupied with the generic blurring in *Othello* and *Antony and Cleopatra* (chapters 3 and 4). She calls *Othello*, for example, "a terrifying completion of the comedies" (p. 110). See also Madelon Sprengnether, "Annihilating Intimacy in *Coriolanus*," in *Women in the Middle Ages and the Renaissance: Literary and Historical Perspectives*, ed. Mary Beth Rose (Syracuse: University of Syracuse Press, 1986), pp. 89–111. She sets *Coriolanus* in the larger context of Shakespeare's tragedies, which "demonstrate, with a terrible consistency, the ways in which love

kills" (p. 89). Charles R. Forker considers a large group of Elizabethan love tragedies in "The Love-Death Nexus in Elizabethan Renaissance Tragedy," *Shakespeare Studies* 8 (1975): 211–30. G. K. Hunter makes some intelligent observations about love tragedy in his new volume in the Oxford History of English Literature. Romeo and Juliet, for example, "are caught up (as we are) into the pleasures of a poetry that lifts them out of the day-to-day contingencies of the plot, a poetry in which they (and we) discover that Petrarchan tropes can become real experiences" (*English Drama 1586–1642: The Age of Shakespeare*, Oxford: Clarendon Press, 1997, p. 444). See also Celia R. Daileader, *Eroticism on the Renaissance Stage: Transcendence, Desire, and the Limits of the Visible* (Cambridge: Cambridge University Press, 1998).

2. Denis de Rougemont, *Love in the Western World*, tr. Montgomery Belgion, rev. ed. (New York: Pantheon, 1956), p. 53. First published in 1938. See also his *Love Declared: Essays on the Myths of Love*, tr. Richard Howard (New York: Pantheon, 1963).

3. See Rosalie L. Colie, "*Othello* and the Problematics of Love," chapter 3 of *Shakespeare's Living Art* (Princeton: Princeton University Press, 1974). Colie acknowledges that "It was not altogether easy to make a tragedy of a love story, traditionally the stuff of comedy" (p. 135). She looks at *Othello* from the perspective of *Romeo and Juliet* and the commonplaces of love derived from the Petrarchan sonnet writers, but the plays "unmetaphor" these commonplaces—that is, they realize the fictional, conventional images in terms of dramatic experience. Michael Bristol interestingly explores the ritually farcical ideas behind *Othello* in "Charivari and the Comedy of Abjection in *Othello*," in Linda Woodbridge and Edward Berry, eds., *True Rites and Maimed Rites: Ritual and Anti-Ritual in Shakespeare and His Age* (Urbana: University of Illinois Press, 1992), pp. 75–97. Edward A. Snow puts a valuable emphasis on sexual issues (especially sexual fantasies) in "Sexual Anxiety and the Male Order of Things in *Othello*," *English Literary Renaissance* 10 (1980): 384–412.

4. See Avraham Oz, "What's in a Good Name? The Case of *Romeo and Juliet* as a Bad Tragedy," in Charney, ed., *"Bad" Shakespeare*, pp. 133–42. Oz takes a strong generic point of view about *Romeo and Juliet*, for example: "It has many moments of fine melodrama, which would not have been bad had Shakespeare meant his play to be a melodrama. But the play seems to have aspired for more: from the very outset it raises in us overt expectations for tragic stature."

5. See Linda Charnes, "What's Love Got to Do with It? Reading the Liberal Humanist Romance in *Antony and Cleopatra*," in Shirley Nelson Garner and Madelon Sprengnether, eds., *Shakespearean Tragedy and Gender* (Bloomington: Indiana University Press, 1996), pp. 268–86. First published in *Textual Practice* 6 (Spring 1992). Part of it also appears in Linda Charnes's book, *Notorious Identity: Materializing the Subject in Shakespeare* (Cambridge: Har-

vard University Press, 1993), chapter 3. Charnes makes a spirited attack on liberal humanist critics of the play, whose work "is always implicitly coded male (regardless of the anatomical sex of its practitioner) because it is a view—possible only from a position of total cultural entitlement—in which gender and class differences are 'transcended' in great literature's embrace of a 'universal' human nature" (p. 270). See also Linda Fitz's witty article, "Egyptian Queens and Male Reviewers: Sexist Attitudes in *Antony and Cleopatra* Criticism," *Shakespeare Quarterly* 28 (1977): 297–316.

Catherine Belsey has some perceptive observations on "Cleopatra's Seduction" in Hawkes, ed., *Alternative Shakespeares* vol. 2, pp. 38–62. Cleopatra "makes hungry / Where most she satisfies" "by promising what she frequently, but not predictably, fails to deliver, by being inconsistently *elsewhere*" (p. 42). See also the illuminating essay of Phyllis Rackin, "Shakespeare's Boy Cleopatra, the Decorum of Nature, and the Golden World of Poetry," *Publications of the Modern Language Association* 87 (1972): 201–12, and Laura Levine, *Men in Women's Clothing*, chapter 3.

6. Gayle Greene has very shrewd things to say about Othello as a lover in "'This That You Call Love': Sexual and Social Tragedy in *Othello*," in Barker and Kamps, eds., *Shakespeare and Gender*, pp. 47–62. First published in *Journal of Women's Studies in Literature* 1 (1979): 16–32. Greene's remarks on Othello's sexuality get to the heart of the tragedy: "Implicit in Othello's language is a suspicion of sexuality and the physical being of woman and man, which Iago turns easily to loathing" (p. 53). For a more historically based view of Desdemona see Lena Cowen Orlin, "Desdemona's Disposition," in Garner and Sprengnether, eds., *Shakespearean Tragedy and Gender*, pp. 171–92. First published in *Private Matters and Public Culture in Post-Reformation England* (Ithaca: Cornell University Press, 1994), chapter 4.

CHAPTER FIVE: ENEMIES OF LOVE

1. Meredith's essay is reprinted in Wylie Sypher, ed., *Comedy* (Garden City, N.Y.: Doubleday Anchor, 1956). Meredith is forward-looking in his insistence that pure comedy can only flourish "where women are on the road to an equal footing with men, in attainments and in liberty—in what they have won for themselves, and what has been granted them by a fair civilization" (p. 32).

2. See the full discussion of sexual issues in *Venus and Adonis* in Kahn, *Man's Estate*, chapter 2.

3. John Donne, "The Exstasie," in Gardner, ed., *The Elegies and The Songs and Sonnets*, p. 61.

4. See the masterful discussion of this sonnet in Stephen Booth, *An Essay on Shakespeare's Sonnets* (New Haven: Yale University Press, 1969), pp. 152–68. See also Helen Vendler, *The Art of Shakespeare's Sonnets* (Cambridge: Harvard University Press, 1997).

5. There is an excellent, full chapter on *All's Well* in Neely, *Broken Nuptials*, chapter 2. She also has a good deal to say about *Measure for Measure*. See also Peter Erickson, *Rewriting Shakespeare, Rewriting Ourselves* (Berkeley: University of California Press, 1991), chapter 3 on *All's Well*.

6. See the introduction to the Arden edition of *Twelfth Night*, eds. J. M. Lothian and T. W. Craik (London: Methuen, 1975). There is a valuable discussion of the criticism of the play and a helpful scene-by-scene analysis. The editors try to redeem Orsino's first speech about love "even if we do also suspect him of luxuriating in it" (p. lxii). A typical comment about Orsino is Valerie Traub's statement that he is "more in love with love than with any particular object" (*Desire and Anxiety*, p. 135).

7. See Eric Partridge, *Shakespeare's Bawdy: A Literary & Psychological Essay and a Comprehensive Glossary* (New York: Dutton, 1960). In his brief summary of the bawdy in all of the plays, Partridge says that in *Romeo and Juliet* "Mercutio and the Nurse sex-spatter the most lyrically tragic of the plays" (p. 53).

CHAPTER SIX: GENDER DEFINITIONS

1. Two recent collections of essays on gender are particularly valuable: Barker and Kamps, eds., *Shakespeare and Gender* and Garner and Sprengnether, eds., *Shakespearean Tragedy and Gender*. Stephen Orgel's essay, "Nobody's Perfect: Or Why Did the English Stage Take Boys for Women?" offers an excellent account of gender anxieties in the Elizabethan theater (in Ronald R. Butters, John M. Clum, and Michael Moon, eds., *Displacing Homophobia: Gay Male Perspectives in Literature and Culture* [Durham: Duke University Press, 1989, pp. 7–29]). This volume reprints *South Atlantic Quarterly* 88 (1989). See also Orgel's stimulating and original book, *Impersonations: The Performance of Gender in Shakespeare's England* (Cambridge: Cambridge University Press, 1996).

2. See Janet Adelman, "'Born of Woman': Fantasies of Maternal Power in *Macbeth*," in Garner and Sprengnether, eds., *Shakespearean Tragedy and Gender*, pp. 105–34. First published in Marjorie Garber, ed., *Cannibals, Witches, and Divorce: Estranging the Renaissance* (Baltimore: The Johns Hopkins University Press, 1987). See also Adelman's important study, *Suffocating Mothers: Fantasies of Maternal Origin in Shakespeare's Plays, "Hamlet" to "The Tempest"* (New York: Routledge, 1992). She makes an important point that Lady Macbeth is a female temptress allied with the witches. This is a subject more fully developed in Deborah Willis, *Malevolent Nurture: Witch-Hunting and Maternal Power in Early Modern England* (Ithaca: Cornell University Press, 1995), chapter 6 on *Macbeth*. See also Kahn, *Man's Estate*, chapter 6. Kahn emphasizes the similarity in the definition of manliness between Macbeth and Coriolanus. Gender issues in *Macbeth* (and related plays) are

cleverly defined in D. W. Harding's essay, "Women's Fantasy of Manhood: A Shakespearian Theme," *Shakespeare Quarterly* 20 (1969): 245–53. See also Dennis Biggins, "Sexuality, Witchcraft, and Violence in *Macbeth*," *Shakespeare Studies* 8 (1975): 255–77. Biggins shows how much the language of the witches is drenched in sexuality.

3. Sarah Siddons, the sister of John Philip Kemble, played Lady Macbeth for forty years, from 1777 to 1817. She played Volumnia, also in Kemble's productions, from 1806–11. See Carol Jones Carlisle, *Shakespeare from the Greenroom: Actors' Criticisms of Four Major Tragedies* (Chapel Hill: University of North Carolina Press, 1969), pp. 397–410. The New Variorum Edition of *Macbeth*, ed. Horace Howard Furness, Jr. (New York: Dover, 1963; first published 1873) has a long selection from Mrs. Siddons's "Remarks on the Character of Lady Macbeth," pp. 472–77.

In the course of her compelling essay, " 'Anger's My Meat': Feeding, Dependency and Aggression in *Coriolanus*," in Murray M. Schwartz and Coppélia Kahn, eds., *Representing Shakespeare: New Psychoanalytic Essays* (Baltimore: Johns Hopkins University Press, 1980), pp. 129–49, Janet Adelman makes acute observations on Volumnia as "not a nourishing mother" (p. 130). See also Kahn, *Man's Estate*, chapter 6, where the link between Macbeth and Coriolanus is developed. Another powerful commentary, psychoanalytically oriented, is in Sprengnether, "Annihilating Intimacy in *Coriolanus*," in Rose, ed., *Women in the Middle Ages and the Renaissance*, pp. 89–111.

4. Christopher Marlowe, *Tamburlaine the Great*, ed. J. S. Cunningham, The Revels Plays (Manchester: Manchester University Press, 1981).

5. See Andrew S. Cairncross's introduction to the Arden edition of *The Third Part of King Henry VI* (London: Methuen, 1969), p. xli.

6. Antiopa is Theseus's first Amazon wife, according to the early legends. Statius in his *Thebiad* has Theseus returning with Hippolyta as his wife. Both accounts are in Plutarch's "Life of Theseus," which Shakespeare used as a source. See Jeanne Addison Roberts on the Amazons in *The Shakespearean Wild: Geography, Genus, and Gender* (Lincoln: University of Nebraska Press, 1991), pp. 125–31. See also Paster, *The Body Embarrassed*, pp. 234–38. The article by Celeste Turner Wright, "The Amazons in Elizabethan Literature," *Studies in Philology* 37 (1940): 433–56, is comprehensive.

Louis Montrose has a wide-ranging, psychoanalytically oriented article on Elizabethan images of Amazons in "*A Midsummer Night's Dream* and the Shaping Fantasies of Elizabethan Culture," in Margaret W. Ferguson, Maureen Quilligan, and Nancy J. Vickers, eds., *Rewriting the Renaissance: The Discourses of Sexual Difference in Early Modern Europe* (Chicago: University of Chicago Press, 1986), pp. 65–87. There is a longer version of this article in *Representations* 44 (1983): 61–94. Montrose points out that the second volume of William Painter's *The Palace of Pleasure* (1567) begins with a seven-page account of the Amazons and their "Woman's Commonwealth." See also Simon Shepherd, *Amazons and Warrior Women: Varieties of Feminism in Seventeenth-Century Drama* (New York: St. Martin's Press, 1981), especially chapter 1, "Warrior Meets Amazon."

7. See Katharine Usher Hunderson and Barbara F. McManus, *Half Humankind: Contexts and Texts of the Controversy about Women in England, 1540–1640* (Urbana: University of Illinois Press, 1985).

CHAPTER SEVEN: HOMOEROTIC DISCOURSES

1. See Constance Brown Kuriyama, *Hammer or Anvil: Psychological Patterns in Christopher Marlowe's Plays* (New Brunswick, N.J.: Rutgers University Press, 1980). In the second sentence of her preface, Kuriyama states that her book "began with a conviction that our tendency to ignore or minimize Marlowe's homosexuality was effectively limiting our understanding of his work" (p. ix). See also Jonathan Goldberg, *Sodometries: Renaissance Texts, Modern Sexualities* (Stanford: Stanford University Press, 1992), chapter 4 on Marlowe, and Joseph A. Porter, "Marlowe, Shakespeare, and the Canonization of Heterosexuality," in Butters, Clum, and Moon, eds., *Displacing Homophobia*, pp. 127–47.

2. See the extensive discussion on authorship and collaboration in the introduction to Eugene M. Waith's Oxford edition of *The Two Noble Kinsmen* (Oxford: Oxford University Press, 1989). Jeffrey Masten has a complex discussion of the homoerotic in *The Two Noble Kinsmen* (and also in *The Two Gentlemen of Verona*) in *Textual Intercourse: Collaboration, Authorship, and Sexualities in Renaissance Drama* (Cambridge: Cambridge University Press, 1997), Cambridge Studies in Renaissance Literature and Culture, 14. See especially chapter 2.

3. Bruce R. Smith argues strongly against a binary view of sexuality in early modern England in favor of a continuum of sexual behavior. This would help to explain what appear to us to be large inconsistencies and contradictions. See "L[o]cating the sexual subject" in Hawkes, ed., *Alternative Shakespeares*, pp. 95–121. See also his essay, "Making a difference: Male/male 'desire' in tragedy, comedy, and tragi-comedy," in Susan Zimmerman, ed., *Erotic Politics: Desire on the Renaissance Stage* (New York: Routledge, 1992), pp. 127–49. Valerie Traub's complex essay, "The (in)significance of 'lesbian' desire in early modern England," is also in this volume, pp. 150–69. Traub uses the term "female homoeroticism" throughout her article and in her book, *Desire and Anxiety*. Jean E. Howard's essay in *Erotic Politics* is ostensibly about *The Roaring Girl*, but she offers general reflections on prevailing misogynistic attitudes and fear of women's sexual appetites ("Sex and social conflict: The erotics of *The Roaring Girl*," pp. 170–90).

4. See chapter 2, note 6.

5. See Joseph Pequigney, "The Two Antonios and Same-Sex Love in *Twelfth Night* and *The Merchant of Venice*," in Barker and Kamps, eds., *Shakespeare and Gender*, pp. 178–95, and Cynthia Lewis, " 'Wise Men, Folly-Fall'n': Characters Named Antonio in English Renaissance Drama," *Renaissance Drama* N.S. 20 (1989): 197–236.

6. See Pequigney's article, "The Two Antonios," in Barker and Kamps, eds., *Shakespeare and Gender*. He goes out of his way to reject traditional homoerotic arguments for Antonio in *The Merchant of Venice*.

7. Gregory W. Bredbeck has extensive commentary on *Troilus and Cressida* in *Sodomy and Interpretation*, chapter 2. See also Traub, *Desire and Anxiety*, especially chapter 3.

8. See Joseph Pequigney, *Such is My Love: A Study of Shakespeare's Sonnets* (Chicago: University of Chicago Press, 1985). See also Bredbeck, *Sodomy and Interpretation*, pp. 167–80 (under the title "The Shakespearian Sodomite"), and Eve Kosofsky Sedgwick, *Between Men: English Literature and Male Homosocial Desire* (New York: Columbia University Press, 1985), chapter 2 on Shakespeare's *Sonnets*. There is a long, balanced discussion of this subject in Bruce R. Smith's book, *Homosexual Desire in Shakespeare's England*, chapter 7.

9. The whole issue is interestingly discussed in Di Gangi, *The Homoerotics of Early Modern Drama*, especially in chapter 2, "The Homoerotics of Marriage in Ovidian Comedy."

CHAPTER EIGHT: LOVE & LUST: SEXUAL WIT

1. See the elaborate notes on Sonnet 129 in Stephen Booth's edition, *Shakespeare's Sonnets* (New Haven: Yale University Press, 1977), pp. 441–52. See also Vendler, *The Art of Shakespeare's Sonnets*.

2. See Coppélia Kahn, "The Rape in Shakespeare's *Lucrece*," in Barker and Kamps, eds., *Shakespeare and Gender*, pp. 22–46. First published in *Shakespeare Studies* 9 (1976): 45–72. Kahn draws our attention to the "curious fact that Lucrece acquires a moral stigma from *being* raped" (p. 23) and that "Tarquin considers the rape a violation not of Lucrece's chastity but of Collatine's honour" (p. 31).

3. In *The Arte of English Poesie* (1585?), George Puttenham calls hendiadys "the figure of Twynnes" eds. Gladys Doidge Willcock and Alice Walker (Cambridge: Cambridge University Press, 1936), p. 177. Hendiadys is authoritatively discussed in George T. Wright's article, "Hendiadys and *Hamlet*," *Publications of the Modern Language Association* 96 (1981): 168–93. ·

4. Frankie Rubinstein's big book, *A Dictionary of Shakespeare's Sexual Puns and Their Significance* (London: Macmillan, 1984), is full of brilliant insights and wild speculations based on etymology. E. A. M. Colman, *The Dramatic Use of Bawdy in Shakespeare* (London: Longman, 1974) is more authoritative. Eric Partridge's *Shakespeare's Bawdy* (first published in 1948) is personal and

enthusiastic. The most recent study is Gordon M. Williams, *A Dictionary of Sexual Language and Imagery in Shakespearean and Stuart Literature*, 3 vols. (London: The Athlone Press, 1994). A condensed version of this book is Gordon Williams, *A Glossary of Shakespeare's Sexual Language* (London: The Athlone Press, 1997).

5. See Richard David's introduction to his Arden edition of *Love's Labour's Lost* (London: Methuen, 1968). "That *Love's Labour's Lost* is an imitation of Lyly's plays is as much a commonplace of criticism as that it is a satire on Lyly's affected language, his 'Euphuism'" (p. xxx).

6. See Adelman's *Suffocating Mothers*. She pursues with relentless energy her theme of "fantasies of maternal malevolence, of maternal spoiling, that are compelling exactly as they are out of proportion to the character we know, exactly as they seem therefore to reiterate infantile fears and desires rather than an adult apprehension of the mother as a separate person" (p. 16). Another powerful study of misogynistic themes in Shakespeare is Neely, *Broken Nuptials*. Her views are complex. The long introduction sets forth ideas on which the book is based, for example: "Deidealization, as it prepares the way for marital sexual union, activates the misogyny that coexists with idealization" (p. 6). See also Leslie A. Fiedler, *The Stranger in Shakespeare* (London: Croom Helm, 1973), chapter 2, "The Woman as Stranger."

7. See Samuel Taylor Coleridge, *Shakespearean Criticism*, 2 vols., ed. Thomas Middleton Raysor (London: Dent, 1960), I:211.

8. See Johannes Fabricius, *Syphilis in Shakespeare's England* (London: Jessica Kingsley, 1994). Fabricius makes much use of *Timon, Hamlet,* and *Troilus and Cressida*. There are splendid illustrations in the book.

9. See Charles J. Sisson's British Academy lecture, "The Mythical Sorrows of Shakespeare," *Proceedings of the British Academy 1934* 20 (1935): 45–70.

Plautus, 5
Plutarch, 93, 96, 145, 153, 223
Polanski, Roman, 138
Porter, Joseph A., 224
Priapus, 194, 198
problem plays, 5, 63–78, 115, 210, 218
proverbs, ix, 9, 46, 147, 156, 163, 188,
    216–17
psychoanalysis, 3, 223–24
puns and wordplay, 7, 37–38, 52–53,
    83, 93, 117, 120–1, 125, 146,
    151–52, 178, 181–208, 225–26;
    "capricious," 37; "country," 77;
    "dear," 47; "feigning," 38; "fond,"
    32; "front," 94; "goats"/"Goths,"
    37; "palmer," 83; "pride," 109;
    "sluggardized," 111–12; "stuffed,"
    42; "waste"/"waist," 182; "will,"
    155, 177
Puritans, 2, 64
Puttenham, George, 225
Pyramus and Thisbe, 30–32

Quilligan, Maureen, 217–18, 223

Rackin, Phyllis, 221
Ranald, Margaret Loftus, 216–17
rape, 14–15, 17–21, 50, 56, 59, 117,
    122–23, 141, 144, 162, 167, 181,
    183, 208, 225
Rape of Lucrece, The, 17–21, 117–18,
    123, 144, 154, 181–84, 187, 198,
    211, 225
Raysor, Thomas Middleton, 226
rhetoric, 34, 37, 43, 49, 97, 169, 187,
    189
Richard II, 37, 81, 134–35, 148–49
Richard III, 6, 127–31
Roberts, Jeanne Addison, 223
romance and the romantic, 5, 46, 55,
    61, 70–72, 80, 88, 95–97, 99, 101,
    106, 153, 167–68, 188, 193–97,
    208, 210–11, 214

Romeo and Juliet, 2, 4–5, 22–24,
    81–88, 96, 98–100, 105–6, 116,
    119–22, 147–49, 192, 208, 210,
    212, 219–20, 222
Rose, Mary Beth, 219, 223
Rosenblatt, Jason P., 219
Rubinstein, Frankie, 187, 225

Saslow, James M., 216
satire and the satirical, 4–5, 7, 9,
    12–13, 21–23, 25, 35, 38, 42, 49,
    63, 73, 78, 88, 101, 109, 120–21,
    125, 173, 206, 209, 211, 217,
    226
satyr, 198
scapegoats, 88
Schanzer, Ernest, 218
Schoenbaum, S., ix
Schwartz, Murray M., 223
sculpture. *See* painting
Sedgwick, Eve Kosofsky, 225
self-love, 6, 44, 111, 116–19, 131,
    160
sexual innuendo. *See* double entendre
sexual words, 68, 225–26; "baiser,"
    191; "bear," 92; "blood," 38, 43,
    64–65, 74, 76, 125, 137, 140, 182,
    196–97, 216; "caret," 192; "case,"
    190, 192–93; "circle," 192;
    "cliff"/"cleft," 202; "cloy," 91;
    "cock," 53; "cods," 188, 193; "coy,"
    108; "count" (=gown), 190–91;
    "country," 77, 185–86; "cut," 117,
    190; "desire," 168, 177; "die," 89;
    "disedge," 77–78; "do it," 138;
    "dribbling dart," 115–16; "edge,"
    77; "fit," 160; "fitment," 194;
    "focative," 192; "foot"/"foutra,"
    190–91; "hit," 120, 123, 189–90;
    "keys," 193; "kicky-wicky,"
    114–15; "lap," 77; "leap," 191;
    "manly marrow," 114; "mark,"
    189; "medlar," 120; "Mountanto,"